TOWARD A REVOLUTION
IN MILITARY AFFAIRS?

TOWARD A REVOLUTION IN MILITARY AFFAIRS?

Defense and Security at the Dawn of the Twenty-First Century

Edited by
Thierry Gongora and Harald von Riekhoff

Contributions in Military Studies, Number 197

Greenwood Press
Westport, Connecticut • London

Library of Congress Cataloging-in-Publication Data

Toward a revolution in military affairs? : defense and security at the dawn of the
    twenty-first century / edited by Thierry Gongora and Harald von Riekhoff.
        p.   cm.—(Contributions in military studies, ISSN 0883–6884 ; no. 197)
    Includes bibliographical references and index.
    ISBN 0–313–31037–8 (alk. paper)
        1. Military art and science—History—20th century—Congresses.   2. Information
    warfare—Congresses.   3. Operational art (Military science)—Congresses.   I. Gongora,
    Thierry.   II. Von Riekhoff, Harald, 1937–   III. Series.
    U42.T69   2000
    355′.009′04—dc21   99–055176

British Library Cataloguing in Publication Data is available.

Library of Congress Catalog Card Number: 99–055176
ISBN: 0-313–31037–8
ISSN: 0883–6884

First published in 2000

Greenwood Press, 88 Post Road West, Westport, CT 06881
An imprint of Greenwood Publishing Group, Inc.
www.greenwood.com

Printed in the United States of America

The paper used in this book complies with the
Permanent Paper Standard issued by the National
Information Standards Organization (Z39.48–1984).

10 9 8 7 6 5 4 3 2 1

Copyright Acknowledgments

The editors and publisher gratefully acknowledge permission to reprint from the following:

Chapter 3 by Martin Libicki is a shortened and edited version of a paper that was originally published by the Institute for National Strategic Studies and the National Defense University Press in
August 1995.

Chapter 9 by Glenn Buchan is an edited version of a paper previously published by RAND in
1998 (P-8015).

Portions of chapter 10 by Andrew Latham were originally published as "The Contemporary Restructuring of the US Arms Industry: Toward 'Agile Manufacturing.' " Reprinted by permission
from *Contemporary Security Policy*, vol. 18, no. 1. © Frank Cass & Co. Ltd., 1997, 900 Eastern
Avenue, Ilford, Essex IG2 7HH.

Contents

Acknowledgments

This book is based on revised versions of papers presented at a conference held in Quebec City (October 3–4, 1997) by the *Institut québécois des hautes études internationales* (Université Laval). In preparing this conference and book we became indebted to many institutions and people. The conference was cosponsored by the Research Group in International Security (Université de Montréal/McGill University), the Royal Military College of Canada, and the security studies programs of Carleton University (Ottawa) and Queen's University (Kingston). The Canadian Department of National Defence also made a special financial contribution to the organization of the conference through its Security and Defence Forum. The conference also became a success thanks to the contribution of many individuals, including Robert J. Art, Hervé Coutau-Bégarie, Maude Dubois, Michel Fortmann, David Haglund, Fen O. Hampson, Michael A. Hennessy, Stéphane Lefebvre, Albert Legault, Dean Oliver, Lili Réhel, and Joel J. Sokolsky. Finally, we would like to thank our editor at Greenwood Press, Heather Ruland Staines, for her unrelenting support and patience, as well as Bobbie Goettler and Élise Lapalme who did a splendid work in preparing the manuscript.

The book contains three pieces which were previously published in part. Martin Libicki's *What Is Information Warfare?* is a shortened and edited version of a paper that was originally published by the Institute for National Strategic Studies and the National Defense University Press in August 1995. An earlier and shorter version of Andrew Latham's chapter appeared as "The Contemporary Restructuring of the U.S. Arms Industry: Toward 'Agile Manufacturing'" in *Contemporary Security Policy*, in April 1997. Material from this article is reprinted here by permission from *Contemporary Security Policy*, vol. 18, no. 1, © Frank Cass & Co. Ltd, 1997, 900 Eastern Avenue, Ilford, Essex (UK) IG2 7HH. Finally, a draft version of Glenn C. Buchan's chapter appeared as a RAND research note (P-8015) in 1998.

Acronyms

AAMRC	Agile Aerospace Manufacturing Research Center
AF/ASC	Air Force's Aeronautical Systems Center
AIMS	Agile infrastructure for manufacturing systems
AJAs	Assembly jig accessories
AM³	Affordable multi-missile manufacturing
AMI	Agile manufacturing initiative
AMS	Academy of Military Science [People's Republic of China]
ARPA	Advanced Research Projects Agency
ARPA/NSF	Advanced Research Projects Agency/National Science Foundation
AT&T	American Telephone and Telegraph
AWACS	Airborne warning and control system
BAOR	British Army of the Rhine
BDA	Battle damage assessment
BMP	Best manufacturing practices
BMPCOE	Best Manufacturing Practices Center of Excellence
C^2	Command and control
C^2W	Command-and-control warfare
C^3I	Command, control, communications, and intelligence
C^4I	Command, control, communications, computing, and intelligence
C^4ISR	Command, control, communications, computing, intelligence, surveillance, and reconnaissance
CAD	Computer-aided design
CAE	Computer-aided engineering
CALS	Computer-assisted logistics support
CAM	Computer-aided manufacturing
CAPP	Computer-aided production planning
CAT	Computer-aided testing
CDMA	Code-division multiple access
CD-ROM	Compact Disk/Read-Only Memory
CFE	Conventional armed forces in Europe

CIA	Central Intelligence Agency [United States]
CICA	Competition in Contracting Act
CIM	Computer-integrated manufacturing
CJCS	Chairman of the Joint Chiefs of Staff [United States]
CJTF	Combined joint task force
CLF	Canadian land forces
CNN	Cable News Network
CREST	Centre de recherche et d'études sur les stratégies et technologies [France]
CTIB	Commercial technology and industrial base
CTPID	Center for Technology, Policy and Industrial Development
CW	Communication warfare
CyW	Cyberwarfare
DBS	Direct broadcast satellite
DES	Digital encryption standard
DMDC	Defense Manpower Data Center [United States]
DND	Department of National Defence [Canada]
DOD	Department of Defense [United States]
DSMC	Defense Systems Management College [United States]
DSTO	Defence Science and Technology Organisation [Australia]
DTIB	Defense technology and industrial base
DVE	Distributed virtual environment
ECM	Electronic countermeasures
EcoW	Economic warfare
ECRC	Electronic Commerce Resource Center
EIW	Economic information warfare
ELINT	Electronic intelligence
ESECS	European security study
EU	European Union
EW	Electronic warfare
FASA	Federal Acquisition Streamlining Act
G7	Group of Seven
GDP	Gross domestic product
GES	Government electronic systems
GNP	Gross national product
GPS	Global positioning system
HARM	High-speed Anti-Radiation Missile
HSM	High-speed machine
HW	Hacker warfare
IBW	Intelligence-based warfare
IISS	International Institute for Strategic Studies
IntelW	Intelligence warfare
IR	Infrared
ISO	International Organization for Standardization
ISR	Intelligence, surveillance, and reconnaissance
IW	Information warfare
JAWS	Joint attack warfare strategy
JCS	Joint Chiefs of Staff [United States]
JDAM	Joint Direct Attack Munition
JDW	Jane's Defence Weekly
JITM	Just-in-time manufacturing
JSTARS	Joint Surveillance and Target Attack Radar System
LAI	Lean aircraft initiative

LEM	Lean enterprise model
LMTAS	Lockheed Martin tactical aircraft systems
LRET	Low-rate expandable tooling
LRPW	Long-range precision weapon
MADE	Manufacturing automation and design environment
MDAS&T	McDonnell Douglas advanced systems and technology
MDC	McDonnell Douglas Corporation
MILSATCOM	Military satellite communications
MIT	Massachusetts Institute of Technology
MOP	Memorandum of policy
MORF	Ministerstvo Oborory Rossiyskoy Federatsii [Ministry of Defense of the Russian Federation]
MPRI	Military Professional Resources Incorporated
MTR	Military-technical revolution
N/C	Numerically controlled
NAMP	New aircraft and missile products
NASA	National Aeronautics and Space Administration [United States]
NASDAQ	National Association of Securities Dealers Access Quotation
NATO	North Atlantic Treaty Organization
NII	National information infrastructure
NIST	National Institute of Standards and Technology
NOA	New operational art
NRC	National Research Council [United States]
NSA	National Security Agency [United States]
NTIB	National technology and industrial base
OASD	Office of the Assistant Secretary of Defense [United States]
ONA	Office of Net Assessment [United States]
OODA	Observe, orient, decide, act
OUDA	Office of the Undersecretary of Defense for Acquisition [United States]
PGM	Precision-guided munition
PKE	Public key encryption
PLA	People's Liberation Army
PsyW	Psychological warfare
R&D	Research and development
RAM	Random access memory
RAND	Research and development (Corporation)
RBA	Revolution in business affairs
RMA	Revolution in military affairs
ROA	Revolution in operational art
SAR	Synthetic aperture radar
SDI	Strategic Defense Initiative
SOF	Special operations forces
SR	Surveillance and reconnaissance
STAR	Committee on Strategic Technologies for the Army [United States]
START	Strategic Arms Reduction Treaty
TEAM	Technologies enabling agile manufacturing
TQM	Total quality management
UAV	Unmanned aerial vehicle
UN	United Nations
UNPROFOR	United Nations Protection Force

TOWARD A REVOLUTION
IN MILITARY AFFAIRS?

Introduction: Sizing up the Revolution in Military Affairs

Thierry Gongora and Harald von Riekhoff

The notion that we are engaged in a revolution in military affairs (RMA) is part of common knowledge among defense and military analysts. This consensus, however, hides a significant degree of debate about the nature of the RMA, its likely development, and its implications for various nations, the future of warfare, and defense policy. This introduction and the following essays provide viewpoints on the subject structured around the following themes: (a) the substance of the RMA; (b) different national perspectives on the changing nature of warfare and defense; and (c) the impact of the RMA on power projection and defense industries. Considered as a whole, this collection of essays deals with broad aspects of the RMA, rather than with specific technologies and concepts of operations. This was a conscious choice based on the opinion that broad issues are likely to be the most enduring and important for an understanding of the phenomenon; while technologies and operational concepts will keep developing in ways that make any analysis quasi-obsolescent as soon as it is published. In short, we choose to study the train of the RMA from a distance rather than to study its engine and cars from a few feet as they whiz past.

IS THE RMA A TRUE REVOLUTION?

We often take for granted the existence of the RMA in order to discuss more practical and pressing issues that stem from it, but it is useful to stand back and discuss the nature of the phenomenon. According to the standard definition offered by Andrew Marshall, Director of the Office of Net Assessment (U.S. DOD), an RMA "is a major change in the nature of warfare brought about by the innovative application of new technologies which, combined with dramatic changes in military doctrine and operational and organizational concepts, fundamentally alters the character and conduct of military operations" (McKitrick et al. 1995, 65). This definition has been rightly praised for stressing the fact that military-technological innovation is not enough to create an RMA; it also requires doctrinal and organizational innovations. But Marshall's definition can also be criticized for its vagueness; what constitutes "a major change in the nature of warfare" indeed? Neo-Clausewitzian analysts, for instance, could argue that there has never been a major change in recorded history, since war has always been about the pursuit of political ends through violent military means; and no amount of technological development will ever change that (Howard 1994). Conversely, some analysts could claim that the real RMA we are witnessing is not about information technologies and advanced conventional weaponry, but about the end of the Clausewitzian era, when nation-states made war for political purposes, and the rise of a new mode of warfare in which war is disconnected from *raison d'État* and can be a way of life rather than an instrument of politics (Keegan 1993; van Creveld 1991).

Determining whether the current changes qualify as an RMA therefore depends on the criteria used to determine what constitutes "major" or "revolutionary" change, a point reflected in contributions to this volume. Rogers sees in the current changes an RMA that could lead to a military revolution; Marsh, on the other hand, categorically asserts that no RMA has yet occurred. Although Rogers's and Marsh's arguments can be seen as poles apart, they actually have more in common than meets the eye. Rogers makes a distinction between an RMA and what military historians call a military revolution.[1] Military revolutions are periods of military transformation that are so intense that they have consequences beyond the realm of warfare, affecting social, economic, and political domestic structures, and international orders. Although RMAs are usually the precursors of military revolutions, they do not lead to such developments systematically. As Rogers argues, RMAs that did not change the balance between offense and defense (in direction, not just in degree) also failed to become military revolutions. He thinks that the current RMA shifts the balance in favor of offense decisively, notably because of the increased role of airpower in military operations. This development could have a series of consequences, as Rogers notes, in terms of change in the fundamental elements of military power: a large population and economic base may matter less in the future than the quality of standing forces, and the vitality of the high-tech sector of the economy. Rogers remains, however, cautious about the broader social and political implications of this development, noting that the increasing importance of information, knowledge, and intellectual resources in generating military power might create a barrier to the diffusion of the RMA to nations with authoritarian regimes. This point is important. Past military innovations originating from the West were intimately connected with the broader Western institutional framework, creating a barrier to the effective adoption of the Western way of warfare by other civilizations (Ralston 1990). Rogers also argues that the transition to smaller professional military forces might create a gap between societies and armed forces; a prospect likely to deteriorate civil-military relations. This trend might be offset, however, by the fact that military reserves will continue to play some role in the future, given the costs of an all-professional force, and that the military-civilian divide might erode in the field of manufacturing, as Latham points out, as well as in the skills and educational background of military and civilian personnel.

A good case for not qualifying the current changes in military affairs as revolutionary is presented by Marsh, who makes the point that although information technologies are dramatically enhancing military capabilities, these improvements are essentially taking place within a traditional, doctrinal, and intellectual framework that limits what can be done. While Rogers thinks the RMA might unleash sociopolitical change that could cause a military revolution, Marsh reverses the causality and argues that the real revolution will come from the erosion of the sociopolitical order associated with state sovereignty as a result of the rise of virtual communities based in distributed virtual environments (DVEs). Defense of territory and sovereignty would thus lose meaning, undermining the very function of armed forces. This scenario is futuristic, but it relates to a broader concern over the decline of the nation-state and interstate wars among analysts of military and security affairs (Desch 1996; van Creveld 1991, 1996). A fundamental change in the nature of armed conflict (e.g., low-intensity and terrorism instead of interstate), in its likelihood (e.g., dramatically reduced because of the obsolescence of major wars and the spread of democracy), or in the actors likely to be involved (e.g., increased role for nonstate actors) portend the possibility that the RMA as presently configured, that is, as an improved way of waging conventional wars, could end up with little or no strategic utility as the RMA is being preempted by a revolution in the nature of armed conflict.

This alternative scenario for the future has its merit in terms of counterbalancing a tendency to discuss the RMA in a political vacuum, but it overstates the case for the marginalization of conventional warfare. Although the prospects for a war among the major powers are reduced since the end of the Cold War, and might remain low for a variety of emerging structural reasons, limited wars involving a major power, or regional powers, remain a distinct possibility, particularly in the Middle East, and in East and South Asia. It is also premature to claim that the prevalence of nonstate actors and of civil wars in conflict trends since 1945 sounds the knell of state sovereignty and defense. After all, most protracted conflicts around the world are still about the control of territory and political authority, often for the purpose of creating a new state; these wars are waged by forces that often rely on conventional weapons, organizations, and tactics; and finally, once in power, the new rulers tend to restructure their guerrilla or militia units into regular armed forces. The RMA may not prove a panacea, as Buchan points out, but it would still be a positive development if it meant that war would be less likely in the future (if, as Buchan argues, conventional invasion would be less feasible)[2] and if it translated into more options in the application of military force in low-intensity conflicts or operations other than war.

Some analysts, like Géré and Bi, take a third approach, instead of arguing for or against fundamental changes in military technology, or in the nature of conflict, they talk about a new operational art (NOA) or a revolution in operational art (ROA). For Géré, the NOA is an attempt to achieve information dominance over the enemy and to wage battle from a distance, thus eluding contact with enemy forces. The NOA, however, is made possible by the contemporary RMA, that is, the transformation of weapon systems, military organizations and operations through the integration of information technologies. When information technologies are integrated into a coherent system that includes modern weapon systems operated by highly trained personnel, they provide force multipliers to military formations, allowing them to perform more complex maneuvers, to fire accurately at longer range, and to experience a higher degree of situational awareness compared to their opponents.

Some of these developments are not new. Precursors of the RMA can be found in military operations during the War in Lebanon in 1982 (e.g., Israeli air operations over the Bekaa valley), the Vietnam War (e.g., the use of guided bombs to strike bridges in North Vietnam), or even the Second World War if one considers aircraft carrier operations in the Pacific or the air defense system of the Battle of Britain. Perhaps what is more peculiar to the post–Gulf War period is that the information revolution is no longer confined to air warfare and naval operations, it increasingly affects land warfare, the environment that until now has remained the most difficult in terms of command and control of forces, performance of complex maneuvers, detection of friendly and enemy units, and accurate fire (Freedman 1998, 12). Recent U.S. efforts to integrate information technologies into the structure and equipment of ground units (the process of digitization) show impressive results despite the experimental nature of such formations. In one exercise, performed in November 1997, a digital formation (the U.S. 4th Infantry Division) showed that "[c]ompared with currently deployed forces, the digitized 4ID inflicted more than twice as many enemy casualties, in half the time, over three times the normal battlespace, using 25 percent fewer combat platforms" (Hewish 1998). Such gains in "military productivity" are what Western armed forces will seek in the twenty-first century to make up for their decreasing size.

Since information technologies are at the heart of the current RMA, it was inevitable that the argument would be made that information itself is the instrument of, or the medium through which, war will be waged. The notion of information warfare, however, has its limit as an analytical category. Since information can be almost anything, information warfare can also mean almost anything, from striking headquarters or communication systems with conventional weapons, to hacking computer systems, to conducting propaganda and psychological operations, or even to committing atrocities to instil panic in the enemy's population. As a result, it is difficult to prove that information is not a decisive factor in warfare. Libicki's *What Is Information Warfare?*, reprinted here as a chapter, is a salutary essay that takes most of the hot air out of a set of issues relating to the increased dependence of modern societies and militaries on information systems. A parallel with the earlier experience of airpower is worth making in this regard. When the military potential of airpower emerged early in the twentieth century, wild predictions were made about its potential and the vulnerability of industrial societies to even a few strategic bombardment raids. The historical experience, however, showed that strategic bombardment was not a simple concept to carry out, and that modern societies and economies were more resilient to its effects than had been initially anticipated. It is likely that information warfare, as an independent area of operations with a potential for decisive strategic results, will know the same lack of achievement for most of the twenty-first century. Attacks on information systems might not even achieve results comparable to what an air offensive can now do at the strategic level, if, as Libicki argues, information operations are not a form of warfare, a type of operations, or an arm comparable to land, sea, and air forces, and operations.

Nevertheless, the information infrastructure of nations will be increasingly "securitized," that is, the object of a discourse aiming at presenting the issue of the security of information systems—and of *cultures* in the case of the more encompassing version of the discourse—as so essential as to warrant the use of force and other extraordinary measures to insure their integrity.

Determining whether the RMA represents a revolutionary change depends on one's definition of "revolutionary," but also on the level one is looking at. From the very broad level of the fundamentals of strategy, the current changes seem like ripples on a calm sea; or to use another image, one could argue that the new operational art made possible by the RMA would be comprehensible to Clausewitz or Napoleon, if they were still among us. At the level of the men, women, and organizations in charge of translating the technological potential of the RMA into new weapons, information systems, doctrines, and forms of organization, however, these developments certainly qualify as a sea change; and a Napoleon or Clausewitz would marvel at the command, control, and communication systems, logistics, firepower, protection, and mobility put at the disposal of armies and staffs nowadays.

Military revolutions in the past have also coincided with fundamental changes in weapon production techniques (Krause 1992). For instance, the developments in metallurgy that made possible the founding of early artillery guns were essential to the military revolution associated with the end of the Middle Ages and the beginning of the Renaissance (Rogers 1995b, 64–73). The powerful, mobile artillery thus created transformed war on land and sea in Europe, and paved the way for the European conquest of Asian states (Parker 1988, 115–45). Similarly, the application of industrial-age techniques to the production of weapons and supplies allowed the fielding of mass armies from the second half of the nineteenth century on, and the waging of total wars subsequently.

Are we on the threshold of a similar shift that would lead us beyond the parameters of industrial-age arms manufacturing? Latham argues that recent developments in the arms industry portend of such change. The implementation of "agile manufacturing" in the field of weapon production promises to decouple rate and volume of production from unit costs, thus allowing the production of smaller batches of technology-intensive weapon systems, and might lead to the creation of a national technology and industrial base (NTIB), in which defense production would no longer rely on a few defense industrial firms, but on networks of firms that would transcend the commercial/military industrial divide characteristic of defense production during the Cold War. As Latham argues, the U.S. government plays a key role in this process of defense industrial transformation, a fact underlined by the nomination in November 1997 of Jacques S. Gansler, a firm believer in agile manufacturing, as Under Secretary of Defense for Acquisition and Technology.

Increased reliance on commercial off-the-shelf procurement, the effort to restructure defense production along the lines of the most innovative manufacturing and organizational practices in the private sector, and the erosion of the commercial/ military industrial divide look promising in terms of savings and shorter weapon design and production cycle. It is not yet clear, however, that we have overcome the parameters of industrial-age arms manufacturing when we consider megamergers in aircraft and defense industries on both sides of the Atlantic, and the cost of developing and procuring future aircraft such as the F-22, the Joint

Strike Fighter (JSF), or the RAH-66 helicopter. Perhaps all that the new production techniques will yield are savings that will mitigate the cost of future acquisitions, but without stopping the trend toward increased cost for each new generation of weapon systems. The example of the Dreadnought, early in the twentieth century, is instructive. This new class of battleships was built using new production techniques that yielded significant savings. The Dreadnought made obsolete all existing battleships with its speed and firepower, for a cost increase of only 10 percent; nevertheless, the cost of subsequent classes of battleships soared again, and the total cost of acquiring a fleet based on such ships remained a significant burden on the defense budgets of Britain and Germany (Massie 1991). An upheaval in arms manufacturing is in progress, and history will tell us whether it will prove to be a revolutionary transformation of the way we develop, produce, and procure weaponry.

Historically, each past military revolution has translated into increased defense costs. The end of medieval warfare brought the introduction of more expensive types of fortifications and the acquisition of costly artillery. The industrial revolution, although it allowed the cheaper production of some items like firearms, also caused an overall increase of defense costs by making possible war on a much greater scale. The RMA is also likely to increase the cost of defense through the introduction of generations of more sophisticated equipment. Defense establishments are therefore trying to cope with these increased costs by reducing the number of personnel and weapons, on the assumption that the RMA will bring gains in military productivity that will compensate for the decrease in the size of armed forces. The other main solutions to the problem of defense financing and management have been the transfers of the latest private sector management techniques to the (public) defense sector and a trend toward a privatization of support services. So far, the new management techniques associated with what is sometimes called the revolution in business affairs (RBA)[3] have failed to impress. The U.S. example, arguably a large and wealthy defense establishment where great savings could be expected, shows that private-sector best practices are: (a) difficult to implement; (b) not necessarily applicable to the specific context of defense management; and (c) likely to take time to produce savings, which will fall short of the financial requirements of defense modernization (Dahlman and Roll 1997; Khalilzad and Ochmanek 1997, 4). Nevertheless, the new management techniques and models of organizations associated with the RBA are widely presented as models for emulation to the defense organizations and armed forces of countries engaged in the transition toward the RMA and might be a fruitful source of examples for the military that are looking to new solutions to adapt their organization to the information age, as long as the process of borrowing and emulation takes into account the specific conditions under which armed forces operate and which preclude a complete reproduction of private sector solutions.

Outsourcing and privatization in defense have made inroads in such fields as maintenance services on military facilities, catering for troops on foreign deployment, the management of air training facilities and programs (e.g., the NATO Flying Training in Canada program run by a private sector consortium in collaboration with the Canadian government), and have been used or are considered in such sensitive areas as military assistance (e.g., MPRI contract with Croatia and

Bosnia) and the transport of weapons and munitions such as tanks or naval ordnance. This trend, when linked to increased activities by private security firms in sub-Saharan Africa and in weak states around the world (Shearer 1998), could substantiate a case for considering the "privatization of defense and security" as a growing feature of the RMA. It is still too early, however, to tell whether these signs are passing trends, marginal phenomena limited to specific niches, or the beginnings of a post-Westphalian era where the state no longer has a monopoly of the means of warfare.

NATIONAL PERSPECTIVES

One cannot escape the central role of the United States in discussing national perspectives about the RMA. The present U.S. position as the sole global power, established with the end of the Cold War, has been reinforced by the introduction of RMA technologies and doctrines. Unlike the short-lived monopoly of atomic weapons, U.S. primacy in the RMA sphere promises to continue unchallenged for at least another twenty years, if not longer. One merely needs to cite a few elementary facts to establish the scope of U.S. dominance of the field. U.S. investment in intelligence collection, surveillance, and reconnaissance (ISR), particularly space-based aspects of the so-called system of systems, exceeds that of all other nations combined, and the United States also leads in C⁴I and precision force (Nye and Owens 1996, 28). U.S. R&D expenses in information technology exceed those of the rest of the world. When it comes to dominant situational awareness, the United States, to cite Libicki, has the "world's best eyes" (Libicki 1998, 414). In the foreseeable future, no country or group of countries can match U.S. hegemony in the RMA sphere. As a consequence, all wars in which the United States chooses to become involved will inevitably assume the nature of asymmetric conflicts (Freedman 1998, 34).

In the contemporary politico-strategic environment, the United States enjoys not only an unprecedented freedom of choice in deciding whether to participate in a war, but it could also opt increasingly in the future for a new form of involvement in regional conflicts without the risks of direct physical presence on the battlefield. As Nye and Owens argue, using the analogy of extended nuclear deterrence, the United States could share its dominant situational knowledge with its allies and friends instead of committing troops (Nye and Owens 1996, 27). Similarly, Libicki speaks of vertical coalitions whereby the United States would provide intelligence and systems assistance to threatened parties in whose security it had a stake (Libicki 1998, 420). The example of the Iran-Iraq War where the United States provided valuable intelligence to the Iraqis in order to contain Iranian offensives may well point to the future (Freedman 1998, 71).

For the United States the advantage of such flexible coalition arrangements is readily apparent; however, for potential recipients it may prove to be a problematic solution for regional conflicts. To many, information assistance will seem like a poor ersatz for the physical presence of U.S. forces in the region, both for their deterrent and actual combat value. Also, some nations may be reluctant to rely on a U.S. information umbrella, as suggested by Nye and Owens, and Libicki, for fear that critical intelligence might be doctored or withheld. They may therefore prefer to construct their own C⁴ISR systems, if it is within their national capability. During the 1999 NATO air operation over Yugoslavia, some European allies complained that they had no direct access to U.S. satellite information. At the Cologne summit in June 1999, European Union (EU) members therefore decided to revive an earlier, derailed initiative to build a European reconnaissance satellite (Johansen and Rispens 1999, 32). Finally, one has to recall the end phase of UNPROFOR, the UN peacekeeping operation in Bosnia, to realize that a functional division of labor, as envisaged under the information umbrella scheme, can generate considerable political tension. NATO allies with troops on the ground in Bosnia came to resent the advice and pressure of their U.S. ally whose forces were not involved and thus not at risk as a consequence of proposed actions. If political disagreements could originate in the close-knit NATO framework, its occurrence should *a fortiori* be anticipated in the context of much more loosely structured coalitions.

In terms of the international hierarchy of power, the RMA has definitely reinforced the dominant global strategic position of the United States. If we cluster countries on the basis of the role played by the RMA in realizing their politico-strategic interests, we can identify four distinct groupings in addition to the unique U.S. position: first, the United States's principal NATO allies, Australia and Japan; second, "peer competitors," that is, Russia and China, with no other candidates in sight; third, "niche competitors" consisting mainly of developing countries with a capability to make selective use of some RMA technologies; and, finally, the large residual cluster of states with minimal prospects or inclination to adopt RMA technologies. The best strategy of this last group is to avoid involvement in conventional wars in which RMA technology is likely to figure prominently or, failing that, to minimize damage from the RMA by resorting to a strategy of deception and camouflage.

Second Tier RMA Users

For members of this tier, the RMA poses a delicate mixture of opportunities and challenges. On the one hand, as Buchan correctly observes, the RMA promises to improve the effectiveness of the members' armed forces at a time when defense budgets and force size are generally shrinking. On the other hand, the RMA raises the problem of coping with the qualitative gap between the members' own national forces and those of their U.S. ally, a gap which threatens to undermine future allied interoperability. Problems of interoperability surfaced during the Gulf War despite the overall success of the operation, and a marginalization of NATO allies without a capacity for air strikes with precision-guided munitions was evident during Operation Allied Force over Yugoslavia in the spring of 1999.

If this qualitative discrepancy is allowed to continue, rank-and-file NATO allies risk a de facto disenfranchisement in future alliance decision-making. As well, the United States might be dissuaded from embarking on collective engagements with allies that are incapable of operating in an RMA environment. Faced with such gloomy prospects, U.S. allies, at least the more powerful ones, may be expected to buy their RMA subscription, as Freedman styles it, and "to make an effort to stay abreast of these technologies and adopt them where possible, if only for the purpose of interoperability and to gain access to US policy-making at times of crisis and war" (Freedman 1998, 72).

France

As François Géré points out, the RMA poses some significant challenges for France in terms of force structures, defense industrial policy, and commitments to international bodies such as NATO or the EU. Many of these challenges are not specific to France, but rather representative of those facing European powers, what is perhaps peculiar to France is the fact that the transition to a post–Cold War security and defense policy started later than in other European countries, such as Britain and Germany, in particular in regard to reductions in defense budgets and consolidation of defense industry. As a result post–Cold War "defense downsizing" in France collided with the subsequent defense effort required to adapt French defense to the new strategic environment and the RMA.

The French government came up with a new defense white paper in 1994, but the real "revolution" in French defense policy was unleashed by a series of decisions made in 1995–96 (Heisbourg 1997, 27). The new defense policy translated into a willingness to consider greater integration in NATO's military structures, a military strategy oriented toward force projection in the context of multinational coalitions, a transition to smaller armed forces and an all-volunteer force, and a restructuring of defense industry to consolidate French industrial assets and promote the emergence of a European defense industrial base. The aim is to restructure French defense over the short (i.e., 2002) to long term (i.e., 2015), but this goal is hampered by reduced defense expenditures that do not provide sufficient resources to meet the objectives (Tiroch 1997). The resource problem is further exacerbated by the fact that France, which has only recently moved to an all-professional military force, has yet to undertake substantial manpower reductions to free up additional investments for its RMA strategy.

So far France has tried to maintain a domestic production capability in all major weapon systems, but its increasing difficulties in developing and producing new major defense systems (ex: aircraft carrier, advanced fighter, space systems) on a national basis indicate the inevitablity of greater European defense integration. As a group, the European countries that are both members of NATO and the EU spend less on defense and are shorter of power projection capabilities than the United States; but they maintain more defense manufacturers and models of main weapon systems.[4] A major consequence of the RMA in Europe is the creation of a strong impetus to reorganize defense on a transnational basis, so that Europeans can get the means to assume a greater role in the promotion of defense and security in Europe. As Géré concludes, the RMA cannot be conceived and developed in France, and in Europe as a whole, in exactly the same manner as in the United States. The proper course for France to follow is to select certain RMA niches, not to rival the United States by pursuing the entire RMA spectrum, and to develop these in full partnership with its European allies.

Britain

Next to the United States, Britain is the nation most committed in word and deed to the RMA. Britain's relative advantage in the RMA field over its European allies can be attributed to several factors. First, Britain has had a longer experience with an all-volunteer force, which better suits the needs of the RMA, than France and most other NATO countries. Second, Britain has become Europe's center for high-technology research and has civilian expertise in many core technologies relevant to the RMA (Richter 1999, 54). Finally, Britain has been the most enthusiastic and supportive partner of the United States in coalition operations like Desert Storm (1991), Desert Fox (1998) and Allied Force (1999). In order to retain this highly prized special relationship with the United States, it is absolutely essential that Britain retains full interoperability with its American ally on whom, among others, it depends for satellite navigation, strategic reconnaissance, and support for its Trident submarines (McInnes 1998, 841).

The incumbent Labor government has been a vigorous promoter of the RMA, which not only suits British military interests but also corresponds with Prime Minister Blair's broader political goal of transforming his country into a more modern, technologically oriented, "cool Britain" type of society. While still in opposition, Labor had stressed the importance of maintaining a high-technology defense sector, and has pursued this policy while in office. In 1998 the Blair government issued a defense white paper, entitled *Strategic Defence Review*, which outlined a long-term defense program up to the year 2015 (Ministry of Defence [UK] 1998). The white paper deliberately addresses the RMA issue and throughout is imbued by its underlying philosophy. The white paper emphasizes flexibility, joint operations and strategic mobility, and the ability to project British power globally, thus giving it a comparative advantage "to punch above its weight" (McInnes 1998, 826).

The planned re-equipment of its armed forces to ensure military success at a minimum cost to British lives creates a financial dilemma, as the Labor government has reduced the defense budget without a corresponding cut in the size of forces. To square this circle, the British government has launched a "smart procurement" initiative intended to cash in on the opportunities offered by the RBA. In particular, the initiative seeks to cut British procurement costs by enhanced collaboration with allies, increased use of commercial technology, and the exploitation of lean and agile manufacturing techniques (McInnes 1998, 843).

Australia

The preoccupation with the RMA is by no means confined to the principal allies of the United States. To take the example of a middle power, Australia has taken a very positive view of the RMA and regards it as a welcome opportunity to gain a competitive edge over regional rivals. As one Australian defense official noted, "'Third Wave' warfare has washed over the ADF [Australian Defence Force] like a tsunami. Everyone is talking about it, writing papers on it or attending conferences on it" (Dunn 1996). As a result, investments in information systems are prioritized whether one looks at the long-term Takari program designed to digitize the Australian armed forces (DSTO 1997) or the fact that official defense policy documents underline "knowledge edge" as a priority in the acquisition of new equipment and systems (Department of Defence [Australia] 1997a; 1997b, 56–60). As in Britain and the United States, the effort of Australian authorities to implement a significant force modernization in an era of limited defense budgets has led to a reform of defense management influenced in part by the RBA. The report of the Defence Efficiency Review in March 1997 became the basis of the Defence Reform Program, an initiative with far-reaching consequences since it included a streamlining of the military and defense top echelons, increased jointness for the armed services, a reorganized acquisition service and other management reforms designed to produce savings that would be reinvested in new major equipment acquisitions (Defence Efficiency Review 1997; Department of Defence [Australia] 1997a). Accordingly, Australia's RMA potential in the Asia-Pacific region is second only to the United States, and equal to Japan in overall technological development capabilities, but ahead of Japan in communications and simulation technology (Dibb 1997–98, 111). Placing Australia ahead of Japan in its RMA potential may seem surprising in view of the latter's enormous economic strength, but it is an opinion that is shared by other analysts who have argued that "Japan is prevented more by political and cultural constraints than by technological ones from transforming itself into a power that can take advantage of the RMA" (Hashim 1998, 443).

Canada

The RMA has made slower progress in Canada than in Australia. In view of Canada's proximity to the United States, the integrated North American continental economy, and the long tradition of military cooperation betwen the two nations, one would have expected the RMA to have made greater inroads in Canada than has occurred so far. The Department of National Defence (DND) has been slow to explore the RMA and has failed "to identify a comprehensive strategy regarding it" (Richter 1999, 1). This general caution surrounding the RMA and its slow adoption by the Canadian forces must be attributed to a combination of factors: the general downsizing of forces and brutal reduction in defense spending; the preoccupation of the military establishment with internal reform and public relations after a series of scandals; and the Liberal government's distinct preference for low-key, low-expense, and low-intensity peacekeeping or humanitarian missions, a preference that is both ideologically and fiscally motivated.

Critics, both within DND and outside, have warned that with their present equipment, Canadian land forces would be unable to operate on a par with their U.S. or British allies in a medium-to-high intensity conflict scenario (Gongora 1998, 7). The problem of interoperability is less serious for the Canadian navy and air force: the Halifax-class patrol frigates are capable of operating in an increasingly digitized naval environment, and the CF-18 fighters have been upgraded to handle precision-guided munitions and as a result were able to take part in NATO's Operation Allied Force in 1999. There is evidence that since 1998 DND has embarked on a more serious and systematic study and planning of the RMA for

Canadian forces, for since that year several studies and reports on the subject were prepared by DND. More significantly, in 1998 an operational working group on the RMA was formed in DND (Richter 1999, 24), and the Defense Management Committee mandated a distinctly Canadian perspective on the RMA and RBA for the year 2010 and beyond (Leggat 1998).

Assessments of the prospects of a successful adoption of the RMA by Canadian forces vary considerably. On the whole, members of DND appear optimistic. They derive much of their optimism from the assumption that Canadian forces will do well as long as they buy the right U.S. equipment and can "plug" into U.S. systems (Richter 1999, 24). Some nongovernmental observers share this optimism. Shadwick notes that the diversification of defense industries into the commercial field occurred in Canada before other developed industrial economies followed the same trend. The "already-existing civil-military mix, and interactions, within Canada's high-technology sector could bode well for the RMA/RBA era" (Shadwick 1998, 7). Gongora believes that Canada's essential RMA requirements may be attainable, for Canadian forces have more modest requirements and do not have to acquire the complete range of deep and precision strike systems sought by U.S. forces (Gongora 1998, 7–8). Other analysts have taken a more skeptical view of Canada's prospects. Richter regards Britain, Australia, and Israel as being better positioned to adopt RMA strategies than Canada. The incentive to adopt RMA strategies is weakened by the fact that Canadian forces will most likely be called upon to perform peacekeeping operations or humanitarian missions where RMA technologies are less relevant. Even if Canada should decide to direct its energy and resources into the RMA field, "the prognosis is not favorable. Canada's small defence establishment, limited research and development infrastructure, and niche-oriented technology sector do not bode well for the applicability of information technologies in the defence sector" (Richter 1999, 50).

"Peer Competitors"

The second category of states affected by the RMA consists of so-called "peer competitors," notably the Russian Federation and China. In the short term at least, the term "peer" is more an honorary designation than an accurate reflection of reality, for neither Russia nor China is in a condition to challenge the United States in high-intensity conventional warfare.

Russia

The relative Russian retardation in the RMA is not without historical irony, for as Kipp and other analysts have pointed out, the concept, which dates to the late 1970s, is a Soviet invention. During his tenure as chief of the Soviet General Staff (1977–84), Marshal Nikolai Ogarkov and his deputy General Makhmut Gareev began to write about the RMA with reference to the emerging new generation of nuclear weapons and advanced high-precision conventional weapons that called for a rethinking of basic military-political and operational-strategic problems. Marshal Ogarkov was painfully aware that the new trend favored the United States with its superior technological base and thus put in doubt the hard-earned strategic parity between the Soviet Union and its U.S. rival. Ogarkov's prescience was not welcomed by his political masters and contributed to his downfall in 1984. Although Soviet military analysts had studied the new physical principles of the RMA for more than a decade, to observe its successful application during the Gulf War came as profound shock, all the more as most of the destroyed Iraqi equipment was of Soviet origin and thus underscored Russian vulnerability. As Kipp observes, the Soviet/Russian General Staff saw the Gulf War as a watershed, comparing it to the breakdown of the Napoleonic warfare paradigm in the Franco-Prussian War.

Senior Russian officers have explored the different facets of the RMA, and in particular joint operations, information warfare, and precision weapons, and how these relate to Russian national security. Despite their continuing intellectual involvement and sophisticated understanding of the RMA, actual progress in undertaking the necessary technological and organizational changes has been delayed. The West is making the transition to information societies; achieving an information society is still a distant vision for Russian reformers. Russia's ongoing internal crisis has significantly delayed the pace of reform (Kipp 1998). The immediate preoccupation of the Russian military is naturally with its mere survival as a functioning institution. This has rendered the RMA somewhat irrelevant for the present. Russian defense planners rely on nuclear deterrence to deter foreign aggression and on a constellation of military and paramilitary formations (over which their control is sometimes dubious) to provide internal security, while postponing the acquisition of modern technology until the middle of the decade (i.e. 2005).

There is general consensus among analysts that Russia is unable to implement the RMA under the present conditions (Dibb 1997–98, 108; Hashim 1998, 438–40). Russia's defense is still caught in a spiral characterized by declining military budgets, delayed force reductions and equipment acquisitions, and deteriorating readiness and morale. Consequently, it will take years to carry out the transition to a smaller volunteer force with advanced weaponry (Freedman 1998, 70). Despite this assessment, there is little reason to doubt that in time Russia will make the RMA transition. Its prized status as a great power, technological sophistication in several key sectors (e.g., reconnaissance satellites, electronic warfare, precision weapons), as well as its long-standing intellectual interest in the RMA, all point in that direction. Finally, as Kipp reminds us, there is Russia's historical tradition of belatedly adapting to foreign initiatives from a disadvantaged position by creating a distinctly Russian solution.

China

As is the case with Russia, the interest in the RMA is present and is sustained by China's determination to rank as a great power, but it is still far removed from meeting the technological or organizational conditions of membership in the RMA club. China has taken a keen interest in the RMA and information warfare since the Gulf War and there exists an extensive Chinese literature on these related subjects, which shows an increasingly distinct Chinese perspective (Thomas 1998).

But as Bi demonstrates, the interest of Chinese military thinkers in limited war, combined operations, and high-tech weapons can be dated to the 1980s, and despite a clear evolution this literature has not yet provided a comprehensive and viable operational art. The Chinese case shows that writing about the RMA need not mean being able to implement it. China lacks information technologies and precision weapons, its military scientific and technological infrastructure lags behind the West by at least a decade; and its authoritarian political culture may well preclude the adoption of new forms of organizations and of doctrines required for successfully implemening the RMA (Hashim 1998, 440; Huxley and Willett 1999, 75–76).

Despite these limitations, it is likely that in the future China will be able to incorporate certain aspects of the RMA to its advantage. Like other developing countries, China might eventually opt for a less comprehensive RMA menu designed for two purposes: to counter key U.S. systems that are essential for power projection (e.g., aircraft carrier) and information operations (e.g., AWACS and JSTARS) and to improve the PLA's regional power projection capabilities. Although China's military-industrial complex meets the PLA's basic equipment needs, many obstacles remain before it can tap the growing civilian R&D pool so essential to defense manufacturing under the RMA (Gurtov and Hwang 1998, 299–300). While China is unlikely to match the United States or Japan in RMA sophistication, its efforts and the input of Russian military technology transfers could improve the regional balance of power in its favor (Dibb 1997–98, 108).

"Niche Competitors"

The third category consists of "niche competitors" that will emerge mostly from developing countries with a reasonably sophisticated technological infrastructure and often with closed or partially closed societies. Unlike "peer competitors" whose military outreach capacity would presumably be global, "niche competitors" would operate in a regional context. Overall, developing countries may be regarded as the losers insofar as the RMA will become another contributing factor that widens the chasm between themselves and the developed world. Yet some analysts, including Rogers and Buchan, believe that rather than being the losers in the RMA sweepstakes, certain developing regional powers could become effective "niche competitors." This status could be achieved by selectively adopting some RMA technologies, combining them with conventional technologies, and developing the appropriate tactics and politico-military strategies. By engineering such a mix of technologies, countries like India, Iran, or a post-sanction Iraq might acquire a decisive advantage over any regional adversary. Beyond this achievement, "niche competitors" might even be in a position to inflict costly damage on full-scope RMA powers and thus deter U.S. attempts to project military power for limited purpose and at low cost (Cohen 1996, 53).

The key to success in becoming a "niche competitor" is a selective and imaginative combination of old and new technologies, rather than the full-scale introduction of RMA technologies, which is hardly a realistic option for developing countries. Some of the principal components of the RMA, for example, digitization, computer processing, global positioning systems, and systems integration, are readily available to anyone with money and the willingness to use them (Nye and

Owens 1996, 28). In terms of marginal utility, the gains that "niche competitors" can make "by utilizing readily available information technology may be more significant than whatever new capabilities the United States gains by riding the crest of information technology" (Libicki 1998, 414).

But other observers, particularly those who have made a systematic comparative analysis of regional powers, are more skeptical about the prospects of achieving "niche competitor" status. India has made a careful study of the Gulf War, which was particularly unsettling insofar as in size and quality India's armed forces were comparable to the defeated Iraqi forces. The pessimistic lesson from the event was that "because of its startling new technology, the United States can destroy a military force the size of India's without suffering much more than a metaphorical scratch. There is, therefore, simply no deterrent to American armed action against India" (Rikhye and Singh, 1994, 107).

Other non-Western countries who studied the Gulf War came up with an equally bleak picture about transforming their large but outdated conventional forces into smart high-technology forces capable of selectively exploiting some promising areas of the RMA (Hashim 1998, 443). Dibb strikes a similar note when he concludes that of all the countries in the Asia-Pacific region, only Australia, Japan, Singapore, and possibly Taiwan, are currently embarked on an RMA path (Dibb 1997–98, 96). For the rest of the countries of the region, the RMA is not a priority, or an available option, and they are more interested in acquiring weapon platforms rather than defense systems.

THE WAY AHEAD

A fundamental point must be reiterated in the analysis of the RMA: this revolution is shaped by the United States. U.S. defense expenditure and military R&D effort outclass those of all other great powers.[5] Perhaps we would not talk of an RMA if it were not for the United States trying to outrun itself in order to maintain the qualitative edge it enjoyed in conventional warfare during the 1990s. The RMA as a concrete phenomenon, instead of a set of technological potentialities, is therefore heavily influenced by the U.S. strategic context; notably, the necessity of developing a formula for power projection that would work under more difficult conditions than the ones found in the Gulf in 1990–91, when U.S. forces were able to get in the theater and to prepare a counteroffensive over a period of several months without any countermeasures taken by the enemy. In seeking these improved power projection capabilities, the United States does not intend to develop specific weapon systems and operational concepts that would make obsolete most of the systems in its current arsenal, since this would compromise the readiness of forces in the transition period. As a result, the United States is proceeding cautiously in the implementation of the RMA, investing in the modernization of existing types of weapon platforms and organizations rather starting from scratch. This approach falls short of what earlier analysts of the RMA would have liked to see carried out (Bracken 1993; Mazarr 1994). According to such a perspective, the current period of relative international peace could have been an opportunity to develop totally new forces and operational concepts rather than to invest in those in place.

While the dynamics of U.S. defense policy definitely shapes the configuration of the RMA in terms of technological and doctrinal developments, as well as its pace, the latter is also affected by the level of rivalry between the great powers. Historically, military technology tends to stagnate in the absence of interstate rivalries; this is why, in part, from the fifteenth to the nineteenth century, Europe, with its system of rival powers, produced more military innovations than the great empires of Asia, which tended to be more militarily conservative once established. Rivalries between states are not absent from the post–Cold War international system, but it is difficult to find, or foresee, a level of rivalry between major powers sufficient to trigger a spiral of insecurity and an age of boundless military innovation. The United States enjoys a clear edge in most indicators of power, and most of the industrial and scientific resources to develop RMA-related military technologies are based in the U.S. economy and other advanced economies whose states are allied to the United States. Remaining challengers are either nominal "peer competitors" like Russia or China, which are unlikely to pose a global challenge before at least another ten years, or "niche competitors," which could challenge the United States on a regional basis, or compete with it in a few specific military technologies. In addition, this search for the next global military challenger to the United States assumes that cycles of hegemonic struggle and their attending RMAs are inevitable; but this may not be true anymore. It is possible that the development of the international system has reached a stage where war between major powers is obsolete, and the resort to force in relations between states declines as democracy spreads over the globe (Mueller 1989; Russett 1993).

The present characterization of the RMA as an incremental process of improvements in military forces in an international environment that remains favorable to U.S. predominance is representative of the prevalent view, abroad, of the relation between the RMA and the United States. In short, the RMA would lend to the United States increased power projection capabilities at the expense of regional and great powers in Eurasia; in addition, a division of labor might emerge in which the United States would contribute high-tech capabilities such as long-range precision strike, global logistics, and information dominance, while regional allies would provide the bulk of the troops, a prospect likely to cause tensions in an alliance like NATO as pointed out before. In the United States, paradoxically, the outlook for the profits to be reaped from the RMA is often more pessimistic. Buchan and Rogers, for instance, argue that the RMA could be exploited by middle or regional powers to develop significant military capabilities, that the RMA may benefit more these powers than the United States, and that the result may be more multipolarity than U.S. leadership of world affairs. In the United States the optimistic vision of the RMA seems to give way to the nightmarish prospect of asymmetric conflicts.

Although it is true that many regional and great powers that fear U.S. military intervention will seek to adapt the RMA to the specific task of deterring and countering U.S. power projection, the United States is also working on developing its own counter-initiative to these counter-power projection strategies. The *Joint Vision 2010* doctrine, as well as some recent technological solutions for early-entry forces, clearly show that the U.S. military do not expect the next regional war to present conditions for power projection as auspicious as those found in the

Gulf conflict of 1990–91 (CJCS 1996; Hewish 1996). In this competition for maintaining, or denying, power projection, the United States is favored to a large extent because its defense effort is in a class by itself, and the post-Vietnam American military have proved their ability to innovate and to maintain a high level of intellectual competence.[6]

Asymmetries in conflict can be found at the levels of technologies and tactical combat, of strategies, and of commitment or interests. The subject is therefore vast; and it is difficult to deny its impact on the outcome of conflicts. It is also difficult, however, to generalize about the subject, because so much depends on the specifics of each category, or even instance, of asymmetry. Perhaps Freedman provides the most concise treatment of the subject when he argues that the international strategic scene is now characterized by an asymmetry in capabilities that favors more U.S. involvement in foreign conflicts; while an asymmetry of interests favors, on the contrary, a policy of noninvolvement since so few contemporary conflicts seem to put in jeopardy key U.S. interests and therefore warrant the commitment of U.S. forces with the attending risk of casualties (Freedman 1998, 34–35). This tension between conditions favorable to U.S. intervention and the absence of strategic interests worthy of putting U.S. lives at risk makes more sense of the current situation than the argument about a post-heroic age in which all decisions on U.S. intervention are determined by an overwhelming concern for U.S. casualties (Luttwak 1996).[7] Recent history shows that the American public's attitude toward military casualties is more complex than a simple aversion. It reflects a weighting of "benefits and costs" heavily influenced by the degree of consensus among the political elite (Larson 1996). In addition, as Géré points out, the preservation of human capital is a necessity for armed forces that rely on highly skilled military professionals, and this can be an additional reason for being prudent in deciding to commit troops; but it is not by itself an obstacle to action.

In conclusion, the RMA, defined as the process of transformation of weapon systems, military organizations, and operations through the integration of information technologies, has the potential to provide much improved conventional military power to the nations that can afford it. This transformative process is led by the United States and creates a host of challenges for other nations. Close allies of the United States have to join the RMA in order to maintain interoperability between their forces and those of the United States; otherwise, they face the possibility that their alliance with the United States could become more unbalanced than it is currently. Nations that perceive the RMA as a potential instrument for increased U.S. military intervention will seek to develop countermeasures to deter or defeat this improved conventional military power. The range of asymmetric responses to the RMA is very broad since it encompasses political measures, strategy, tactics, military organizational structures, and specific weapons. In practice, the variety of asymmetric responses adopted by other nations will be constrained by the need for most governments to maintain conventionally structured armed forces for the purpose of state sovereignty (defense of territory and monopoly of violence domestically). The RMA may not reach the proportions of a full-fledged military revolution in the first quarter of the twenty-first century, but it will represent a significant challenge for the defense establishments and armed forces of the world.

NOTES

1. This distinction has also been made by another colleague of Rogers, Williamson Murray, who draws the conclusion that a military revolution is a phenomenon of such scope that armed forces cannot do much but "hold on and adapt to trying and difficult times" (Murray 1997a, 72). Two other analysts, Metz and Kievit, have also underlined the difference between minor and major RMAs (the latter being what historians call military revolutions) and the fact that major RMAs cannot be controlled, instead they require a capacity for adaptation (Metz and Kievit 1995, 9–10).

2. The assertion by Buchan that conventional invasions will be less feasible in the face of smart munitions appears to contradict Rogers's assertion that the RMA is shifting the balance between offense and defense in favor of the former. This contradiction points out the limits of analysis based on offense/defense balance. While this type of reasoning makes sense in the context of a single level of analysis, for instance when applied to nuclear doctrines and strategic nuclear weapons, this notion loses some of its value in the analysis of conventional war. The fact is that it is difficult to extrapolate from the tactical balance between offense and defense to the upper levels of war. For instance, while the tactical balance between offense and defense moved in favor of the defense from the mid-nineteenth century on, leading to the strategic impasse of the Western front in 1914–17, the tactical defense was used to conduct operational and strategic offensives with success in other wars and theaters (notably the American Civil War and Franco-Prussian War). Likewise, in the initial phase of the Arab-Israeli War of 1973, the Egyptian army used the defensive capabilities of air defense and antitank missiles to lead its offensive across the Suez Canal and into the Sinai. In the present case the RMA favors the defense at the strategic and operational levels if we assume that it will be used by status quo powers to deter or defeat aggression by revisionist powers (Buchan's argument); as for the tactical balance, one could make the case that it favors offense as Rogers argues (with reference to the Gulf War).

3. The impact of information technology on corporate organizations has led to a revolution characterized by a "flattening" of organizational structures, an "informating" or digitization of management and production, and a new focus on "core competencies" that are sources of competitive advantages while other functions are outsourced (Fukuyama and Shulsky 1999).

4. The eleven countries that are both members of NATO and the EU have, as a group, a GDP roughly in the same category than the United States. In 1997, however, their defense expenditures equaled 59 percent of what the United States spent on defense (IISS 1998, 295). In 1995 Europe had three times as many defense manufacturers as the United States for a global defense equipment budget half the size of that of the United States. Similarly, four models of main battle tanks were produced in Europe compared to one in the United States, sixteen models of armored vehicles compared to three, and eleven models of frigates compared to one in the United States (Schmidt and Dussauge 1997, 78). The limited power projection capabilities of European countries is a recurrent theme in the literature on European defense (O'Hanlon 1997; Schake, Bloch-Lainé, and Grant 1999, 25–27).

5. In 1997, for instance, U.S. defense expenditure amounted to $272,955 million, which is slightly under the combined defense expenditures of NATO European countries, China, and Russia ($273,914 million) (IISS 1998, 295–97). U.S. expenditure on military R&D in 1996 ($37,000 million) was more than twice superior to the combined military R&D effort of China, France, Germany, Great Britain, Japan, and Russia ($14,090 million) (Arnett 1998, 268–69).

6. As a rough measure of the intellectual competence of the U.S. military, one can mention that 90 percent of U.S. military officers held a university degree in 1996 (DMDC 1996). Other analysts, however, think that the U.S. military still lack a firm commitment to

professional military education and a willingness to examine past military performance with objectivity (Murray 1997b; Watts and Murray 1996, 410–12).

7. The concern for military casualties, noted by many analysts as a key feature of contemporary U.S. defense policy, or even of defense policy-making in all contemporary democracies, has in fact a long history in U.S. strategic culture. In the 1840s Dennis Hart Mahan, the military thinker who influenced the generation of officers who fought the American Civil War, argued that the offensive tactical doctrine prevailing at the time in Europe was inappropriate to the U.S. Army, notably because its disregard for life would be inacceptable in a military system where soldiers were also voters (Hagerman 1988, 9). This concern for waging war with as few casualties as possible became a feature of U.S. military leadership, strategy, and tactics to a much greater extent than in other Western armies in the nineteenth and twentieth centuries. Nevertheless, this concern did not prevent Americans from participating in several wars and from sustaining high casualties in some battles during these two centuries.

2

"Military Revolutions" and "Revolutions in Military Affairs": A Historian's Perspective

Clifford J. Rogers

A few years ago I edited a collection of essays entitled *The Military Revolution Debate* (Rogers 1995a), which dealt with various aspects and interpretations of Michael Roberts's famous thesis on the radical changes in European warfare that took place in the sixteenth and seventeenth centuries. I was a little surprised when the first review of the book came out in a journal that usually does not emphasize the military history of that era—*Airpower Journal*. Not long thereafter, the volume was also reviewed by Eliot Cohen in *Foreign Affairs*, another publication that usually has a somewhat more contemporary focus (Cohen 1995; Petersen 1995).

The reviews themselves made it pretty clear why airpower historians and students of current foreign policy have taken such an interest in the book: because of the vigorous ongoing debate about the putative "revolution in military affairs" or "RMA," which many believe we entered with the Gulf War, when stealth technology, precision-guided munitions, and other military applications of advanced computer technology seem to have made a fundamental change in the very nature of warfare. Mindful of Thucydides' observation that the future will resemble the past, even though it will not reflect it, political scientists have therefore been eager to find historical precedents for this RMA, the study of which ought to bring valuable insights to the analysis of the military present and future. Since some of the best historians in the business have now spent more than four decades investigating "the Military Revolution," which Michael Roberts argued took place between 1560 and 1660, and have produced an extensive and important body of scholarship on the subject, it is only natural that this material has generated so much interest from people not otherwise much concerned with the geometry of the *trace italienne* style of fortification or the tactical reforms of Maurice of Nassau.[1]

Some military historians with an interest in twentieth-century developments, like Andrew Krepinevich, have also made significant contributions to this discourse. Building in part on my idea (Rogers 1995b) that the development of Western military might over the years since 1300 has followed a pattern similar to the biological model of punctuated equilibrium evolution (i.e., with long periods of gradual, incremental evolution punctuated by episodes of short, sharp, radical change), Krepinevich (1994b) has proposed a long series of RMAs, each of which potentially offers valuable insights into the current military transformation:

- Infantry Revolution (fourteenth century);
- Artillery Revolution (fifteenth century);
- Fortress Revolution (sixteenth century);
- Revolution of Sail & Shot (sixteenth century);
- "The" Military Revolution (seventeenth century; linear warfare);
- Napoleonic Revolution;
- Land Warfare Revolution (railroads and rifles; American Civil War through World War I);
- Naval Revolution (circa 1850–World War I) (engine-powered steel ships, etc.);
- Interwar Revolutions in Mechanization, Aviation, and Information;
- Nuclear Revolution.

MILITARY REVOLUTIONS AND REVOLUTIONS IN MILITARY AFFAIRS

What I propose to do here is not to elaborate my own version of such a list, nor to expound on the punctuated equilibrium evolution model, nor yet to focus on the current RMA in the light of its predecessors (though I will do some of that at the end). Rather, I want to suggest a distinction between "RMAs" and "Military Revolutions," and to highlight some of the questions and issues that such a perspective brings to the foreground. Let me begin with definitions. To my mind, an RMA is simply a revolutionary change in how war is fought—a change that can often be recognized by the ease with which "participating" armed forces can defeat "nonparticipating" ones. An often-cited example is the blitzkrieg style of warfare developed by the Germans in the interwar period and unleashed against Poland and France in 1939–40 with startling consequences (Doughty 1998; Fitzsimonds and van Tol 1994, 25, 29).

Some, but by no means all, RMAs have extremely wide-ranging implications for social, economic, and political structures, balances of power, and other areas outside the realm of the armed forces. A good example is the Artillery Revolution of the early fifteenth century (Rogers 1995b).[2] A mass of technical improvements created gunpowder artillery capable of knocking down the walls of the castles and fortified towns that dominated the military geography of medieval Europe, thus reversing the balance between offense and defense in siege warfare, which had formerly been strongly weighted against the attacker. The implications of this tactical-level military change rippled out a very long way, both within and outside of the conduct of war. First, somewhat ironically, this radical improvement in the craft of siege warfare led to a great relative decline in the importance of sieges and a complementary rise in the decisiveness of field battles. Before the Artillery Revolution, as Pierre DuBois wrote at the opening of the fourteenth century, "[a] castle can hardly be taken within a year, and even if it does fall, it means more expenses for the king's purse and for his subjects than the conquest is worth. Because of these lengthy, dangerous and arduous sieges, and because battle and assaults can be avoided, leaders are apt to come to agreements which are unfavorable to the stronger party" (DuBois 1936, 3; Verbruggen 1997, 306).

After the Artillery Revolution newly vulnerable stone walls no longer gave weak armies great leverage with which to resist strong ones. This was noted by Francesco Guicciardini when the Artillery Revolution was brought to Italy by Charles VIII in 1494. The Florentine historian observed that the slowness and uncertainty of siege warfare had once made it almost impossible to dispossess the ruler of a state; but now that improved artillery had taken the art of war and "turned it upside-down, as if by a sudden storm," and "the siege and taking of a city became extremely rapid and achieved not in months but in days and hours," victory on the battlefield became tantamount to victory in war, for "whenever the open country was lost, the state was lost with it" (Guiccardini 1964, 20; Parker 1988, 10). Since small states usually found it impossible to resist large ones in open battle, leaders were no longer "apt to come to agreements which are unfavorable to the stronger party."

Thus the strategic as well as the tactical balance in siege warfare was shifted in favor of the offensive. Both these changes brought great advantages to the few powers with the resources to maintain both large siege trains and also powerful armies spearheaded by a substantial element of professional soldiers serving in permanent standing formations like the *compagnies d'ordonnance* instituted in France and Burgundy in the late fifteenth century. This, in turn, effected a major change in the political relationship between the "core" and the "periphery" in much of Europe, that is, between the apparatus of the central state and regional interests and local powers that often opposed it. The threat of rebellion lost much of its force, because it no longer "mean[t] more expenses for the king's purse and his subjects than the conquest is worth" to put down a rebellion. This led to what S. E. Finer called a "coercion-extraction cycle," with the central state using its military might to extract more tax revenues from unwilling provinces, and then using the new tax revenues to purchase a further increment of armed power, and so on (Finer 1975, 96). Philip de Commines, writing at the time, recognized part of this circular dynamic when he referred to "a prince who is powerful and has a large standing army, by the help of which he can raise money to pay his troops" (de Commines 1906, 387), though he did not make the connection between the Artillery Revolution and the coercive power of a standing army. The same considerations also changed the balance between the emerging large nation-states and their smaller or more divided neighbors, for the latter, too, lost the ability to rely on the strength of the passive defense to defeat the offensive drives of their more powerful adversaries. Thus, by the early sixteenth century (when the introduction of the *trace italienne* fortress again reversed the balance between offense and defense in siege warfare), the royal government of France had reasserted its control over Normandy, Gascony, Brittany, and Burgundy and invaded Italy, which had also been entered by the other two European "gunpowder empires"—Spain, which had just used a French-style artillery train to complete the five-hundred-year *reconquista* of Iberia by driving the Moors out of the strongholds of Granada, and the Ottoman Empire, which had made good use of massive bombards and a huge army in conquering its neighbors on all sides, including the massively fortified capital of the Byzantine Empire in 1453 (Cook 1993; McNeill 1982, 95–99).

So, out of the small seed of technical and tactical changes in siege warfare, there emerged (by a process of gross simplification, no doubt) the centrally governed nation-state, equipped with a large standing army and provided with greatly increased revenues; and also the beginnings of the modern European map, with a united France, an insular England, a Christian Iberia, and a religiously and ethnically mixed Balkans. When an RMA bears consequences on this scale, I term it a true Military Revolution.

The question that immediately presents itself is whether the current RMA is, in fact, the start of a full Military Revolution. The importance of that question should be obvious. While contemporaries have fairly frequently been able to recognize RMAs as they happened, they have rarely if ever been able to anticipate the scale or the direction of the consequences that transform some RMAs into Military Revolutions, perhaps because the broader concept is a recent invention. The value of doing so for the next Military Revolution, however, would be proportionate to the magnitude of the changes initiated by it, which would by definition be very great. A study of past RMAs that did or did not become Military Revolutions should provide some approaches to take and highlight some questions to ask as we try to determine which category our present RMA falls into. Such a study should also help us understand and anticipate in what direction this most recent RMA might take us if it is, in fact, one of the greater upheavals like the Infantry Revolution of the fourteenth century or the Artillery Revolution of the fifteenth.

Let us start by considering some RMAs that remained largely limited to the domain of Mars. Possible examples of this phenomenon include the adoption of smaller bronze cannon firing cast-iron balls in France in the second half of the fifteenth century, the tactical reforms of Maurice of Nassau and Gustavus Adolphus, the adoption of the flintlock musket and socket bayonet at the end of the seventeenth century, the switch to the Minié ball rifle in the 1840s–1860s, the further switch to breech-loading cartridge rifles from the 1860s, and, as already noted, the development of the blitzkrieg. This list is limited to land warfare, but other RMAs could easily be adduced for naval and air warfare—the introduction of the ironclad or the dreadnought, for example, or of radar.

It may at first seem strange that I have headed this roster of RMAs with the changes in late-fifteenth century artillery, when I had already used the Artillery Revolution of the fifteenth century as an example of a true Military Revolution. The contradiction is apparent rather than real, however, and in fact this is an excellent illustration of the difference between the two categories. The Artillery Revolution, the full military revolution, occurred in the *early* fifteenth century (in the decades on either side of 1430), when giant stone-throwing bombards, using newly developed corned powder and manufactured with longer barrels than fourteenth-century guns, became capable of knocking down castle walls with relative speed and ease. The consequences of this overturning of the balance between offense and defense have already been dealt with above.

Between twenty and forty years after this set of developments, artillery design underwent another period of rapid improvement. It was discovered that cast bronze muzzle-loaders were structurally much stronger than the wrought-iron "hoop and staves" guns that had effected the Artillery Revolution. Thus, they could, without bursting, handle a stronger charge of powder, one that took full advantage of the potential of corned powder and that, furthermore, could effectively propel a dense cast-iron ball. Since iron has roughly triple the specific gravity of stone, that meant that a given size (bore) of cannon could now strike with triple the kinetic energy of its stone-firing predecessor. Rather than using this change to construct massive bombards firing five-ton iron balls, European gunsmiths emphasized relatively smaller cannons that retained much of the "punch" of the larger bombards but because of their size were much easier and faster to transport, and could be manufactured in larger quantities. These guns were also cast with trunnions, which made it possible for them to be used with modern gun-carriages, which were easier to maneuver, quick to deploy, and could be pulled by smaller teams of horses. Siege trains thus gained increased effectiveness and much-enhanced mobility (Dubled 1976). It was guns of this sort with which Charles VIII took Italy by storm in 1494. Yet, though these changes dramatically changed the craft of the artillerist, were unambiguously far superior to the older style, and made it possible for commanders to conduct campaigns of conquest with greater speed and on a larger scale than previously possible, the basic difference they made was nothing so fundamental as "the new guns can knock down walls; the old ones couldn't." (They did have somewhat of that effect in Italy, but that was essentially a matter of the Artillery Revolution finally reaching the peninsula, rather than a consequence of the switch from bombards to bronze cannon.) Thus, though they might qualify as having effected an RMA (perhaps only barely), the new bronze guns certainly did not bring about a Military Revolution.

The adoption of the flintlock musket and the socket bayonet is another good example of an RMA that was not a Military Revolution. The flintlock was a weapon far superior to the matchlock it replaced (Boyle 1677, 30–31, 38). It took some forty-four individual movements to load and ready a matchlock, so that a soldier could probably fire only once per ninety seconds or so. The flintlock greatly simplified this procedure by replacing the slow-burning fuse or "match" with a flint-and-steel mechanism as the agent of ignition, a change that at least doubled, and probably tripled, the rate of fire the typical infantryman could achieve. About the same time as the flintlock came into general use, Europe saw the invention and spread of the socket bayonet, which gave fusiliers the ability to resist cavalry attacks without the support of the pikemen who had until then been provided for that purpose (Black 1994, 39–41; Mork 1967, 37–46; Nosworthy 1990, 39–44).[3] Once the pikemen in a unit (typically 33 percent of the formation in the 1670s) (Boyle 1677, 24–25)[4] were rearmed with flintlocks, a given number of soldiers could thus deliver around four times as much fire as an equivalent unit of pikemen and matchlock musketeers.[5] This dramatically increased rapidity of fire made it possible to make infantry formations much thinner without compromising the ability to deliver constant fire along the front. By the mid-eighteenth century, the typical line of infantry had shrunk from ten deep to just three or four deep.[6] The elimination of the pikemen also greatly changed the tactical problems faced by the small-unit commander, the organization of formations, and the appearance of the battle. For a variety of technical reasons, the change from matchlock to flintlock also increased the extent to which drill could speed up firing, giving a major advantage to the best-trained and most-drilled troops, like the feared Prussian infantry of Frederick the Great. Where troops armed with flintlocks and bayonets came up against troops still employing matchlocks, the former were sometimes successful even against heavy odds—as with Eugene of Savoy's victories over the Ottomans.[7] Thus, by the definition suggested above, the change could be seen as an RMA.

Despite all this, however, it is difficult to identify any really significant changes off the battlefield caused by the adoption of the flintlock. Despite Jeremy Black's suggestion to the contrary,[8] it did not (by my definition, at least) cause any sort of Military Revolution within Europe, though it could be argued that it at least contributed to a revolution in the military balance between "the West and the rest." Still, a general historian of Europe presented with the details of a "flintlock RMA" might well be forgiven for asking "so what?"

One reason for the limited impact of the advance to flintlocks, and to cast-bronze muzzle-loaders, is that each of these developments *reinforced* rather than *reversed* the standing balance between offense and defense. Ever since the battles of Pavia and la Biccoca in the early sixteenth century, it had been clear to most European generals that a frontal attack on a prepared enemy meant horrendous losses to the enemy's firepower; this was one of the primary factors contributing to the defense-minded and maneuver-driven campaigns typical of the "age of limited warfare." Increases in firepower tend normally to favor the defense (since a motionless and often partially covered defender can employ that firepower much more effectively than can a soldier marching forward in an attack), and so the introduction of the flintlock simply reinforced this tendency—at least when it was a question of flintlock-armed army against flintlock-armed army. Similarly, the predominance of attack over defense in siege warfare initiated by the development of really effective bombards in the early-mid-fifteenth century was strengthened rather than challenged by the developments in artillery that came later in the century (before being reversed a few decades later by the introduction of the *trace italienne*). This suggests that one of the first questions we should ask of a new technology or technique that seems to have made the old style of warfare obsolete is whether it represents a difference in direction or just one in degree.

Jean de Bloch (also known as Ivan or Jan Bloch), a Polish "defense intellectual" writing at the turn of the twentieth century, considered the advent of the flat-trajectory, smokeless powder magazine rifle to be a genuinely revolutionary development (de Bloch 1993, 2, 11, 17, 28, 39, 120). The new rifles, he argued, would have had a radical effect on tactics, command and control, and even recruitment, because the extended range and lethality they brought to the battlefield demanded dispersed troop formations rather than dense attack lines, and this in turn required a different style of leader and a different type of soldier, one with more independence and intelligence. Even if adaptations of this sort were made, however, he considered that the new weapons made it impossible for direct attacks against a dug-in enemy to succeed without cripplingly high casualties. Thus, he thought, (though he did not use the precise term) there was a true Military Revolution coming, for the exceedingly high costs of aggressive victory made offensive strategy irrational, and so made war unlikely or even impossible (de Bloch 1993, 2–3, 20–22). Of course, despite the solid logic of his case, *every* major belligerent in the First World War went on the offensive in 1914: the Germans launched the Schlieffen Plan; the French Plan XVII led them to make a doomed attack into southern

Germany; the Russians attacked East Prussia; the Austrians attacked Russia (Howard 1986). In the East, where the space-to-troops ratio was higher, the offensives were sometimes successful, but in the West, after the initial run of the Germans' Great Wheel, the defensive strength of the cartridge rifle fired from entrenchments soon proved itself every bit as great as de Bloch had predicted. In 1915 the "Massacre of the Innocents" [*Kindermord*] at Ypres and the disastrous French offensives in Arras and Champagne wrote out that lesson in rivers of blood. And yet, in 1916, 1917, and 1918, great offensives at the Somme, Verdun, Passchendaele, and so forth, continued to be the order of the day.

If de Bloch had reflected a little more deeply on the American Civil War and the Franco-Prussian War, he might have anticipated this seeming paradox of perversity (as some contemporary commentators on his thought did).[9] In those two wars, which saw the first massive struggles between armies equipped with, respectively, rifled muskets and breech-loading rifles, the great difficulty and extraordinarily high cost of frontal assaults against entrenched enemies had already been well demonstrated, from Malvern Hill, Gettysburg, and Cold Harbor to Gravelotte-St. Privat—as de Bloch was well aware. Yet in each of those cases the side with the larger army had proven willing to suffer those losses, to make attack after attack despite the casualty rates, and eventually had been able to secure an aggressive victory regardless of the tactical superiority of the defense. The same was true after the Minié ball had given way to the rimfired brass smokeless powder cartridge: in the Russo-Japanese war and the Balkan Wars of the early twentieth century, victory went to the more aggressive side, though it came at horrendously high cost in blood. The tactical "revolution" of the magazine rifle was thus essentially one of "the same, only much more so," and so the strategic/political level Military Revolution anticipated by de Bloch did not appear.

Of course, the impact of the improvements in the infantryman's arms would have been much greater if any one nation or group of nations had been able to maintain a monopoly over them. The Crimean War offered various examples of the ways in which one-sided enjoyment of a superior technology could make it possible for the possessor to accomplish military feats that would otherwise have been impossible. French and English troops armed with Minié ball rifles were able to storm successfully positions that would have been impregnable if the Russians too had been so equipped. If the Russians had been able to employ steam power with anything like the effectiveness of the Allies, then there is little possibility that the expeditionary forces could have won the war. Yet such technically based advantages have almost invariably been very short-lived, as the defeated side and anyone else paying attention has scrambled to adopt or adapt the "revolutionary" technology.

Thus, another important question to ask about an RMA is how easily it can be copied by those who are initially disadvantaged by it. Assuming the blitzkrieg was indeed an RMA, it nonetheless had no chance to effect a lasting Military Revolution, because it was adapted and adopted by all the great powers within a very few years after its introduction. The fourteenth-century Infantry Revolution, by contrast, gave a long-standing advantage to certain nations—for example, the English and the Swiss—to the cost of other powers, such as France, who could not or would not copy her neighbors' innovations because of the extraneous (i.e., nonmilitary) implications of making the nation's defense dependent on the armed populace. The government of Charles VI of France, for example, began a program of encouraging the common people to practice with the longbow or crossbow, but then canceled the effort when the King realized that the common archers "if they had been gathered together, would have been more powerful than the princes and nobles" (Juvenal des Ursins 1838, 385). The more intimately an RMA is intertwined with particular social, political, or economic structures, the more difficult it will be to replicate and the more likely it will be to develop into a true military revolution. This helps explain why RMAs like the Infantry Revolution or the French Revolution that are *not* based primarily on technological innovations are significantly more likely to be true Military Revolutions, causing changes that are extended rather than extinguished by the spread of the revolution.

Recent work on historical RMAs—Krepinevich's article, for example—has tended to focus on the victories won or defeats suffered because one or another nation has succeeded or failed in making the military adjustments necessary to exploit a new weapon, tactical system, or style of warfare. This is certainly a subject worthy of study, because even if (as seems often to be the case) such "monopoly" RMAs are very fleeting, rarely lasting beyond a single war (if even that long), nonetheless the outcome of that single war is no trivial matter for the nations involved. For an RMA to become a Military Revolution, however, it must make changes that endure beyond the monopoly period, that have great effects on the nature of war *among* militaries who have already adopted the new warfighting techniques on both sides. The advantage brought to the offensive over the defensive, and the strong over the weak, by the Artillery Revolution, for example, applied equally whether only the aggressor possessed the new artillery or whether both sides did. The Duchy of Burgundy was one of the leaders in the new technology, indeed was *the* leader (DeVries 1998; Garnier 1895), but this was largely irrelevant in a consideration of the impact of effective artillery on the balance of power between the Duchy and the Kingdom of France, because the key effect of the Artillery Revolution was to change the basic ways in which military strength was measured and compared. Before the Artillery Revolution, fortifications and a "negative aim" (to use Clausewitz's term for a defensive intent) were arguably even more important components of strength than a large and well-trained army, but after the Artillery Revolution, because fortresses no longer gave a small army such great leverage to resist a large one, the size and quality of the field army, the ability to prevail in open battle, became crucial. Thus, whether or not the Duchy had a large, powerful, up-to-date siege train, whether or not, indeed, that siege train was superior to the one possessed by the King of France, the relative size and wealth of the two entities meant that the Artillery Revolution put the Duchy at a relative disadvantage. Similarly, the harnessing of the whole nation to the purposes of war that emerged from the French Revolution fundamentally changed the balance of power between large, populous states such as France and smaller ones such as Prussia, and this differentiation endured even after Prussian reforms remodeled the Hohenzollern army some distance along French lines. The military consequences of the French revolution made small states relatively insignificant in the European system—no more could the Netherlands be a great power, as in the time of the Eighty Years' War, nor Sweden as in the Thirty Years' War, nor even Prussia as in the Seven

Years' War. (It is true that Prussia defeated the much more populous Austrian Empire in 1866, but this was in large part due to a brief monopoly RMA advantage, in that the Prussians had the breech-loading Dreyse needle guns, which fired much faster than the Austrian muzzle-loaders and—even more importantly—could be fired from a prone position [Wagner 1899, 122–24]. Even with that advantage, the Prussians in 1866 could not have held off Russia, Austria, and France combined, as they had done in the Seven Years' War.) Only in the later nineteenth century, as parts of the unified nation-states of Germany and Italy, could smaller powers like Prussia or Sardinia regain their influence on the international stage. When we look at the current RMA, it may be more important to think about how it will affect global balances of power *after* its components have been universally adopted than to worry about who will get an initial advantage during its emergence.

A related issue is the question of whether or how an RMA alters the balance of military power *within* a participating society—in other words, how an RMA changes the answer to the query "Who fights?" The most obvious example would be the Infantry Revolution of the fourteenth century (Rogers 1995b, 58–64). After the victory of the Flemish militiamen at Courtrai in 1302, infantry forces composed of soldiers drawn from the common people (as opposed to the martial aristocracy) rapidly came to dominate the battlefields of Western Europe. The Scots, imitating the Flemings, demolished the chivalry of England at Bannockburn in 1314; the English then adopted the Scottish practice of fighting on foot and destroyed a French army at Crécy in 1346; by Poitiers ten years later even the French normally fought on foot (Gray 1836, 142; le Baker 1889, 143). Men-at-arms drawn from the gentry and nobility continued to play a very important military role (acting as cavalry during a campaign, but almost invariably dismounting for battle), but now they shared the martial limelight with men of the lower classes. This was rather less true in France than elsewhere, because, as noted above, the French monarchy recognized that such a shift in military enfranchisement inevitably would bring a shift in political strength, and so the French kings impeded the progress of the Infantry Revolution in France (and partly in consequence suffered a long string of grim battlefield defeats, from Crécy and Poitiers to Agincourt and Verneuil). In England, Switzerland, Scotland, and the Low Countries, on the other hand, the rising military importance of the commons did indeed contribute greatly to the growth of what by medieval standards were "democratic" institutions, such as the House of Commons in England. The Commons met as a separate body for the first time in 1332, just after the battle of Dupplin Moor, the first of the great battlefield victories won primarily by English archery; by the 1350s (after Crécy), the Commons had gained parliamentary powers at least equal to those of the Lords; and in the 1420s (in a reaction to an obtaining system that was even more wide open) the property qualification that entitled a freeman to vote in Parliamentary elections was set at £2 of land income per year, a remarkably low level (less than a semi-skilled laborer might earn in a year) that was, however, identical to the level that, by the Statute of Winchester, obliged a man to own a bow and serve in the royal host as a foot archer when summoned (Rogers 1995b). There was clearly a strong connection there between military and political participation. Just so, the rise of the hoplite phalanx in the seventh century B.C. led directly to the political rise of the small-farmer class from which the hoplites were drawn (and of the "tyrants" they supported) at the cost of the aristocrats who had up until then dominated Greek society—and warfare (Andrewes 1956, 31–38; Forrest 1966, 94–97, 104–5).[10]

The French Revolution had a similar effect. The massive broadening of military participation in French society was a concomitant of the extension of political franchise to the populace; neither could have survived without the other.[11] An opposite case would be the Norman expansion of the eleventh century, which was so rapid, so extensive, and accomplished by so few men that it might well be accounted an RMA (Douglas 1969). Over less than half a century, Norman knights extended their sway over England, Calabria, Apulia, Sicily, and Palestine. Military power was concentrated into the hands of a relatively small number of men who could afford the costly warhorses and the expensive armor and equipment of the knight, and these same knights grasped more and more power in society at the cost of the lowest (and to an extent the highest) strata of society. The general pattern, in other words, is that *ceteris paribus* changes in "who fights" (very often changes sparked by technological or tactical innovations) will lead more or less directly to corresponding changes in "who rules" (Andreski 1968).

CONCLUSION

So then, we have before us a number of questions to address to the current RMA. First, does it involve a military "change in direction" or is it rather "the same only more so?" Will it mainly be important during the interval in which it can be used as a monopoly advantage, or does it involve changes that will continue to be of great significance even after it has been adopted on all sides? Does it change the balance between offense and defense? Between small states and large, populous ones? Does it change the balance of the components that must be considered in order to assess a nation's military strength? How readily can it be copied or adapted by current "nonparticipants"; to what extent will that require changes in their social, cultural, or economic structures as opposed to just their military ones? Does it mean a major difference in the answer to the question "who fights" within a society? In sum, are we seeing a mere RMA or the start of a true Military Revolution?

Since my area of expertise is really fourteenth- and fifteenth-century military history, it would doubtless be wise of me to leave the answers to those questions to people who know more than I do about current developments in military technology. On the other hand, my more distant perspective on the current RMA may give me a certain advantage in seeing the forest rather than the trees. So, with that *caveat lector*, I will venture a few thoughts on the subject.

In my opinion, the current RMA is indeed likely to become a full Military Revolution. It seems to have all the key ingredients. First, judging by the Gulf War (and even taking into account the many peculiar factors that separate that conflict from any we are likely to see in the near future), the new style of warfare does not seem to be a case of "the same only more so." A case for the opposite viewpoint could certainly be made—for example, noting that there were more PGMs dropped during the Vietnam War than during the Gulf War, that stealth technology could be seen as "ECM only more so," and so on. It seems to me that those points, however, only illustrate that the current *revolution* in military affairs, like all others, is built on a long foundation of *evolutionary* change. Furthermore, the Vietnam War, like the other wars of the twentieth century, was fundamentally a ground war, in which airpower was an extremely important auxiliary to the land forces, but still an auxiliary nonetheless. Perhaps, as a nonspecialist in this area, I have been misled by the "CNN version" of the war, but it does seem to me that we may finally have reached the stage that airpower enthusiasts from Douhet onwards have constantly, if heretofore inaccurately, proclaimed: the point at which airpower surpasses land power as the *primary* determinant of victory or defeat in warfare. This is not to say that armies will be unimportant in the new military environment, any more than the Infantry Revolution made cavalry insignificant, or the French Revolution made standing armies of professional soldiers unnecessary. Yet if it proves true that airpower (including cruise missiles, attack helicopters, etc.) surpasses armor and infantry forces as the decisive element in future wars, that will clearly represent a change in direction rather than being just "the same only more so."[12]

It is obvious that Allied airpower in the Gulf was so effective in part because it was able to act virtually unopposed by the Iraqi air force. The war would certainly have been very different (as future wars presumably will be very different) if *both* sides had possessed stealth technology, precision cruise missiles, JSTARS, and the other high-tech components of the current RMA. Still, I do not think we are looking at a case like the Seven Weeks' War of 1866, where one-sided employment of a key new military technology led to a decisive victory, but also led to the immediate adoption of the new technology (breech-loading rifles) by the defeated side and essentially to a restoration of the previously obtaining military environment. It is difficult to imagine what the first war fought on both sides by participants in the current RMA will be like, but I can see little prospect of its being in any sense a restoration of the military status quo ante.

One reason for this conclusion is that the new technologies deployed in the Gulf War imply a major change between the offense and the defense, just as did the Artillery Revolution of the fifteenth century. In general in warfare, increases in sheer firepower tend to favor the defense, while advances in speed, mobility, and surprise favor the offense (Clausewitz 1984, 357–93, 523–28). Airpower is an inherently offensive component of military force, partly because it can largely ignore terrain (one of the greatest sources of strength for the defensive in land warfare), and partly because of its speed. Airplanes effectively hidden by stealth technology share the great offensive advantages possessed by all planes in preradar days (Brodie 1965, 85–87; Douhet [1942] 1983, 8–9, 16–19, 52–55). Missiles, too, have these advantages and have long had them without greatly impacting the actual *conduct* of war; the difference now is that precision-guided missiles have plenty of impact combined with enough discrimination to make their use politically acceptable.[13] It is possible to imagine new technologies like orbiting directed-energy weapons that could conceivably reverse this situation just as radar reversed the otherwise probably insurmountable advantage of the offense in air warfare, but barring some such radical development it is likely that the reduced effectiveness of the defense and the increased advantages to be gained by surprise attacks in starting wars will be key elements of the developing Military Revolution.[14]

Another reason why the current RMA seems likely to develop into a full Military Revolution is that it does imply a change in the fundamental components of military power. For quite a long time now, indeed arguably ever since the American and French Revolutions, the two most important components of a nation's warfighting potential have been its population and the strength of its economy; the size and skill of its standing forces have been somewhat less important, though of course still quite important and in some cases decisive. The emerging style of warfare strongly emphasizes quality over quantity, that is to say, it greatly increases the importance of the standing forces as opposed to the population as a whole, and of the high-tech sector of the economy as opposed to the economy as a whole. This is all the more true because the standing forces have always been of greater importance in short wars than in long ones, and the current RMA, with its emphasis on the offensive and on surprise attacks, will likely increase the prevalence of short, sharp wars (like the Six-Day War or the Hundred Hours phase of the Gulf War) over drawn-out contests of national strength and determination like the World Wars. This opens up the possibility for smaller, more militaristic states to play in the military major leagues (even in offensive wars rather than defensive ones) in a way they have generally not been able to do since the French Revolution, provided of course that they have a higher proportion of their economies in the high-tech sectors and are willing to invest higher proportions of their GNP in standing military forces. This should tend to break the military dominance of the superpowers (including potential superpowers like China and Russia) in favor of a broader group of "great powers," as in the pre–World War II world.

The problems posed for the defense by the new technologies may also prove, rather counterintuitively, to favor the small over the large, the weak over the strong. There are two basic reasons for this. The first is the increased importance of surprise, which is a commodity equally available to large and small powers; thus its relatively greater significance means a relatively smaller portion of the military equation in which strong powers have the advantage over weak ones (assuming both possess the new technologies).

The second is that, like nuclear weapons, precision-guided cruise missiles and stealth aircraft make it very difficult for even the "winning" side in a war to prevent serious harm to its home front. In land warfare a strong aggressor may hope to push all the fighting into enemy territory and keep its own rear essentially inviolate, but between two participants in the current RMA this will not be the case. It may be that, again like nuclear weapons, this will reduce the usefulness of military force (or the threat of military force) as an instrument of aggressive policy, because a powerful nation that might be willing to risk its troops in pursuit of a foreign policy goal might not be willing to risk its power grid, its transportation system hubs, its defense industrial and research facilities, its computer networks (assuming that these too are easier to attack than to defend), and so on. On the other hand, similar considerations may lead to increased use of military force by nations who are willing to accept the political costs of launching surprise attacks in pursuit of aggressive aims; this in turn suggests that one of our key priorities in "managing" the coming military revolution should be to increase the political costs of such actions by strengthening and emphasizing the world community's opposition to such actions.

Let us now look at the coming Military Revolution from a somewhat broader perspective, viewing stealth technology, cruise missiles, precision guidance systems, and associated developments as just specific examples of the more fundamental basis of the revolution—the application of information technology to warfare—so that we also include advanced biotechnology and "information warfare" as elements of the new style of warfare. We can then immediately see two other ways in which the coming Military Revolution will be likely to change the basic components of national military power. First, warfare based on biotechnology and computer programming would require extraordinarily low capital investment (relative to the costs of aircraft carriers and B-2 bombers). This is another aspect of the shift from quantity to quality, and therefore another factor that will tend to favor the small against the large. If the Taiwanese military were by chance to assemble a team of a half-dozen extraordinarily talented computer programmers and put them to work on developing computer viruses, for example, they might conceivably be able to gain a degree of "military" power disproportionate to Taiwan's economy, population, natural resources, economic strength, and so forth (i.e., the traditional measures of national strength). Biotechnology, more frighteningly, offers similar possibilities for states relatively poor in material resources. Note how this conception requires a certain readjustment of what we understand by the term "military," though I think the requirement is justified. Second, these same possibilities illustrate how the institutions that advance, develop, and distribute *knowledge* will come to play a more and more important role in determining a nation's power. This suggests that another key step in managing the coming Military Revolution will be to add even more emphasis to education, and especially to university systems, as vital to national defense as well as to economic prosperity.

The increased importance of intellectual versus material resources in the new military environment may perhaps turn out to be a barrier to the worldwide expansion of the current RMA, one that could favor the Western democracies much as the Infantry Revolution favored England, Flanders, and Switzerland relative to France. Just as the French monarchy refused to embrace the Infantry Revolution because of its political implications, so it may be that authoritarian governments may be unwilling to take the steps required to develop the vibrant intellectual environment necessary to full participation in the Information Revolution and its military concomitant. Perhaps I am being naive, but it seems to me that there is a certain independence of mind and intellectual flexibility demanded in the computer sciences that would be fundamentally problematic for authoritarian regimes to cultivate.

Finally, we come to the question of "who fights." As already noted, the general tendency of the new style of warfare seems to be to emphasize the role of the standing military, which has the highly technical and specific skills to manage modern instruments of violence. As already noted, the general historical pattern is that those who fight also rule—in class terms at least, if not in individual ones. Thus, in the twentieth century, when governments have had to enlist the participation of their entire nations in order to fight wars, the state has almost invariably set itself up as the champion of the masses (whether via democratic institutions, "National Socialism," or "People's Republics"). In America the need for the contributions of women and African Americans in the two World Wars does much to explain the success of the suffrage and civil rights movements (though of course the connections are complex ones). Does this mean that if we move to a world of armies in which conscript infantrymen are of little importance, while highly educated professionals are the key element of victorious militaries, that there will be less and less pressure on governments to make sure the poor and uneducated are included in the national consensus? Does it suggest that the growing amount of room for women in the armed forces will provide a continuing impetus for women's equal rights? I will not venture to attempt an answer to those questions, but I think they are worthy of consideration. I would also suggest that there is somewhat of an inherent tendency for standing armies to separate themselves more and more from their civilian societies, and that over the past two centuries one of the strongest countervailing forces has been the armies' awareness that in major wars they would have to accommodate large numbers of "recent civilians" and incorporate them into the military structure. The coming Military Revolution will tend to undermine that countervailing force and may therefore contribute to what some observers already consider a developing trend of increasing divergence between the armed forces and the civilian world. This is a possibility that needs watching.

In sum, there seems to be a good chance that the current military developments stemming from advances in information technology will be the start of a genuine Military Revolution—an epoch-making change in the nature of warfare with consequences extending to social structures, and to the ways in which states measure, acquire, and utilize power, consequences that will endure after the monopoly phase of the Revolution in Military Affairs has passed. In thinking about the impact of new technologies, we should not focus just on ensuring that we are the first to adopt them or the most successful at adapting to them; we should also think about how they will affect the balance between offense and defense, between strong states and weak ones, and so on, *after* they have become tools widely available in the world military environment. Forewarned may in the long run be even more important than forearmed.

NOTES

My thanks to Thierry Gongora and Fred Kagan for thought-provoking comments on drafts of this paper. The views expressed herein are those of the author and do not purport to reflect the position of the United States Military Academy, the Department of the Army, or the Department of Defense.

1. For the scholarship on the early modern Military Revolution, see the essays in Rogers (1995a).

2. It should be noted that there is an error in the article's discussion of the technology of the artillery revolution, which I will take this opportunity to correct. On page 69 I indicated that the hooped-staves manufacturing method was a fifteenth-century innovation, when in fact it was in use by the 1370s (albeit not for guns of the scale and proportions of the 1420s). See Peter Burkholder (1992) for a thorough and well-crafted discussion.

3. Nosworthy states that the flintlock "effectively doubled" the rate of fire to two rounds per minute, and Black agrees. The implied rate of fire for the matchlock of one shot per minute is probably too high, however, though different historians give widely varying figures. Mork (1967, 42, 46) suggests a rate of fire of at best one shot per ninety seconds for the

matchlock at the end of the seventeenth century, compared to a rate of two or three shots per minute with a flintlock in the eighteenth century. See also Parker (1988, 17–18). If we allow the musketeer the high rate of one shot per minute, and take the low figure of two per minute for the flintlock, the calculation is as follows: 100 men armed one-third with pike as per Boyle (1677, 24–25) could fire sixty-six shots per minute; 100 all armed with fusils could fire 200 per minute, a ratio of 3:1.

4. Pike fell to 20–25 percent by the 1650s (Parker 1988, 18); by the end of seventeenth century a ratio of 15–20 percent pike was standard.

5. 1.5 times as many soldiers firing (from two-thirds to three-thirds of the formation) three times as fast (from once per 90 seconds to once per 30 seconds) equals 4.5 times the volume of fire. If we take an initial formation of only 20 percent pike, the increase in firepower is 1.25 x 3= 3.75.

6. Three-rank batallion formations had been used on occasion since the early eighteenth century, but the French army's standard (regulation) deployed depth went from six ranks to five in 1693, to four in 1740, and to three only in 1754. Frederick the Great changed his army's standard formation from four deep to three deep between 1740 and 1742 (Nosworthy 1990, 74, 94, 187, 199, 206).

7. For example, at the battle of Peterwardein, Eugene defeated a Turkish army double the size of his own, and inflicted two casualties for every one his troops suffered, thanks in part to his troops' use of flintlocks (Black 1995, 101; Henderson 1964, 44, 223–24). Mork, however, points out that French armies employing matchlocks won some victories over Anglo-Dutch forces equipped with flintlocks (Mork 1967, 49-50).

8. "The development of the socket bayonet, of the flintlock musket, and of improved warship design brought about qualitative changes in warfare at least as important as those of Roberts' period, and arguably more so, with their consequence of a rise in the tactical importance of massed firepower in both land and naval warfare" (Black 1994, 7).

9. For example, note the comment of Major-General C. E. Webber in de Bloch (1993, 103): "History in every way proves that the fear of wholesale destruction has never been a deterrent of war." Note also the remarks of Admiral E. R. Freemantle (de Bloch 1993, 106).

10. For a measured critique of this view (which nonetheless accepts that "men who wanted a change… were given the strength to insist on it when they first fought in a phalanx"), see Salmon (1977, 100).

11. Similarly, the government of the people established by the American Revolution was accompanied by a heavy reliance on an army of the people, that is, on a militia system that demanded the participation of all adult white freemen between the ages of eighteen and forty-five (Millet and Maslowski 1984, 79–80, 89–90).

12. Reading Robert H. Scales (1993) helped convince me that this was the case, despite the author's emphasis on the importance of the highly trained and extraordinarily competent soldiers of the U.S. Army in that conflict.

13. Of course, the ballistic-missile/nuclear warhead combination (mainly because of the latter rather than the former element of the pair) has had a great impact on the conduct of war, in that it has compelled the Great Powers to limit their military efforts in various ways in their efforts to avoid escalation to nuclear Armageddon. The impact on national strategy and military resource allocation has also been great, but my point is that nuclear missiles have not been used, and so have not had much direct effect on the conduct of war, whereas non-nuclear missiles have been used, but until recently lacked the power or precision to be of great importance.

14. It is also possible, however, that improved detection technologies will eliminate the effectiveness of stealth technology, and some combination of countermeasures will prove able to protect many targets from precision strikes so effectively that the current RMA will prove short-lived.

3

What Is Information Warfare?

Martin C. Libicki

In recent years, a concept known as "information warfare" has become popular within certain circles of the U.S. defense establishment. The concept is rooted in the undisputable fact that information and information technologies are increasingly important to national security in general and to warfare specifically. According to this concept, advanced conflict will increasingly be characterized by the struggle over information systems. All forms of struggle over control and dominance of information are considered essentially one struggle, and the techniques of information warfare are seen as aspects of a single discipline. Those who master the techniques of information warfare will therefore find themselves at an advantage over those who have not; indeed, information warfare will, in and of itself, relegate other, more traditional and conventional forms of warfare to the sidelines. If it takes information warfare seriously enough, the United States, as the world's preeminent information society, could increase its lead over any opponent. If it fails to do so, proponents argue, it may be at considerable disadvantage, regardless of strengths in other military dimensions.

Coming to grips with information warfare, however, is like the effort of the blind men to discover the nature of the elephant: the one who touched its leg called it a tree, another who touched its tail called it a rope, and so on. Although some parts of the whole are closely related in form and function (e.g., electronic warfare and command-and-control warfare), taken together all the respectably held definitions of the elephant suggest there is little that is *not* information warfare.

This essay examines that line of thinking and indicates several fundamental flaws while arguing the following points:

- Information warfare, as a separate technique of waging war, is an analytically weak concept. There are, instead, several distinct forms of information warfare, each laying claim to the larger concept. Seven forms of information warfare—conflicts that involve the protection, manipulation, degradation, and denial of information—can be distinguished: (1) command-and-control warfare (which strikes against the enemy's head and neck); (2) intelligence-based warfare (which consists of the design, protection, and denial of systems that seek sufficient knowledge to dominate the battlespace); (3) electronic warfare (radioelectronic or cryptographic techniques); (4) psychological warfare (in which information is used to change the minds of friends, neutrals, and foes); (5) "hacker" warfare (in which computer systems are attacked); (6) economic information warfare (i.e., blocking information or channelling it to pursue economic dominance); and (7) cyberwarfare (a grab bag of futuristic scenarios).[1]

- The several forms of information warfare range in maturity from the historic (that information technology influences but does not control) to the fantastic (which involves assumptions about societies and organizations that are not necessarily true).

- Although information systems are becoming important, it does not follow that attacks on information systems are therefore more worthwhile. On the contrary, as monolithic computer, communications, and media architectures give way to distributed systems, the returns from many forms of information warfare diminish.

- Information is not in and of itself a medium of warfare, except in certain narrow aspects (such as electronic jamming). Information superiority may make sense, but information supremacy (where one side can keep the other from entering the battlefield) makes little more sense than logistics supremacy.

As Anne Wells Branscomb has pointed out, "in virtually all societies, control of and access to information became instruments of power, so much so that information came to be bought, sold, and bartered by those who recognized its value" (Branscomb 1994, 1). Branscomb could have added stolen and protected as well.

COMMAND-AND-CONTROL WARFARE (C²W)

MOP-30, the Joint Staff's pronouncement on command-and-control warfare (C²W), argues its objective is to decapitate the enemy's command structure from its body of command forces.[2] U.S. forces demonstrated mastery of information warfare in the Gulf War by destroying many physical manifestations of Iraq's command-and-control structure. These operations have frequently been pointed to as *the* reason why the bulk of the Iraqi forces were ineffectual when U.S. ground forces came rolling through (although carpet bombing helped). Decapitation can be accomplished by a blow to the head or by severing the neck, each thrust serving a different tactical and strategic purpose.

Antihead

Gunning for the commander's head is an old aspect of warfare. Examples abound, from the ancient practice of seizing the enemy's king to the death of Admiral Nelson, shot by a shipboard sniper, the employment of sharpshooters against opposing generals during the American Civil War, the downing of Admiral Yamamoto's plane in April 1943, strategic nuclear targeting theory, and attempts to find Saddam Hussein during the Gulf War or Mohammed Aideed in Somalia. Historically, commander's accessibility has kept shifting,[3] but the most recent change has been the transformation from the commander to the command center. Today's command centers are identifiable by copious, visible communications and computational gear (and the associated electromagnetic emissions), the physical movement of paper and other official supplies, plus enough comings and goings of all sorts to differentiate these centers from other venues of military business.

An attack on a command center, particularly if timed correctly, can disrupt operations even without hitting a high-ranking enemy commander. Despite the known disadvantages of single-point vulnerabilities, most commerce in messages tends to circulate within very small spaces. Fusing data and distributing them to harmonize everyone's situational awareness requires either a central set of ganglia or a major redesign of legacy systems. Determining the location of a command center permits juicy targets to come within gunsight—an opportunity rarely passed up.

Iron bombs are not the only way to attack command centers. Systems can be disabled by cutting off their power, introducing enough electromagnetic interference to make them unreliable, or by importing computer viruses, yet none of these means is foolproof or cost-effective compared with iron bombs on target. Most soft-kill weapons require knowing the location of the target. Although some of them have a larger effective radius than conventional munitions, the difference is limited and finding before firing remains equally essential.

How long will command centers remain vulnerable? Bunkering can protect headquarters, but at the cost of mobility (and newly perfected penetrating ordnance requires deep and comparatively immobile bunkers). Control of the signature of the command center may be a better strategy. Computers can be shrunk to the desktop, emissions of communications gear masked by electronic clutter (both deliberate and ambient) or off-loaded through multiple redundant cables or line-of-sight relays away from headquarters, and paper will yield to the paperless, perhaps optical, society (someday). Networks can generally be decentralized. Comings and goings and congregations that create valuable targets can be reduced through videoconferencing and whiteboarding. Power supplies can be supplemented by bunkered generators or, more ingeniously, by relying on dispersed photovoltaic collectors for electricity (which should be scattered so their presence will not reveal the command center). These means can keep command centers indistinguishable from any other inhabited space. Failing this result, the degree to which an enemy is hurt by being struck will depend on backup architectures (e.g., which nodes supply what information, what information is vital for battlefield decisions).

Antineck

Modern militaries have been knit by electronic communications since the mid-nineteenth century and by radioelectronic communications since the 1920s. Cut these communications and command-and-control is disabled, which, again, is old in warfare (up to a third of Union troops in the American Civil War were used to protect communications and transportation lines). What is new is the size of the communications load in the information age. Air defense systems, for instance, work better when integrated across facilities than when each facility works independently. The extent to which operations depend on the flow determines whether efforts to cut communications are worthwhile.

Cutting communication links requires knowing how the other side communicates. If its architecture is written in wire, the nodes (e.g., the AT&T building in downtown Baghdad) are easily identified and disabled. Like command centers, communications systems can be crippled by attacks on generators, substations, and fuel supply pipelines (e.g., gas lines into power plants), such as U.S. forces carried out in the Gulf War. If the architecture is electromagnetic, often the key nodes are visible (e.g., microwave towers). If satellites are used for transmission and signalling, then communication lines can be jammed, deafened, or killed.

The impact of attacks depends on how far the other side has progressed from the mainframe era. A communications grid composed of many small elements rather than a few large ones radiates less and casts smaller shadows over the landscape; it offers greater redundancy and compounds the enemy's targeting problems. Deliberate redundancy, of course, is more efficient than accidental.[4] Systems that replicate message traffic multiply the likelihood of a message getting through in highly degraded conditions, even if redundancy reduces the system's overall capacity. Additional robustness can be protected by new technologies such as spread-spectrum (to guard against burst errors in heavy jamming environments) and sophisticated error-correction techniques (e.g., trellis coding). A strategy of redundancy still leaves the management problem of distinguishing vital bit flows from merely useful ones. Bureaucratic, rather than technological, factors may determine the vulnerability of any data-passing system.

To What Effect?

The potential influence of C^2W on the outcome of conflict is predicated on the architecture of command relationships among the attacked. Iraq imitated its Soviet mentor, in part for political reasons (Iraqi society is ruled through convictions, rather than conviction). Cutting or thinning the links between head and body could easily be predicted to immobilize the body. Front-line Iraqi troops were sitting ducks for U.S. air and ground attack and showed little creative response.

Clearly, a rigid opponent like Iraq is only one end of a long continuum of possibilities. Other societies may allow local commanders more autonomy. Although the North Vietnamese also were hierarchically organized, their units were capable of long periods of untethered operations. An attack on central authority could conceivably release field commanders to demonstrate an initiative that would more than compensate for any lack of coordination resulting from chaos at the center.

The opposite also merits thought: if the center can be induced to come to terms, the last thing wanted is for peripheral forces to continue to fight. Future General Robert E. Lees, one hopes, would surrender whole armies rather than free them to fight on in guerrilla campaigns. Consider the difficulties in Bosnia: although Belgrade signed a peace agreement in July 1994, the Bosnian Serbs refused to sign and continued to fight (unless Belgrade's signature was deceptive). Decapitating a military may make it less effective but more troublesome. Much of what passes for strategy to control nuclear war consists of persuading an opponent to cease operations prior to global conflagration. Attacks on command-and-control thus make sense only if enemy forces are acting under positive (e.g., don't fire until I tell you) rather than negative control. Otherwise, the strategy could backfire.

INTELLIGENCE-BASED WARFARE (IBW)

IBW occurs when intelligence is fed directly into operations (notably, targeting and battle damage assessment), rather than used as an input for overall command and control. In contrast to the other forms of warfare discussed so far, IBW results directly in the application of steel to target (rather than corrupted bytes). As sensors grow more accurate and reliable, as they proliferate in type and number, and as they become capable of feeding fire-control systems in real time and near real time, the task of developing, maintaining, and exploiting systems that sense the battlespace, assess its composition, and send the results to shooters assumes increasing importance for tomorrow's militaries.

Despite differences in cognitive methods and purpose, systems that collect and disseminate information acquired from inanimate systems can be attacked and confounded by methods that are effective on C^2 systems. Although the purposes of situational awareness (an intelligence attribute) and battlespace visibility (a targeting attribute) are different, the means by which each is realized are converging.

Offensive IBW

Sharp increases in the ratio of power to price of information technologies, in particular those concentrated on distributed systems, suggest new architectures for gathering and distributing information. Tomorrow's battlefield environment will feature a mixed architecture of sensors at various levels of coverage and resolution that *collectively* illuminate it thoroughly. In order to lay out what may become a complex architecture, sensors can be separated into four groups: (1) far stand-off sensors (mostly space but also seismic and acoustic sensors); (2) near stand-off sensors (e.g., unmanned aerial vehicles [UAVs] with multispectral, passive microwave, synthetic aperture radar [SAR], and electronic intelligence [ELINT] capabilities, as well as similarly equipped offshore buoys and surface-based radar); (3) in-place sensors (e.g., acoustic, gravimetric, biochemical, ground-based optical); and (4) weapon sensors (e.g., infrared, reflected radar, and light-detection and ranging [lidar]). This variety of sensors illustrates the magnitude and complexity of the task for those who would try to evade detailed surveillance. Most forms of deception work against one or two sensors—smoke works for some, radar-reflecting paint for others, quieting for yet others—but fooling overlapping and multivariate coverage is considerably more difficult.

IBW portends a shift in what intelligence is useful for. Usually, the commander uses intelligence to gauge the disposition, location, and general intentions of the other side. The object of intelligence is to prevent surprise—a known component of information warfare—and to permit the commander to shape battle plans. The goals of intelligence are met when battle is joined; when one side understands its tasks and is prepared to carry them out while the other reels from confusion and shock—thus, situational awareness. The side that can see the other side's tank column coming can dispose itself more favorably for an encounter. The side that can see each tank and pinpoint its location to within the effective radius of an incoming warhead can avoid engaging the other side directly, but can fire munitions to a known, continually updated set of points from stand-off distances. This shift in intelligence from preparing a battlefield to mastering a battlefield is reflected in newly formed reporting chains for this kind of information. Although the direct reporting chain to the national command authority will continue, new channels to successively lower echelons (and, eventually, to the weapons themselves) are being etched. An apparent loss in status perceived by the intelligence apparatus (thus one resisted) is turning out to offer a large gain in functionality.

The task of assessing what individual sensor technologies will have to offer over the next decade or so is relatively straightforward; globally available technologies will come in many types for use by all. The task of translating readings into militarily useful data is more difficult and calls for analysis of individual outputs, effective fusion of disparate readings, and, ultimately, integration of them into seamless, cue-filter-pinpoint systems. If the Army's demonstration facilities at Ft. Huachuca are indicative, the United States has done a good job of manually integrating sensor readings in preparation for the next step—which is automatic integration. Automation removes the labor-intensive search of terrain and takes advantage of silicon chip's ability to double in speed every two years. Automatic integration will depend, in part, on the progress (always difficult to predict) of artificial intelligence.

Defensive IBW

Equally difficult to predict (or to recognize when they succeed) are defenses developed to preserve invisibility or, at least, widen the distance between image and reality on the battlefield. IBW systems can be attacked in several ways. On one hand, an enemy would be well advised to make great efforts against U.S. sensor aircraft (such as AWACS or JSTARS). On the other, using sensors that are too cheap to kill may be wiser (e.g., it is expensive to throw a $10,000 missile against a $1,000 sensor). Sensors can also be attacked by disabling the systems they use (e.g., hacker warfare), and their systems can be overridden or corrupted (e.g., electronic warfare).

The most interesting defense, in relation to likely opponents of the United States in the next ten or twenty years, would be to use a variant of the traditional cover (concealment) and deception with an admixture of stealth (which, being expensive, is unlikely to see widespread use even in the U.S. inventory). When sensor readings are technically accurate (that is, when the readings reflect reality), countering IBW requires distorting the links between what sensors read and what the sensor systems conclude.

In high-density realms (e.g., urban areas, villages crowded together, forests, mountains, jungles, and brown water) counterstrategies may rely on the exploitation or multiplication of the confusing clutter. In lower density realms—plains, deserts, blue water—a man-made object, particularly a military one, will stand out as not belonging there, so, to avoid becoming a target, an object should, instead, resemble the background, rather than ambient man-made clutter. In realms where the assets of daily civilian commercial life are abundant, military assets would need to be chosen so they could be confused with civilian assets, which tend to be more numerous and less directly relevant to the war effort and so are not such valuable targets, contrary rules of engagement notwithstanding.

Decoys, broadly defined, will probably be popular, on the theory that hiding a tree in a forest may be more practical than surrounding it with an obvious brick wall. The success of such measures will vary with the architecture of the IBW systems they are designed to fool. Systems based on multiple and overlapping sensors are more difficult to elude than single-sensor systems.

Information technology can be viewed as a valuable contributor to the art of finding targets; it can also be viewed as merely a second-best system to use when the primary target detection devices—a soldier up close—are too scarce, expensive, and vulnerable to be used this way. Open environments (tomorrow's free-fire zones) aside, whether high-tech finders will necessarily always emerge triumphant over low-tech hiders remains unclear.

ELECTRONIC WARFARE (EW)

Electronic warfare exists to degrade communications, either at the physical basis (via jamming radar or communications) or syntactic basis (by interception or spoofing). Neither type of EW is truly new. In tandem, they underlay Britain's success in defending its island against the *Luftwaffe*. In recent years, as information warfare has acquired a certain cachet, efforts have been made to reinvent EW under this new moniker. Its supposed current rise in status is occurring just as technologies are being developed that will favor the bits (like the bomber of yore) getting through.

Antiradar

A large portion of the EW community deals with radars (both search and target) and worries about jamming and counterjamming. Offense and defense keep coming up with new techniques. Traditional radars generate a signal at one frequency; knowing the frequency makes it easy to jam a return signal. More modern radars hop from one outgoing frequency band to the next. To counter radars, today's jammers must be able to acquire the incoming signal, determine its frequency, tune the outgoing jamming signal accordingly, and send a blur back quickly enough to minimize the length and strength of the reflected signal. Jamming aircraft that are riding in formation with attack aircraft often wipe out return signals (which weaken as the fourth power of the distance between radar and target) by overpowering them, but doing so makes jammers very visible so they must protect themselves. Coalition forces in the Gulf War developed new synergies using jamming aircraft *en masse*. Radars make themselves targets because of their outgoing signals; antiradiation missiles (e.g., the HARM) force radars either to be turned off or to rely on chirping and sputtering. The aborted Tacit Rainbow missile was designed to loiter in an attack area until a radar turned itself on; the outgoing signal gave the missile an incoming beacon, and away it went. As digitization improves, radar can acquire a target by generating a transient pulse and analyzing the return signal before a false jamming signal overwhelms the reflection.

The cheaper digital manipulation becomes, the more logic favors the separation of an emitter from a collector. Emitters, the targets of antiradiation missiles, would proliferate, to ensure the survival of the system and to absorb the strikes from expensive missiles. The emitters would create a large virtual dish out of a collection of overlapping small ones. Because outgoing signals will be more complex, collection algorithms too will grow in complexity, but the ability of jammers to cover the more complex circle adequately may lag. Dispersing the collection surface will also make radars less inviting targets.

Anticommunications

EW against communicators is generally more difficult to wage than EW against radars. The signal strength of communications weakens with the distance to the transmitter squared (versus the fourth power with radar). While radars try to illuminate a target (and therefore send a beam into the assets of the other side), communicators try to avoid the other side entirely and thus point in specific directions. Communicators move toward frequency-hopping, spread-spectrum, and code-division multiple access (CDMA) technologies, which are difficult to jam and intercept. Communications to and from known locations (e.g., satellites, UAVs) can use digital technologies to focus on frontal signals and discard jamming that comes from the sides. Digital compression techniques coupled with signal redundancy mean that bit streams can be recovered intact, even if large parts are destroyed.

EW is also used to geolocate the emitter. The noisier the environment, the more difficult the task. One defense is to multiply sources of background electronic clutter shaped to foil intercept techniques that rely on distinguishing real signal patterns (voice traffic has certain patterns some of which disappear after encryption). A thorough job, of course, requires expending resources to scatter emitters in areas where they may plausibly indicate military activity. Doing so diverts resources from other missions.

As suggested above, the work of finding targets is likely to shift from manned platforms to distributed systems of sensors. Despite the impending necessity of distributed systems, their Achilles' heel is the need for reliable, often heavily used communications links between many sensors, command systems, and dispersed weapons. In sensor-rich environments, EW—expressed by jamming or by soft-kill—can assume a new importance. Interference with communications from local sensors, for instance, can create virtual blank areas through which opposing systems can move with less chance of detection. The success of this tactic critically depends on the architecture of the distributed sensors system to be disrupted. A system that relies *exclusively* on distributed local sensors (intercommunicating or relaying signals by low power to switches) is the most vulnerable. A system that interleaves local and stand-off sensors, particularly where coverage varies and overlap is common, is more robust.

Cryptography

By scrambling its own messages and unscrambling those of the other side, each side performs the quintessential act of information warfare, protecting its own view of reality while degrading that of the other side. Although cryptography continues to attract the best minds in mathematics, sadly for an otherwise long and glorious history, contests in this realm will soon be only of historical interest.

Decoding computer-generated messages is fast becoming impossible. The combination of technologies such as the triple-digital encryption standard (DES) for message communication using private keys, and public key encryption (PKE) for passing private keys using public keys (so set-up communications remain in the clear) will probably overwhelm the best code-breaking computers. In essense, as soon as a key exceeds a certain length (expressed in bits), breaking a code is harder than creating one and becomes increasingly harder as the key lengthens. Any desired ratio between the difficulties of breaking and making codes can be achieved with a long enough key.

Although encryption is spreading on the Internet and all communications are going digital, the transition to ubiquitous encryption will take time. Analog will certainly persist in legacy systems, although its lifetime is limited. Cheap encryption, coupled with signal-hiding techniques such as spread-spectrum and frequency-hopping, will seal the codebreaker's fate.

Digital technologies will make spoofing—substituting deceptive messages for valid ones—nearly impossible. Digital-signature technologies permit recipients to know both who (or what) sent the message and whether the message was tampered with. Unless the spoofer can get inside the message-generation system or the recipient cannot access a list of universal digital keys (e.g., updates are unavailable to that location), the odds of a successful spoof are becoming quite low (e.g., capturing and rebroadcasting GPS signals has some spoofing potential if the recipient lacks an accurate clock).

PSYCHOLOGICAL WARFARE

Psychological warfare, as used here, uses information, not against computers, but the human mind: (1) operations against the national will; (2) operations against opposing commanders; (3) operations against troops; and—a category much respected abroad—(4) cultural conflict.

Counterwill

The use of psychological war against the national will through either the velvet glove ("accept us as friendly") or the iron fist ("or else") is a long and respected adjunct to military operations, with antecedents found in the writings of Thucydides.

The recurrent "peace offensives" and May Day parades of the Soviets showed that they were familiar with its uses, as are we.

The Somali clan leader Mohammed Aideed appears (if symposia hosted by the DOD are an indication) to be a master of the uses of psychological warfare. In a confrontation that cost the lives of nineteen U.S. Rangers in 1993, Aideed's side reportedly lost fifteen times that number—roughly a third of his strength. Photographs of jeering Somalis dragging corpses of U.S. soldiers through the streets of Mogadishu transmitted by CNN ended by souring TV audiences at home in the United States on staying in Somalia. U.S. forces left, and Aideed, in essence, won the information war.

Global broadcasters, CNN a leader among them, ensure that events anywhere on the planet, whether authentic or arranged for show, can be delivered to audiences in many countries. Those CNN broadcasts indicated the immediacy satellites can now provide to news organizations, but, this feature aside, the concept of international news was not invented by CNN. More than twenty-five years ago, the Vietnam War was broadcast nightly to U.S. living rooms, time-delayed for the dinner hour.

The advent of direct broadcast satellite (DBS) may permit one nation, or entity, to address another without getting permission. This capability is now available to anyone at low cost. The two-satellite 150-channel DBS constellation that Hughes Electronics launched over North America, which began service late in 1994, cost roughly $1 billion, and subsequent versions will probably cost less. A DBS transponder over Asia might be profitably leased for an annual fee of perhaps $2 million, well within the range of, say, Kurds, radical Shiites, Sikhs, or Burmese mountain tribes, who could then afford to broadcast their messages to an enormous audience twenty-four hours a day.

Counterforces

The use of psychological methods against the other side's forces offers variations on two traditional themes: fear of death (or other loss) and potential resentment between the trenches and the home front. Getting electronic messages to the other side dates back at least to World War II (e.g., Tokyo Rose). In the Gulf War of 1991, Coalition forces convinced many Iraqis that if they abandoned their vulnerable vehicles they would live longer. The Coalition's persuasiveness was fortified by weapons that had just destroyed such vehicles during the fighting.

The great shift in counterforces psychological operations would come when information technology permits broadcasts of threats or resentment-provoking information to *individual* combatants. When the destruction of a target identified by location can be made near certain, surviving warfare will be a matter of evading detection, rather than evading firepower. What would happen if vehicle operators could be told they had been seen and were about to be targets of deadly munitions unless they visibly disabled the vehicles? The first few times the technique was used, demonstrations, rather than actual attack, might be used to indicate that discovery is the cousin of destruction and that warnings would be ignored at peril to life and limb. With every demonstration, the correlation might become clearer.

Such psychological warfare might save ammunition (and avoid subsequent broadcasts by CNN of a grisly reality). Yet the demonstration must reflect underlying realities, not create them.

Countercommand

Nothing so much suggests the imminence of defeat than confused and disoriented commanders. Confusion and disorientation are cognitive as well as emotional states. Commanders make decisions on the basis of unexpected events. If reality is different from the basis used for decisions, it is difficult and time-consuming to reconstruct a cognitive structure. Simulation, thought experiment, and generalized what-if thinking, which can prepare a commander to recognize wide alternatives (each with its own decision logic), would facilitate coping with the unexpected, but at a high price. Contemplating an assortment of possibilities necessarily detracts from contemplating deeply those presumably probable. Events of low probability are discarded entirely; should they occur, few know how to cope.

The attempt to mislead the other side's commander at the operational level is an important part of information warfare. Historically, such deception has worked best when one side has a good idea of what the other side will and will not do. In World War II, for example, the Germans were convinced that the Allies would try to breach the Atlantic Wall at Calais; the Japanese believed equally strongly that U.S. forces would strike from the Aleutians. In both cases Allied forces played to those fears, keeping the opponent's forces pinned down where the opponent would need them least when the ultimate attack came. Similarly, Iraq was led to believe that the United States would use aerial warfare for only a limited time and only to soften the field immediately prior to ground attack (rather than, as it turned out, for forty days and nights). Iraq also believed that the United States would try to recapture Kuwait from the sea. U.S. quasi-public commentary carried over international media, such as CNN, was shaped to support the first belief; more conventional devices (e.g., having ships sail up and down the coast) supported the second.

Information warfare can also be applied to the everyday task of deceiving opposing bureaucracies—diplomats and spies—about one's intentions and capabilities. Weapons can be said to be more or less efficient than they actually are. A nation's preparations for war can either be highlighted for effect or downplayed for soporific value. Such activity is so common and historical that labelling it warfare rather than the everyday business of statecraft it has always been would prove difficult.

Kulturkampf

Whether cultural struggle is a form of psychological warfare is a rich topic, yet many non-Western nations are disturbed by the extent to which their traditional cultures are being invaded by Western—that is, largely U.S.—popular culture (e.g., fast food, Hollywood movies, clothing). More than one seer has forecast a coming clash of civilizations (Huntington 1993) arising not because countries will take issue with the Madonna but, for example, because her present-day namesake is seen as assaulting a traditional value structure. The trip from fear and loathing to accusations of direct cultural attack is short.

Is "cultural warfare" a form of war (that is, again, policy by other means)? Not as seen from Peoria. First, the entire concept of national culture simply remains alien to most Americans, bred, as they are, to the idea that their nation is defined by norms of political and social behavior, rather than by cultural habits. The U.S. Constitution (with antecedents in English common law) may be the best single expression of this sociopolitical attitude. Americans tend to be impatient with the whole notion of culture, unlike the French, who, at least to American eyes, imbue their language, arts, and cooking with heavy national responsibility. Steeped in national myths of pioneer and immigrant, Americans readily defend the right to pick and choose—or invent—cultural choices rather than settle for one set of them. If the Japanese, say, wish to try to sell Americans calligraphy, family bathing, daikon, or karaoke, they are as welcome as anyone else is to try.

HACKER WARFARE

Winn Schwartau (1994), among others, uses the term information warfare to refer almost exclusively to attacks on computer networks. In contrast to physical combat, these attacks are specific to properties of the particular system because the attacks exploit knowable holes in the system's security structure (such as the tendency of users to employ easily guessed passwords). In that sense the system is complicit in its own degradation.

Hacker warfare varies considerably. Attackers can be on site, although the popular imagination can place them anywhere. The intent of an attack can range from total paralysis to intermittent shutdown, random data errors, wholesale theft of information, theft of services (e.g., unpaid-for telephone calls), illicit systems monitoring (and intelligence collection), the injection of false message traffic, and access to data for the purpose of blackmail. Among the popular devices are viruses, logic bombs (a program designed to destroy a system's software after a predetermined time), Trojan horses (a program designed to weaken defenses from the inside), and sniffers (a program that sits on a host and collects passwords and similarly revealing information).

Is It Real?

It seems excessive, however, to extract a threat to national security from what, until now, has been largely a high-tech version of car theft and joy-riding. Even though many computer systems run with insufficient regard for network security, computer systems can nevertheless be made secure. They can be (not counting traitors on the inside) in ways that, say, neither a building nor a tank can be.

To start with the obvious method, a computer system that receives no input whatsoever from the outside world cannot be broken into. If the original software is trusted (and the National Security Agency [NSA] has developed multi-layer tests of trustworthiness), the system is secure (whether the system functions well is a separate issue). A system of this sort is, of course, of limited value. The real concern is to allow systems to accept input from outside without at the same time allowing core operating programs to be compromised. One way to prevent compromise is to handle all inputs as data to be parsed (a process in which the computer decides what to do by analyzing what the message says) rather than as code to be executed directly. Security then consists of ensuring that no combination of computer responses to messages can affect a core operating program, directly or indirectly (almost all randomly generated data tend to result in error messages when parsed).

Unfortunately, systems need to accept changes to core operating programs all the time. The trick is to draw a tight curtain of security around the few superusers granted the right to initiate changes. Although they might complain, their access methods could be tightly controlled (they might, for instance, work only from particular terminals that were hardwired to the network, which is an option in Digital's VAX operating system). The rapid speed and greater bandwidth of today's computers have made ubiquitous use of encryption and digital signatures possible. A digital signature establishes a traceable link from input back to the user attempting to pass rogue data into the system, and although it will not prevent all tampering (e.g., bugs in the parsing engine), it can eliminate most avenues of attack on a system (a flooding attack is a specific problem but such an attack requires a very fat pipe into a node, and leaves a fat trail to wander back through to catch the malefactors).

Stringent security may make certain innovations in the global network difficult to implement, such as the practice of communicating by exchanging software objects (which bind potentially unsafe executable code to benign data). Systems can (with work) be designed to retain full functionality in face of necessary restrictions. Security comes with costs, particularly if legacy and otherwise reliable operating systems (e.g., Unix) must be rewritten in order to minimize security holes. If the threat is big enough, the dollars spent to protect mission-critical national systems may not seem so large. At present, civilian mission-critical systems can, for policy purposes, be limited to those that run phone lines, energy, and other utility systems, transfer funds networks, and that maintain safety systems.

One reason computer security lags is that incidents of breaking in so far have not been compelling. Although many facilities have been entered through their Internet gateways, the Internet itself has only once been brought down (by the infamous Morris worm). The difficulty in extrapolating from the current spate of attacks on the Internet is that the Internet was designed to trust the kindness of strangers. If it is to be considered a mission-critical system for which compromise is a serious problem, it must evolve and will necessarily become more secure.[5]

Although the signalling systems that govern the nation's telephones have permitted hackers to affect service to specific customers, the system itself has yet to experience a catastrophic failure from attack. None of the few broad phone outages that have occurred has been shown to have been caused by anything other than faulty software. No financial system has ever had its basic integrity become suspect (although intermittent failures occur, such as NASDAQ's frequent problems). An analogy has been drawn between the threat of hacking and the security of the nation's rail system: train tracks, especially unprotected tracks in rural countryside, are easy to sabotage, and with grimmer results than network failure, but such incidents are rare.

Although important computer systems can be secured against hacker attacks at modest cost in usability, that does not mean that they will be secured. Increasing and increasingly sophisticated attempts at hacking may be the best guarantor that national computer systems will be made secure. The worst possibility is that the *absence* of important incidents will lull systems administrators into inattention, allowing some organized group to plot and initiate a broad, simultaneous, disruptive attack across a variety of critical systems. Are today's hackers doing us a favor? Not everyone thinks so; Dorothy Denning, of Georgetown University, has argued that today's volume of random hacking raises the sophistication of hackers, thus raising the cost of recapturing the desired level of systems security. All told, hacker warfare appears to be a problem that is not a problem until it is a problem, when it will shortly cease to be a problem.

Is It War?

Hacker attacks on military information systems can reinforce conventional military operations as well as any other form of information warfare, yet crucial military systems are supposed to be designed with sufficient security and redundancy (and sufficient separateness from the rest of the world) to defeat such attacks (even if unclassified military systems on the Internet are no more secure than comparable nonmilitary systems).

What about attacks on nonmilitary information systems; can they affect the power of the state to defend its vital interests? A flurry of hacker attacks can rival terrorist attacks for annoyance value, and, indeed, can disrupt the lives of more people. Is annoyance without political content an act of war? But hacker attacks are even less likely to force change than terrorist attacks do? Classic insurgency theory uses terrorist attacks to incit government overreaction which then mobilizes people against the government; cyber-repression, if even possible, cannot be so close to people's lives as to induce them into overthrowing the state.

In its ability to bring a country to its knees, hacker warfare is a pale shadow of economic warfare, itself of limited value. Suppose that hackers could shut down all phone service (and, with that, say, credit card purchases) nationwide for a week. The event would be disruptive certainly and costly (more so every year), but probably less disruptive than certain natural events, such as snow storm, flood, fire, or earthquake—indeed, far less so in terms of lost output than a modest recession. Would such a hacker attack prompt the U.S. public to demand the United States disengage from opposing the state that perpetrated the attack, just because of great inconvenience? Probably not.

Should the United States Wage Hacker Warfare?

Defending a nation's infrastructure is the essential but everyday task of bolstering network security. Few doubt that military information systems should be guarded against attack (unclassified open-logistics system are of particular concern); the same is true for mission-critical civilian systems, and perhaps even for the coming national information infrastructure (NII).

Should the government ensure the security of systems critical to the national economy? On the one hand, threatening the economy by targeting its information systems may affect the state. But who should guard the NII? The NSA clearly has the greatest expertise, yet in civilian circles it is also one of the least trusted agencies because of the highly classified nature of most of what it does (and its reputation for opposing the proliferation of encryption technologies whose use would improve security greatly). If and when network security receives more attention, adherence to minimal standards of security may become a precondition for federal regulatory approval (e.g., phone system or power-generation franchises often carry legal obligations for certain levels of assured service), for federal contract approval (e.g., bank systems), or for handling certain records (e.g., personal health data). Care must be taken lest the criteria used to define adequate security reflect military specifications and the array of threats particular to military systems, rather than criteria more appropriate to critical civilian networks.

On the other hand, is information systems security a problem whose solution should be socialized rather than remain private? If a foreign missile hits a refinery that blows up and damages its neighborhood, would the damage be the refiner's fault? No: the problem has been socialized in that the United States has a military to protect it against such attacks. If a gunman hits a refinery tower and causes a similar explosion, would that be the refiner's fault? Yes and no: the problem is partially socialized through public law enforcement. Yet, the refiner—as an owner of potentially dangerous equipment—is reasonably expected to take precautions (e.g., perimeter fencing, security guards). If a hacker on the Internet gains access to the refiner's system and commands a valve to stay open, creating an explosion and damaging the neighborhood, should the refiner be at fault? Yes: it should know everything about its information systems whereas the government may know absolutely nothing. Thus, the refiner should be responsible for protecting its internal systems and ensuring that software-generated events (e.g., software bugs) cannot do catastrophic damage.

The argument against developing a capability for offensive hacker warfare concerns glass houses and stones. The United States is far more dependent on computer systems than other nations are (who would see interruptions of Tehran's telephone service as unusual, for instance). The U.S. edge in perpetrating hacker attacks may be narrower than imagined. Roughly 60 percent of the doctorates granted in computer science and security in the United States are awarded to citizens of foreign countries, two-thirds from Islamic countries or India. Analogies to biological warfare suggest that the United States should stop contemplating certain types of attacks until it has developed antidotes for them. It would be quite embarrassing if a virus intended for another country's computer systems leaked and contaminated ours.

As the world becomes interlinked, most defenses the United States might employ defend not only this country but others as well. Out of the desire to ensure that U.S. corporations' deposits in banks in foreign countries are secure, the United States cannot help promoting operational practices that in turn ensure that the deposits of foreign dictators in the same bank are equally secure. Because hacking is cheap, nations at war might as well see what mischief it can cause, and those that fall victims to such attacks will then have only themselves to blame.

ECONOMIC INFORMATION WARFARE

Information Blockade

The effectiveness of waging economic information warfare through the blockade of information presumes the well-being of societies will become as affected by information flows as they are today by flows of material supplies. Nations would strangle others' access to external data (and, to some extent, their ability to earn currency by exporting data services). Information blockades can be understood as a variant on economic blockades. Cutting off trade in goods can affect the well-being of a country by disrupting production flows and, in the long run, eliminating the benefits of foreign trade. An information blockade works similarly by forcing the target country to work in the dark and, in the long run, by removing the benefits of information exchange. It also limits the ability of the blockaded country to engage in psychological warfare. As a form of blockade, an information blockade lessens the odds of violence by creating less opportunity for physical confrontation (in contrast to, say, boarding suspect ships at sea); and in some aspects it is easier to carry out since information conduits are countable (by contrast, opportunistic smugglers can penetrate the entire length of a border).

But how well can electronic data flows be cut off? Physical linkages, such as copper or wire, can be cut off at the border, in the waters, or at the nearest switch. In World War I, England severed Germany's cable links to the United States. Terrestrial radioelectronic connections can be silenced either by silencing the nearest transmitter (e.g., microwave towers) or by selective jamming. Space-based communications pose a bigger problem. Even if all sources uploading to geosynchronous satellites ceased transmissions (most are institutions, such as phone companies or media services), some services such as direct broadcast satellite would be nearly impossible to block. Free channels would just radiate. In addition, printed material (e.g., technical manuals) could be acquired and even large databases transferred by CD-ROM.

For an information blockade to have power similar to that of an economic blockade, the target nation would need to be dependent on external information flows, although information exchange is only one component of trade. A nation that had lost access to electronic information exchange could be hindered, yet not prevented from conducting trade. Iraq, for instance, could still sell oil. Without real-time access to commodity exchanges or the ability to tap databases on usage patterns, a targeted nation might have somewhat more difficulty writing the most advantageous contract for itself—but that constitutes a far lower loss.

Information Imperialism

To believe in information imperialism means believing in modern day economic imperialism. Thus, trade is war. Nations struggle with one another to dominate strategic economic industries. How does information play in this contest? Although it is difficult in a paragraph to do justice to a complex chain of causality, the logic is as follows. Nations specialize in certain industries; and some industries are better than others. The good industries command high wages and, usually, feature high growth rates. They tend also to be knowledge-intensive; they require and reinforce advantages against which other nations, particularly those with low-wage workforces, cannot easily compete. Acquiring and maintaining a position in these industries is a reinforcing process involving privileged access (on a national basis) to suppliers of information technologies, skilled workforces, markets, and R&D subsidies.

Is this war? Analogies to *Kulturkampf* may be useful here. The United States does not export cultural products with an eye to subverting other cultures; it is something it does at a comparative advantage and wishes to extend through markets in goods and services. The Japanese could argue that, similarly, they do not wish to place the rest of the world into an inferior and dependent technological position. They simply want to make enough money to pay for their imports, and they believe they have a comparative advantage in certain high-technology manufacturing sectors. Whether characterizing trade as nation-to-nation competition is meaningful in an age of multinational corporations remains an open question. Most large manufacturing corporations in the United States and Europe are rapidly losing national coloration—and, in any case, they source components globally. Japanese and other Asian corporations remain noticeably national, but they are moving in the same direction.

CYBERWARFARE

Cyberwarfare is a broad category that includes information terrorism, semantic attacks, simula-warfare, and Gibson-warfare. It is clearly the least tractable because by far it is the most fictitious, differing only in degree from information warfare as a whole. The global information infrastructure has yet to evolve to the point where any of these forms of combat is possible.

Information Terrorism

What would be the information-war equivalent of individual terrorism? Targeting individuals by attacking their data files requires certain presuppositions about the environment in which those individuals exist. Targeted victims must have potentially revealing files on themselves stored in public or quasi-public hands in a society where the normal use of these files is either legal or benign (otherwise, sensitive individuals would take pains to leave few data tracks). Today, files cover health, education, purchases, governmental interactions (e.g., court appearances), and other data. Some are kept manually or are computerized but inaccessible to the outside, yet in time most will reside on networks. Yet, a more plausible response than fear of compromise might be anger at the institutions that permitted files to be mishandled. Before a systematic reign of computer terror could bring about widespread compromise of enough powerful individuals, it would probably lead to restrictive (perhaps welcome) rules on the way personal files are handled.

Semantic Attack

The difference between a semantic attack and hacker warfare is that the latter produces random, or even systematic, failures in systems, and they cease to operate. A system under semantic attack operates and will be perceived as operating correctly (otherwise the semantic attack is a failure), but it will generate answers at variance with reality. A semantic attack presumes certain characteristics of the information systems. Systems, for instance, may rely on sensor input to make decisions about the real world (e.g., nuclear power system that monitors seismic activity). If the sensors can be fooled, the systems can be tricked (e.g., shutting down in face of a nonexistent earthquake). Safeguards against failure might lie in, say, sensors redundant by type and distribution, aided by a wise distribution of decision-making power among humans and machines.

Simula-Warfare

Real combat is dirty, dull, and, yes, dangerous. Simulated conflict is none of those. If the fidelity of the simulation is good enough—and it is improving every year—the results will be a reasonable approximation of conflict. Why not dispense with the real thing and stick to simulated conflict? Put less idealistically, could fighting a simulated war prove to the enemy that it will lose? Unfortunately, in the unlikely event that both sides own up to the capability and number of their systems and the strategies by which these are deployed, would the hiding or finding qualities of these systems be honestly portrayed? Mutual simulation requires adversaries to agree on what each side's systems can do. The reader may be forgiven for wondering whether two sides capable of this order of trust could be even more capable of resolving disputes short of war.

Gibson-Warfare

In novels such as William Gibson's *Neuromancer*, or Neil Stephenson's *Snow Crash*, heroes and villains become virtual characters who inhabit the innards of enormous systems and there duel with others equally virtual, if less virtuous. What these heroes and villains are doing inside those systems or, more to the point, why anyone would wish to construct a network that would permit them to wage combat there in the first place is never really clear.

Summary Assessment

Which forms and subforms of information warfare are real, and which are theoretical constructs? If war is understood as a destructive, extralegal struggle between two forces for control of a state's powers or resources, then *real* forms of information warfare include C²W, EW, IBW, and psychological operations against commanders and forces. Psychological operations against the national will and culture, as well as information imperialism are *arguable* forms of war. Hacker warfare, information blockades, information terrorism, and semantic attacks are *potential* forms of war. Finally, simula-warfare and Gibson-warfare are *unlikely* forms of war in the foreseeable future.

How would the United States fare against a capable opponent in the various (sub-)forms of information warfare? The United States is powerful at antiradar operations, cryptography, offensive IBW, psychological warfare against commanders and forces, and simula-warfare; and it has distinct advantages in *Kulturkampf* and blockading information flows. The United States is *both powerful and vulnerable* when it comes to C²W, defensive IBW, hacker warfare, and techno-imperialism. The United States is *vulnerable* to psychological warfare against the national will, information terrorism, and semantic attacks on computer networks.

Finally, the Table 3.1 lays out which (sub-)forms of information warfare are new in whole or in part and sketches their effectiveness against likely defenses.

LOOKING FOR THE ELEPHANT

Slicing, dicing, and boiling the various manifestations of information warfare produces a lumpy stew. Information takes in everything from gossip to supercomputers. Warfare spans human activities from by-the-rules competition to to-the-death conflict. Some forms of warfare use the human mind as the ultimate battleground; others work just as well even if people go home. Information warfare, in some guises, almost seems to predate organized societies; in other guises, it may continue long after human society has evolved to transcend today's organization whatsoever.

Can information be considered a medium of conflict parallel to other media? If so, is a separate service needed to house information warriors, however defined? There is a certain logic to the argument, for instance, to organize a corps capable of managing the future sensor-shooter system (Libicki and Hazlett 1993). It could develop and organize the elements of the system, oversee their emplacement, interpret sensors data, maintain their integrity, and convey the results generated to the units that need them. This task would encompass IBW directly; the defense of the system would complement other information warfare efforts, such as defensive C² warfare, counter-EW, and antihacker warfare. If information architectures are similar across competing militaries, then this corps may have the best feel for how the other side goes about developing its own sensor-shooter system. Conceivably, this corps would *contribute* to broader efforts in offensive C² warfare, EW, and hacker warfare (just like industrial economists helped pick targets for the U.S. strategic bombing campaign in World War II), but it would not conduct the war.

Table 3.1
Novelty and Effectiveness of (sub-)Forms of Information Warfare

Form	Subtype	Novelty	Effectiveness
C²W	Antihead	Command systems, rather than commanders, are now the targets	New technologies of dispersion and replication suggest that tomorrow's command centers can be protected
	Antineck	Hard wired communication links matter	New techniques (e.g., redundancy, efficient error encoding) permit operations under reduced bit flows
IBW		The cheaper the silicon the more can be thrown into a system that looks for targets	The United States will build the first system of seeking systems, but, stealth aside, pays too little attention to hiding
EW	Antiradar	Around since World War II	Dispersed generators and collectors will survive attack better than monolithic systems
	Anticommunication	Around since World War II	Spread spectrum, frequency hopping, and directional antennas all suggest communications will get through
	Cryptography	Digital code making is now easy	New code-making technologies (DES, PKE) favor code makers over code breakers
Psychological Warfare	Counterwill	No	Propaganda must adapt first to CNN, then to Me-TV (e.g., viewers building their own news from miscellaneous Web sources)
	Counterforces	No	Propaganda techniques must adapt to DBS and Me-TV
	Countercommander	No	The basic calculus of deception will still be difficult
	Kulturkampf	Old history	Clash of civilizations?
Hacker Warfare		Yes	All societies are becoming *potentially* more vulnerable, but good housekeeping can secure systems
Economic Information Warfare	Information Blockade	Yes	Very few countries are yet that dependent on high-bandwidth information flows
	Information Imperialism	Since the 1970s	Trade and war involve competition, but trade is not war
Cyberwarfare	Information Terrorism	Dirty linen is dirty linen whether paper or computer files	The threat may be a good reason for tough privacy laws

Table 3.1 (continued)

Form	Subtype	Novelty	Effectiveness
	Semantic attacks	Yes	Too soon to tell
	Simula-warfare	Approaching virtual reality	If both sides are civilized enough to simulate warfare, why would they fight at all?
	Gibson-warfare	Yes	The stuff of science fiction

As the author can attest, the notion of an information corps falls short of intuitive obviousness. Even true believers understand that many forms of information warfare transcend the DOD: from certain aspects of intelligence collection, to the defense of civilian information systems, to most forms of psychological warfare, to almost all of economic information warfare, and to who knows what percentage of cyberwarfare. No DOD organization, regardless of how broadly constituted, has cognizance of more than perhaps half the territory of information warfare.

Even within that subset, however, the notion of an information warfare corps defined in terms of its medium is problematic. Corpsmen of all stripes tend to see their primary job as facing off against their opposites. Tank crew know that the best weapons to take on tanks are other tanks: ditto for submariners. Fighter pilots may be last to recognize how few countries believe their own jet fighters can win air-to-air engagements with U.S. forces (thus, the Air Force pushes hard for the F-22). Denizens of the U.S. Space Command admit only grudgingly that their role in life is to help air-breathing commanders; given their druthers, they would rather conduct dust-ups with the space systems of other countries.

Unless an information corps is continually oriented to supplying (and protecting) information to support operations (a mission that overshadows the possession of raw firepower in determining conventional engagements), it may be tempted to orient itself against its counterparts. How ironic it would be if an information corps took defeat of the other side's systems as its mission—just when such warfare becomes increasingly difficult to pursue, unproductive of results, and generally irrelevant to outcomes.

Is Information Dominance Possible?

Information warfare admits of the concept of superiority. One side in a conflict may have better access to information than the other. It has more sensors in better places, more powerful collection and analytical machines, and a more reliable process for turning data into information and information into decisions. It can rely on the integrity of command-and-control systems, while the enemy might have only a probabilistic set of weak links over which its messages pass. This state of affairs does not mean that one side's systems can keep the other side from functioning (in contrast to England's ability to bottle up the German surface fleet after Jutland during World War I).

Does the possibility of superiority say anything about supremacy? Only in some cases. One side's jamming device may be powerful or agile enough to block radioelectronic emissions from the other side, yet this superiority would be local and may not imply that its devices can transmit without interference. Because radiation falls off to the square of distance (to the fourth for reflected radar), a wide-area superiority translates poorly into local unintelligibility. Even so, one side might overcome jamming power using such techniques as nulling, directional antennas, or spread spectrum (hiding a narrowband signal in a broadband swath). The result might not be to silence the other side but to reduce its bandwidth to only essential messages. More likely, both sides' bits get through. As for psychological warfare as a zero-sum contest over mind-share, if two messages are opposed to each other, one side's message may dominate the other's. Yet debates tend not to be conducted as a direct clash of opposites but through selective emphasis or de-emphasis. Listeners could also conclude that everyone is lying.

Overarching concepts such as an information warfare corps or information dominance end up having limited application over the entire or even a large segment of whatever falls under the rubric of information warfare. A comparison can be made to "logistics supremacy"; clearly one side's trucks do not prevent those of the other side from getting through. Opposing information systems can probably each expect to go about their business without overwhelming or even corrupting the other.

COMMON THREADS

A few common threads abound among the seven proposed categories of information warfare: (1) the importance of architecture, (2) the opportunistic nature of IW, and (3) the near impossibility of good battle damage assessment (BDA).

Understanding how the other side uses information is critical to knowing what aspect of the enemy to attack. Because success in information warfare is strongly influenced by the quality of intelligence about the other side, most forms of it are highly opportunistic, with effects difficult to predict. Success in decapitating the other side's command structure requires knowing where the command center is (and who is inside it) and where the lines are that run from command to the field. If cryptographic codes are unbreakable, then signals collection requires waiting for opportunities arising from human error, such as talking in the clear or mishandling keys. Computer systems security varies widely, so success in breaking and entering into them also varies widely. The other side's commanders are more easily fooled if they cling to certain prior judgements about the enemy and the battlefield. Luck and circumstance play great roles in information warfare, while brute force seems a smaller factor.

The difficulty of BDA is another thread running through virtually all categories of information warfare. Assessing damage is a frustrating exercise when it cannot be masked or exaggerated—as it can be with human and computer information systems. Was the particular command center identified and destroyed, for instance, really the intended one? Did a virus really disable the computer? How to tell whether a microwave burst really put a tank's electronics out of action? Has every frequency used by a radar been covered by a jamming signal? Some techniques help. The human intelligence that relayed the identity of the command structure may be available to confirm destruction. The crippling of an air defense radar can be assumed by inactivity when one's own aircraft are overhead. Communications sent through secure channels may be diverted into the open when preferred channels are taken out. The destruction of a utility's switch can be inferred by the sudden blackout. Observers can report whether a propaganda barrage against a populace is having an effect. Iraq underestimated how much information warfare it would have to tolerate; it developed clever techniques for exaggerating the extent of bomb damage (even setting off colorful explosives near targets it wanted the coalition forces to believe had been destroyed) but did little to distort the results of attacks on command systems.

An enemy that understands the nature of attacks against it may use techniques to mask the real damage. In hacker warfare, a system whose administrator knows it is under attack can generate false effects. The newly purloined data; were they valuable, or was the enemy's grip purposely loosened so lies may be spread? Files might be established that appear valid, that even correlate to other files, but that are phony—the cyberspace version of Operation Mincemeat (a British ruse in 1943 in which phony invasion plans of Europe were planted on a corpse left for the Germans to find). Replicating fictive digital documents throughout a system is easier than replicating real ones. A system that has been attacked could show false signs of failure by appearing to slow or otherwise appear to be malfunctioning. It may be configured to send garbage through its communications links, rather than real messages. After attack, the system drops the garbage flow and appears to suffer from degraded capacity. With more effort, a system successfully attacked might nevertheless continue to appear healthy by continuing a flow of traffic even though made-up message traffic had to be inserted to make up for the lack of real message traffic.

CONCLUSIONS

First, almost certainly there is *less* to information warfare than meets the eye. Although information systems are becoming more important, they are also becoming more dispersed and, if prepared, can easily become redundant (e.g., through duplication, compression, and error-correction algorithms). Other *commercially employed* techniques, such as distributed networking, spread spectrum, and trellis coding, can ensure the integrity of messages. The growth of networking systems has created new vulnerabilities, but they can be managed once they have been taken seriously. A strategy that strangles the other side by applying pressure on its information pipe may be self-defeating; if the other side's bureaucracy is well understood, it may be defeated even more easily by flooding it with more information than it can handle.

Second, information warfare should not be considered a single category of operations. Of the seven types of information warfare presented here, two—information blockade and cyberwarfare—are notional and a third—hacker warfare—although a real activity, is grossly exaggerated as an element of war viewed as policy by other means. Disregarding these as premature forms of information warfare, and associating EW techniques with whatever ends they support (e.g., C²W, IBW), three forms remain: C²W, IBW, and psychological warfare, each of which can stand as a separate discipline. As it so happens, command-and-control systems are vulnerable because they tend to be centralized, while IBW systems are vulnerable because they rely on communications to unify a decentralized sensor architecture. C²W and IBW are linked in that EW techniques can be used against both command and intelligence systems.

Third, most of what U.S. forces can usefully do in information warfare will be *defensive*, rather than *offensive*. Much that is labelled information warfare is simply not doable—at least under rules of engagement the United States will likely observe for the foreseeable future. Information systems are more important to U.S. forces than they are likely to be to opposing forces; what the United States might do in offensive operations is limited by the restrictive rules of engagement under which it operates, and because the United States's open information systems are by their nature more likely to be understood than systems of other countries.

NOTES

1. Although the information systems required to manage logistics are substantial, they enter into information warfare only if and when an opponent targets the logistics information system to degrade it; similarly, weather collection systems enter information warfare only if they are subject to attack. By contrast, IBW systems are part of information warfare because they are used to read a target that would avoid being read and that often has ways (e.g., cover, concealment, and deception) to distort readings at the source.

2. MOP-30 covers, "the integrated use of operations security, military deception, psychological operations, electronic warfare, and physical destruction, mutually supported by intelligence, to deny information to, influence, degrade or destroy adversary C² capabilities while protecting friendly C² capabilities against such actions."

3. Command effectiveness used to require commanders to oversee and thus remain near the range of combat. In World War I wireline communications enabled commanders to operate beyond the range of enemy arms. Later, the airplane and missile returned the commanders to the target zone.

4. By the Gulf War's end, the number of communications targets left to attack was larger than at the beginning; the Iraqis had many communications systems, more perhaps than even they were aware of, from radio systems that Western oil contractors had left in place to rural telephone systems that routed around major cities.

5. In an important exception to that generalization, the Internet has become a conduit for a large chunk of the DOD's nonsensitive but, in bulk form, essential logistics traffic.

4

Emerging Technologies and Military Affairs

Colonel Howard J. Marsh

INTRODUCTION

Information Age technologies are dramatically enhancing military capabilities and are providing new means in achieving traditional military objectives, but a Revolution in Military Affairs (RMA) has yet to arrive. I hold the view that a true RMA would have to overthrow the existing military order, rendering conventional, chemical, biological, and nuclear weapons redundant.

I will demonstrate that recent advances in technology have, for the most part, been harnessed to twentieth-century doctrinal thought. In the latter part of this chapter, I offer a possible genesis of a true RMA. The erosion of sovereignty through global living in distributed virtual environments (DVEs), along with the dissolution of the modern era international system, could render state-versus-state use of conventional, chemical, biological, and nuclear weapons improbable. A possible collapse of national political sovereignty brought about by emerging technology is the most likely genesis of a Revolution in Military Affairs in the twenty-first century.

My concern, as a long-serving military officer, is that we, the military, are too often transfixed by that which is new, or worse yet, cease the analysis when the direct and urgent consequences of a development are identified. Let us examine the long-term, indirect implications of this strategic determinant called technology.

TECHNOLOGY

I share Martin van Creveld's opening premise in his book, *Technology and War*: "war is completely permeated by technology and governed by it" (van Creveld 1989, 1). Warfare, at least since the introduction of gunpowder in the thirteenth century, has been captivated by technology. Some historians could make a strong case that since the introduction of the wheeled chariot, mankind has been obsessed with the search for that particular technology that would guarantee success on the battlefield. New technology or emerging technology is a long-term constant of warfare. What is different?

In recent years the rate of inventiveness has greatly accelerated, but even the cornucopia of offerings has not yet brought about a Revolution in Military Affairs. Militaries of the post–Cold War era think and resemble their former incarnation of the Cold War era. The world is no longer bipolar—NATO versus Warsaw Pact—but military intellect still thinks in terms of tactical, operational and strategic levels of war and the forms of warfare as a linear continuum. Napoleon would have little difficulty in comprehending the hierarchical structure of regiments, brigades, divisions, and corps prevalent in contemporary armies. Given his penchant for study, he would probably be most impressed to find a library's worth of books stored on CD-ROMs but disappointed to discover that thoughts are still limited by words that have to be read. Contemporary inventiveness has yet to bring about fundamental change to long-existing doctrines.

DOCTRINE

Canadian doctrine, while acknowledging the limitless nature of war, nevertheless uses the finite nature of synthesis and has adopted a *"spectrum of conflict* model to describe the varying states of relations between nations and groups and a *continuum of operations* to describe the range of military responses to peace and conflict (including war)" [emphasis added] (CLF 1996, I-1). This linear model, which excels at capturing all extant types of warfare, has a weakness. It visualizes warfare as a spectrum, much like the electromagnetic spectrum, and like the spectrum of light narrows our thinking to a one-dimensional line. In one direction hostility increases; in the other it decreases. Boundaries have been set around a subject that has no definite limit! This linear doctrinal model makes no allowance for warfare that is outside the spectrum or for the exponential growth of emerging technologies that could change the parameters of thinking about war. As a consequence, military thought related to inventiveness has been largely a sorting exercise. Each new invention is placed somewhere on the accepted spectrum of conflict. The more lethal emerging technologies are assigned to combat functions. The less lethal are assigned to sustainment operations or special operations. The notion that a combination of technologies could so surround the entire doctrinal model as to render it obsolete is an alien thought.

The delineation of warfare into *strategic*, *operational*, and *tactical* has long been espoused and has dominated military thinking for more than a century. Colonel G. F. P. Henderson's 1894 lecture, *Lessons from the Past for the Present*, to the Royal United Service Institution is one of the earliest references in English sources to this three-tiered doctrinal construct that has served the military professional intellect so well in the twentieth century. His thinking is repeated in today's dogma. Canadian Forces Publication (CFP) 300-1, *Operational Level Doctrine for the Canadian Army*, states that this publication is based upon the fundamentals of CFP 300, *Canada's Army* and CFP(J)5(4), *Joint Doctrine for Canadian Forces Joint and Combined Operations*. CFP 300 and CFP(J)5(4) are the strategic level manuals.

CFP 300-1 is the Land Forces' operational level manual. CFP 300-2, *Formation Tactics*, describes how operational level doctrine is put into practice at the tactical level.

As van Creveld has noted, Roman campaigns aside, sometime in the eighteenth century disputes were no longer resolved in a single engagement (van Creveld 1989, 49, 121–23). The practice of nations taking to the field in the morning and running the risk of losing all by evening was replaced by the concept of a protracted series of battles over time and space, that is, a campaign of war. CFP 300-1 devotes three chapters to *campaign design, campaign planning*, and *conducting the campaign*, but the Gulf War land campaign lasted one hundred hours. Western nations have little patience for protracted campaigns. Thanks to communication technology, the international media can present issues in real time and solicit expert opinion in ten minutes. People prefer issues resolved before going to bed. Current writings lead military leadership to believe that campaigns are ended in a textbook manner. Viewing warfare as an "off-on-off" step-function is at odds with the "continuum" model and both are too simplistic for reality. A model finite in comprehension but infinite in accommodation is required. Mathematical theories called *chaos theory* and *fractal geometry* provide means of finding order where the unpredictable—the "fog of war"—is observed. The military concept writers of the twenty-first century, entrusted with the development of military doctrine, would be wise to emulate the mathematicians who endeavor to express reality in finite models (Peitgen, Jurgens, and Saupe 1992).

Canadian doctrine, which is developed in concert with our allies, adopts the U.S. convention of several combat functions at each doctrinal level. This construct referred to as the functional framework "is a tool used by the commander to define the relationship between the functional components necessary to support the campaign design and unify their efforts toward a common goal" (CLF 1996, V-4). At the operational level the functional components, sometimes referred to as combat functions, are: *command, information operations, maneuver, firepower, protection*, and *sustainment* [emphasis added] (CLF 1996, V-5).

Conceptually, the current Canadian doctrine for land operations is but a refinement of much earlier thought. Post–Cold War technologies appear to have been captured and applied to preexisting doctrinal thought. Given the finite nature of the extant doctrinal model, it is not surprising. Much of what is new just does not fit neatly into the finite nature of existing doctrinal models. As Clausewitz warned, "the conduct of war branches out in almost all directions and has no definite limits; while any system, any model has the finite nature of a synthesis. An irreconcilable conflict exists between this type of theory and actual practice" (Clausewitz 1984, 134).

To date Western armed forces have categorized and applied emerging technology to Cold War equipment. Technology has been used as a "force multiplier" to offset the effects of the 1990s downsizing with the hope of preserving combat capability. An examination of the six functional components or combat functions and their related technologies confirms that militaries are evolving, applying emerging technology to familiar ways of doing things.

FUNCTIONAL COMPONENTS AND EMERGING TECHNOLOGY

Command

> From Plato to NATO, the history of command in war consists essentially of an
> endless quest for certainty—certainty about the state and intentions of the enemy's
> forces; certainty about the manifold factors that together constitute the environment
> in which the war is fought,... and last but definitely not least, certainty about the
> state, intentions, and activities of one's own forces. (van Creveld 1985, 264)

Napoleon, Lee, and Slim were outstanding military commanders. As well as
having strong intellects and memories, they all had that cunning ability to "read"
the minds of their enemy and foresee the enemy's intentions. This seemingly
intuitive insight into what would happen next made them heroes in their soldiers'
eyes. They saw the battlefield from its various angles, saw the deployments,
visualized difficulties in moving over various terrain features, and understood the
reactions of men in the "fog of war." They had tremendous three-dimensional,
spatial memories and high-order pattern recognition brains. The Germans coined a
word for this rare natural gift of being intuitively linked to the battlefield
[*Fingerspitzengefühl*] and sought it among their officers. The French use the
expression *coup d'œil*: the almost instinctive capacity to discern through the "fog
of war." For the rest of us mere mortals, maps help in visualizing the terrain.

The history of European warfare discloses the implementation of new
technologies aimed to reduce uncertainty. European commanders during the Middle
Ages conducted warfare without maps. Sketches in the dirt or sand-tables provided
the medium for commanders to convey their intent. The advent of the printing
press and cartography, around the sixteenth century, greatly assisted commanders,
not only in conveying their orders, but also permitted command to be executed
over larger armies on greater expanses of terrain. Between the end of the seventeenth
century and the middle of the eighteenth century armies grew by a magnitude of
ten (van Creveld 1989, 113). The French *levée en masse*, national mobilization,
enabled Napoleon to keep one million men under arms. Effective command of an
army of this size was heavily reliant on accompanying staff and the technologies
of paper, printing, cartography. These communicated the commander's intent, helped
reduce uncertainty, and sustained the force.

Today's commanders are still surrounded by staff and similar technology in
order to reduce uncertainty. Upper level work station computers with at least one
gigabyte of random access memory (RAM) are able to create realistic three-
dimensional views of the "battlespace" from any angle. Computer-generated images
of terrain are replacing the two-dimensional map, but like the map they are simply
a rendition of the actual terrain, albeit a very accurate one. Paper is in the process
of being replaced by data bases, spread sheets, electronic mail, and so on, but few
commanders are comfortable with paperless command posts. Command, with its
accompanying plethora of staff, paper, and the hierarchical command structure
that generates command posts from battalion to army, has changed little in the past
century, and appears to have every intent of maintaining the status quo. Computers

probably cannot take over the moral and psychological dimensions of leadership but they will assist leaders in the analytical aspects of conflict.

As command and leadership find their complete expression in a moral and physical being, it is unlikely that the existing command constructs will change abruptly. Even though computing speeds and computer memory exceed that of most humans, the software required to identify patterns of behavior and activity, synthesize them, and learn from experience are in rudimentary form. Software that fully replicates human thinking would profoundly alter command, but that is decades away. As command has both moral and physical aspects, it may never be automated. Even in *Star Trek*, Data, the android, is rarely permitted command! Solutions and direction derived from mathematical algorithms are too predictable and too easy for an enemy to replicate. Command solely based on computer technology could eliminate that principle of war—surprise.

INFORMATION OPERATIONS

Some aspects of modern warfare such as information operations have definitely altered under the impact of new technologies: "Information operations are not new. In their simplest form they encompass all operations that gain information and knowledge that enhances friendly execution of operations, while denying the adversary similar capabilities by whatever means possible" (CLF 1996, VII-1). Over the centuries there has been a long-term shift away from solely human intelligence gathering means to a greater reliance on electronic gathering means. Prior to the invention of the telescope, circa 1610, scouts would be required to enter the perimeters of enemy encampments to ascertain strengths and intentions. The natural aversion to the dangers of spying has lent impetus to innovativeness, technological and other. Hostage taking, interrogation, and disguise were the mainstays of early information operations. Today, most spying—information gathering—is performed electronically.

Modern information gathering is highly dependent on electronic sensors that can be mounted on a myriad of platforms, man to satellite. These sensors are many and varied, covering most of the electromagnetic spectrum. The emerging technology that is likely to advance information gathering most is the optoelectronic integrated circuit. The microbolometric switch, a parallel technology, performs much the same function by measuring radiant energy. Both devices offer the possibility of converting photons of light into electrons and vice versa. These circuits when manufactured in continuous sheets on polymers and applied to the exterior of equipments would be invisible in the natural light spectrum, because the optoelectronic circuits would emit photons at nonlight wavelengths. Deception is a subset of information operations. The more highly tuned optoelectronic-based sensors would detect every photon and electron emitted. At present there is no technology to counter this level of intrusion. All that exists above absolute zero could be detected. Processing this stream of data into meaningful and timely information, however, will require computing power a million times more capable than today's super computers. Nevertheless, it is not unrealistic to project the attainment of this "all-seeing" sensor and data processor by 2025. Lesser offerings should be available earlier.

It would be interesting to speculate who will be the first to field such a device. The computer industry needs an electron-photon gate to achieve switching speeds in the terahertz range. Multiple, micro-optoelectronic circuits imbedded in polymeric-electrolytic fabrics offer the possibility of chameleon and color-adjustable apparel for the clothing industry. A relatively rudimentary, inexpensive, microbolometric chip operating in the infrared bandwidth would provide vehicle operators with much improved visibility in adverse conditions. My money is on the clothing industry!

Seeing more of the battlefield and knowing the enemy's intent have been the subject of a long-term quest. From Rahab's spies who scouted Jericho prior to Joshua's triumph, through to Hans Lippershey's telescope (1610) and on to spy satellites, the trend of information operations has been obvious—reducing uncertainty, avoiding disclosure. Technology is still subservient to this quest.

Until the advent of the Chappé telegraph in 1794, the passage of information, a subset of information operations, was largely limited to the speed at which armies moved. This system of towers and signals permitted a message to travel 400 kilometers in a day, a performance never attained by mounted relay systems (van Creveld 1989, 155). The electromagnetic telegraph, an early nineteenth-century technology, accelerated the passage of information again. More notably, the sum of telegraph, steam engine, and railway provided a system that greatly enhanced mobilization. This early example illustrates the synergistic effect technologies can have in shaping warfare. The pace increases.

Passage of information in the twenty-first century is again being accelerated by military satellite communications (MILSATCOM) architecture. Not only is information transmitted at the speed of light but extremely high frequencies, 20 to 44 gigahertz (GHz), permit the passage of enormous amounts of data while resisting jamming and providing covert communications.

Information operations have evolved with succeeding advances in technology. As of late, information dominance has been made more difficult because the international media (e.g., CNN) often provide graphic information to the public and the enemy before our military commanders can respond to the new situation, but this falls into the military rubric of psychological operations, a predominantly mid-twentieth-century military necessity. Thirteenth-century Hungarians, however, fearing imminent pillage by Genghis Khan, would argue that psychological operations originated much earlier.

MANEUVER OPERATIONS

Simply put, this is the action of getting to the correct place on time. The military have three subclassifications of maneuver: *strategic*, deploying from home nation to the theater of operations; *operational*, moving within the theater of operations; and *tactical*, maneuvering in contact with the enemy. Until the nineteenth century maneuver had been reliant on organic energy. The leg muscles of both man and horse were the mainstays of maneuver operations.

Energy is required to move mass (armies and their support). Whether mounted or dismounted, whether on land or in the air, maneuver is a function of mass and energy. The amount to be moved and the speed at which it is moved are dependent on the amount of energy available and how quickly that energy can be converted into motion. The two technological great steps forward in maneuver are the introduction of the spoked, hubbed wheel, rotating around a fixed axle (circa 1800 B.C.) and the transition from organic energy (muscles) to chemical energy (machines) (in the nineteenth century) as the primary source of motion.

The lowly bearing and lubrication are critical to every form of maneuver. From the most massive strategic-lift aircraft to the bicycle, from turbine shaft to pedal, none would move without functioning bearings. The genius in Egypt who fabricated chariot bearings from wood and bronze and lubricated his creation with lard is not far removed from the modern engineer who is seeking frictionless bearings. The long-term trend and eventual goal of bearing design is the reduction of friction, eventually to zero. Energy is precious and should not be wasted by mechanical friction—the true enemy of maneuver.

It is not surprising that the ubiquitous bearing, which is present everywhere, enjoys both common and exotic experimentation. New lubricants are no longer based on long linear molecules that fail under heat and pressure, but on soccer ball–like molecules that act like tiny ball bearings within the mechanical bearing. Although this latest advancement in technology will cut the friction level attained by conventional lubricants in half and reduce wear to one-sixth of current levels, it pales in comparison to superconducting bearings whose friction is 100 times less. A free spinning flywheel with such bearings would take a year to stop rotating! The reduction of friction has been a long evolutionary process since bronze and lard lubricated bearings.

Except for the displacement of mounted troops and artillery by the combustion engine in the twentieth century, maneuver operations have advanced at a glacial pace for the last millennium. Historians estimate that the pace at which the Mongols advanced across Asia has only been matched by Patton in World War II—eight miles (12.5 kilometers) a day. At the dawn of the twenty-first century, much is made of finding alternate power sources for land mobility, but for the foreseeable future there is nothing to rival a gallon of hydrocarbon fuel for energy density and quick availability. Maneuver requires horsepower and lots of it. As drag racers know, developing 5,000 horsepower requires "burning" a gallon of fuel a second. Mobile electrical energy devices neither store nor quickly provide this magnitude of energy on frequent demand. Chemical energy, converted in combustion engines to kinetic energy, or chemical energy, converted by fuel cells to kinetic energy, will continue to be the primary power source for maneuver operations.

Although some may argue that the introduction of electronics and situational awareness to vehicles heralds a significant advancement, they are but an evolutionary improvement that ensures more combat power gets to the right place at the right time.

FIREPOWER OPERATIONS

Firepower, like maneuver, is again an energy equation. The objective is to concentrate energy at a vulnerable spot in order to overmatch the resistance of the object being attacked. In its crudest form, the sharp, leading edge of a saber, swinging at 100 miles per hour, has ample kinetic energy to overmatch the molecular bonds of organic flesh and bone. Despite the introduction of gunpowder around the thirteenth century, the organically powered hand-held weapon was the preferred instrument of battle well into the fifteenth century. Sword, spear, lance, and bow competed with the new chemical energy weapon—the cannon and gun—well into the sixteenth century. Even with the introduction of firearms, the process of parting with cold steel was slow: "During the period before 1830 bayonet charges were not infrequent, but their number declined over time. We have the testimony of Napoleon's surgeon general, Larrey, that for every bayonet-wound he treated there were a hundred caused by small arms or artillery fire" (van Creveld 1989, 95). The transition from firepower based on organic energy (e.g., the bow) to chemical (e.g., the cannon) and subsequent refinements to today's high pressure guns and guided weapons has been a long evolutionary process requiring the better part of a thousand years.

Emerging technologies offer greater accuracy, increased lethality, multiple target destruction, and longer ranges, and these, in turn, require greater protection and stealth to ensure survivability. The evolution of firepower is one that is marked by ever increasing concentrations of energy and greater accuracy, which, in turn, permit engagement at longer and longer ranges. In the 1500s destruction of your enemy meant close quarter combat. Now destruction can be meted out by a cruise missile from a distance of hundreds of kilometers. Even a modern missile, however, is only a highly refined chemical energy-based device.

The introduction of directed energy weapons would herald a significant advancement in firepower because energy transfer, rather than being chemical to kinetic, would be electrical to electromagnetic or chemical to electromagnetic. In the final analysis electromagnetic energy will still be transferred to the molecules or atoms of the substance under attack.

For the recipient there is little difference whether the energy arrives by an armor-piercing shell, carrying ten megajoules of kinetic energy, or whether a chemical energy weapon forms a jet of plasma traveling at eight kilometers a second, or whether electromagnetic energy raises the excitation state of atoms in milliseconds; the outcome is the same as being struck by a saber—death. Thus far, Western militaries still view firepower as energy transference.

PROTECTION OPERATIONS

Protection operations, aside from stealth strategies, are the obverse of firepower. Here the aim is to absorb or dissipate the energy of the attacker. The shield was effective in dissipating blows, but it could not be so large so as to prevent the bearer from counterstrokes. Knights first wore mail armor, then adopted plate armor as arrows increased in lethality, but in the process they became so immobile that they often fell victim to ignoble attackers. World War I saw overwhelming firepower in the form of machine guns and artillery. Countering this threat required defensive earthworks. Static trench warfare was the outcome. The introduction of armored fighting vehicles, notably at Cambrai, brought an element of mobility to World War I, but this new capability was not well understood and was therefore trivialized by the Allies. A similar pattern emerged with the introduction of fully developed tanks. Each successive model was more heavily armored. At more than a hundred tons the German Maus was nothing more than a static pillbox that could be bypassed, left for engineers and their explosives. Focusing on the dissipation of attacking energy, the essence of protection, without due consideration for mobility results in immobility. Not heeding this proved costly for the French at the outset of World War II.

Firepower has exceeded protection in the last two centuries. This reality has forced soldiers and their commanders to seek alternative strategies in order to survive. Protection is largely a survivability exercise based on four tenets: avoid detection; if detected, avoid being hit; if hit, minimize damage; and repair quickly. Avoiding detection requires dispersion and stealth. After each major conflict theorists plot the ratio of soldiers per square kilometer. The trend is obvious. Early in the twenty-first century, only a section of soldiers is required to defend the same kilometer of frontage previously defended by a thousand-man regiment in World War I.[1]

Besides dispersion, protection is heavily reliant on avoidance. Optoelectronic circuits that can generate chameleon-like camouflage and sensors that detect incoming attack and respond with "active" armor will most likely become *de rigueur* for armored fighting vehicles. Redundancy of vital systems, including crew, along with vetronics (digitized monitoring of vehicle systems) will enhance survivability and repair, but technologies are unlikely to bring great change to protection operations, although the sustainer's role should be made easier.

SUSTAINMENT OPERATIONS

Contrary to popular thought, future warfare is more likely to be won or lost by the degree of responsiveness and capacity of logistics than by the combat arms. Sustainment is more demanding than the foregoing combat functions. Not only is sustainment a mass and energy equation, but it is equally a system of systems of near limitless complexity. It is easier to fail in this realm. In peacetime entire rifle companies have been rendered *hors de combat* because a soldier mixed potable and nonpotable water. On another occasion, issuing summer-grade diesel in winter rendered a brigade's worth of vehicles immobile for three days! Not a shortage of goods, but a lack of knowledge, is often cited as the Achilles' heel of sustainment operations.

This operational level function should benefit the most from emerging information technology. Space-age sensors measure the physical condition and mental state of every soldier. Vetronics monitor the performance of every vehicle system. This plethora of information is fed to medics and mechanics. The psychological and physical state of the force is assessed second by second. This data is synthesized by software programs that forecast the logistic requirement. Elsewhere the marriage of the International Organization for Standardization (ISO) container, Global Positioning System (GPS), and the cellular telephone provide the logistic command center with the exact contents and location of every resource in the command. Needs and resources can be precisely matched and delivered to the exact location. In the larger scenario sustainment needs can be matched to a nation's resources. Production of goods, recruitment, and training could be harnessed to the military mission, but this has been done before, albeit with the assistance of large bureaucracies.

Even twenty-first century sustainment operations are critical to combat operations and by default reflect the nature of that which they support. A heavy-armor task force requires a heavy sustainment echelon. A light-infantry unit is sustained by a more modest echelon, whereas an electronic warfare unit requires specialized support technicians and accompanying electronic equipments. Except for a moment in history when railways and telegraph shaped the doctrines of mobilization, sustainment has played the "supporting" role. Sustainment operations and sustainment technologies, by their very nature, follow. There is no Revolution in Military Affairs here.

CONCLUDING THOUGHT ON DOCTRINE

The luxury of doctrine-led armies, for the most part, is at an end. The practice of deriving doctrine, then producing equipment to execute that doctrine, requires a clear threat to sovereignty and much national will. Many of the Cold War era equipments are a product of the doctrine-first philosophy. The Swedish S-tank was optimized to fight a battle of attrition from prereconnoitered, hull-down, firing positions. Priority was given to protection, crew survivability, and sustainment. These doctrinal requirements found expression in frontal glacis slopes that approached 70 degrees of obliquity. This angle ensures deflection of all ballistic attacks. A fixed gun that ensured engagements always occurred with only the frontal armor exposed to the enemy, a rearward driving station for hasty retreats to the subsequent firing position, and two shifts of three-man crews to ensure continuous operations.[2] The S-tank design truly expressed Swedish defense doctrine.

The reality of a free world economy, of more than $15.5 trillion, that has more commercial research and development (R&D) activity than the combined defense budgets of the Group of Seven (G7) countries,[3] ensures that, for the foreseeable future, most emerging technologies will come from the commercial sector. Technology will shape doctrine.

THE STAR REPORT: AN EXERCISE IN FORECASTING EMERGING TECHNOLOGIES

For a complete review of the "technology first then doctrine" approach, one has only to review the study of emerging technologies applicable to the military undertaken by the U.S. National Research Council (NRC) on behalf of the Chairman of the Board on Army Science and Technology (NRC 1992). Although almost a decade old, this study offers the student of technology an excellent framework for categorizing the profusion of emerging technologies. The NRC organized a Committee on Strategic Technologies for the Army (STAR) with nine science and technology groups and eight systems panels. These seventeen panels identified twenty-one emerging technologies that are likely to have the most significant impact on land operations in the period 1990–2020. These were classified as "national critical technologies." The heads of the various panels acknowledged the conservative nature of their colleagues. Academics are cautious when it comes to predicting. To overcome this collective reluctance, the committee encouraged panels to employ a bifurcated, predictive model: "optimistic projection" and "conservative projection" became the two branches that bounded their futures.

With the benefit of ten additional years of science and engineering, it is interesting to note that some of the optimistic projections have proven to underestimate advances by an order of magnitude. For instance, the optimistic projection in 1988 for numerical computing power, measured in billion floating-point operations per second (gigaflops), foresaw numerical computing power attaining 100 gigaflops by the year 2000 (NRC 1992, 131). In November 1996 Intel Corporation attained the 200 gigaflops mark in its program to develop a 1,800 gigaflops supercomputer (Rowell 1996).

The original NRC Committee anticipated three difficulties in assessing emerging technologies for land operations: that scientists are conservative in forecasting future performances; that half of the emerging technologies of the late twentieth century were systems as opposed to discrete technologies; and that the synergistic effect of a breakthrough in an unrelated field is rarely, if ever, anticipated until after the discovery. These detracting factors persist, some of them in greater measure today. For all its details, however, the report appears to have had little or no impact on the U.S. Army. The plethora of information and advice probably overwhelmed the U.S. Army senior leadership, or equally, the doctrinal constructs of twentieth-century thinking prevented them from seeing the possibilities.

A PARTING OF WAYS?

Technology and warfare have been constant companions. Their influence on each other is so great that they have become inextricably intertwined. The decade of the 1990s is significant in two respects: the end of the Cold War and the exponential growth of technologies. As wealth and power in the Information Age are largely based on innovation, more and more nations will expend a greater amount of resources on R&D. In turn, R&D produce better tools that further augment the accelerating pace of experimentation. The cycle runs ever faster. This is the dominant trend of emerging technologies—more and faster next year. Military thought of the last 200 years has produced a finite model of doctrine to explain the nature of warfare. This model can no longer accommodate the near limitless explosion of innovation. Emerging technologies are forging new paths without considering military doctrines.

The finite doctrinal models tend to restrict the military practitioner: it requires that technology be classified and made to fit. Thus far Information Age technologies have been applied to existing equipments and used to enhance extant doctrine. This approach is likely to continue into the early part of the twenty-first century, but eventually the geometric progression of increasing inventiveness will not go unnoticed. The fields of biotechnology and quantum technology, in particular, are most likely to prove existing doctrinal thought wanting.

The separation of technology from warfare, because military thought is being outstripped by the rate of ingenuity, is unprecedented. This would herald a new order, albeit a chaotic one, but the separation of technology from warfare does not meet the criteria for an RMA. What could render weapons of mass destruction obsolete?

TECHNOLOGY AND PSYCHE

Previous advances in technology, often unsung, have indirectly affected how people think, administer themselves, and affected national morale. Seemingly innocuous advances have altered the course of military history. Block printing, paper, and double-entry bookkeeping are cases in point: "Between 1500 and 1850, though the techniques of printing did not develop very much, its productivity rose three or fourfold. The spread of printing was critical to the rise of military bureaucracies and of modern armed forces. Equally important was the invention in Italy of double-entry bookkeeping" (van Creveld 1989, 112). Paper, printing, and double-entry bookkeeping, although taken for granted today, provided seventeenth-century European armies the means to record enlistments, administer pay, maintain standards, and measure logistic support for armies with up to 100,000 regulars. Although it is hard to make the case that regular forces were a by-product of double-entry bookkeeping, the converse is true that without an efficient accounting system the maintenance of large armies would have been problematic.

An equally significant advancement occurred in counting. The shift from Roman numerals to Arabic led to the discovery of logarithms by William Napier, and of the decimal system for recording fractions by Simon Stevin (van Creveld 1989, 112). The discovery of logarithms greatly enhanced the speed and accuracy of calculations, ballistic and other. An engineering student raised on seven-digit logarithm tables in the 1960s who witnessed the advent of the pocket calculator in the 1970s can appreciate the impact of Napier's mathematical innovation and the discarding of Roman numerals 300 years earlier. The complacency with which accounting and calculating are executed is so deeply ingrained in our culture that they are now taken for granted.

The twentieth-century dictators Hitler and Stalin understood well the influence of technology on people. Technological advances necessary to construct massive edifices were exploited. The Third Reich massive architectural structures went beyond megalomania. They served as a psychological instrument to intimidate and depreciate the individual. A diminutive personality more readily identifies with the strength of the collective. Stalin did likewise with the so-called "wedding cake" series of seven massive buildings in Moscow to extol the virtues of Communism. Technology, even in supposedly benign form, can be used to shape national will. A technology that is able to affect the psyche of a nation or change society's consensus-building processes can produce grave consequences for the people and a nation's armed forces. Society early in the twenty-first century seems to be in a condition receptive to the changes that could be occasioned by advancing technology.

VIRTUAL SOCIETY

> But only in the last half-year has Internet software arisen that lets groups of people use sight and sound to socialize. This software fosters the mode of communication known loosely as virtual worlds or, more technically, as distributed virtual environments (DVEs) and is inaugurating another new era in technology: the age of social computing. (Braham and Comerford 1997, 18)

The concept of linking simulated experiences is not new. The U.S. Army Simnet, at Ft. Knox, used dedicated high-speed networks to connect simulators. Mock-ups of M1 Abrams tanks replicated crew stations. Vision blocks, optical sights, and display panels were special purpose "computer screens" that displayed real-time graphic images of the simulated world around the tank. The tank driver would advance the tank in this virtual environment through the standard driver controls while the turret crew engaged enemy targets in a computer-generated scenario that extended for miles. Other tanks in the troop were likewise portrayed and care had to be taken to avoid virtual collision or fratricide. After fifteen minutes the simulated wargame seemed very real to participants. In more developed versions simulations of other vehicles, such as attack helicopters, were introduced into the virtual environment. It was an unusual experience to meet and work with other friendly forces in Simnet and at the end of the simulated exercise be denied sharing a beer with a comrade because, in reality, he or she was several hundred miles away. One had more colleagues who shared common values on Simnet than those found in the hangar housing Simnet.

For this author, the luxury of Simnet was restricted to rare visits to Ft. Knox. Very few people, including the Canadian army, could afford the multi-million-dollar computers that generated in real time the visual and audio imagery of a virtual world. Even if purchase of a suite of Simnet simulators was feasible, access to wide-area computer networks with high bandwidth was not available. That was the situation in 1989. But Moore's Law[4]—a geometric progression of computer performance—has radically changed the situation: "Quite suddenly, it seems that the infant technology of DVE is about to leave the sheltered garden of big-budget R&D for the 40 million offices, hotels, and living rooms around the world with access to the Internet" (Rockwell 1997, 26).

Avatar, a Hindu word meaning soul released on earth in bodily form, is the name of an icon depicting an electronic person. Through the eyes of an avatar, it is possible to wander into a virtual city, select and buy virtual real estate, take up residence, and socialize with your avatar, neighbors. Imaginary? According to Rockwell, "AlphaWorld, a distributed virtual environment hosted by Worlds Inc., San Francisco, reveals urban sprawl, virtual style. Over 100,000 people around the globe are registered as 'citizens' of AlphaWorld and many of them have built their own housing, gardens, and portals to other sites on the Internet. Each subdivision is administered by a different user, who maintains property rights" (Rockwell 1997, 27).

What is the political system of this city? What is its territory? Is there a moral foundation to this e-world? Is this a fad? Projecting the growth of this phenomenon should be left to social scientists, but should it mirror the growth of Internet and computer game usage, the 100,000 citizens of AlphaWorld could have 100,000,000 neighbors in ten years.

To date most, if not all, militaries have been captivated by the application of emerging technologies to long-existing principles of war. If modern militaries are so enamored by technology, how is it that this Trojan horse in their midst has gone unnoticed?

PEACE OF WESTPHALIA, 1648

Those who lived through the chaotic years following the Reformation were receptive to change: "At the end of the Thirty Years War, accepting the futility of restoring political and religious unity by force, the European states crafted the Peace of Westphalia in 1648. It is from this we get the modern international system in which political sovereignty and territorial integrity of those states are the highest values" (L. Cook 1994). Clausewitz, more than a hundred years later, reinforced this linkage between political sovereignty and warfare with his famous dictum, *"war is nothing but the continuation of policy with other means"* (Clausewitz 1984, 69).

Even in the latter half of the twentieth century, justification for waging war was generally rooted in terms of the defense of the twin principles of the Peace of Westphalia: territorial integrity and political sovereignty of nation-states. CFP 300, *Canada's Army*, reiterates these dominating themes: "the army's primary purpose is to defend the nation... In addition to defending the nation, the army further promotes and protects Canada's foreign and domestic policy interests" (CFP 300 1997, I-1, I-2). The role of the military is thus set in the context of defending political sovereignty and territorial integrity.

The possibility of a global virtual society displacing national political sovereignty and redefining territorial integrity is very real. Some are, even now, extolling the merits of such an existence because a DVE life-style is less harmful to the environment. DVE devotees need fewer food calories, and fewer hydrocarbons are used in escaping to exotic destinations. And, perhaps, it will herald world peace.

Should our citizens withdraw their support of the modern international system, based as it is on the nation-state, and offer their allegiance to a new political order, initiated by their fondness of virtual global experiences, then the foundation of the military's purpose and the need for weapons of mass destruction would have to be seriously reexamined. Post–Cold War disarmament as covered under the Strategic Arms Reduction Treaty II (START II) and conventional weapons reduction covered under the Conventional Armed Forces in Europe (CFE) Treaty would be minuscule in comparison to that executed by a global government. In such a society the few remaining weapons of mass destruction would be centrally controlled. Nation-states and their militaries, should they exist, would be too closely monitored, possibly by optoelectronic sensors, to permit unauthorized acquisition of twentieth-century weaponry.

CONCLUSION

To date Western military thought has been blinkered by the finite nature of its own doctrinal models. The current practice of linking emerging technologies to existing combat functions has prevented a Revolution in Military Affairs. Combat functions have harnessed emerging technologies; however, the geometric growth of emerging technologies will soon defy categorization. The realization that the profusion of technologies defies classification is likely to herald a new order in military affairs, not a revolution.

Even so, the search for new doctrinal models is likely to pale in comparison to the chaos emerging technologies will wrought on society. If the citizens of the developed world choose to redefine society as a global community comprised of real and virtual lives then nation-state policies, and by inference militaries, will experience profound change. Herein lies the genesis of a true Revolution in Military Affairs. As Clausewitz pointed out, "every age had its own kind of war, its own limiting conditions, and its own peculiar preconceptions... It follows that the events of every age must be judged in the light of its own peculiarities" (Clausewitz 1984, 593).

NOTES

1. The author, as Director Land Force Development, Land Staff (1992–94), had access to data examining troop densities and areas of influence in modern times. During World War I, soldiers were literary shoulder to shoulder, one thousand-plus-man battalions every kilometer of frontage. Currently planners are studying the feasibility of a "technology-enhanced" combat unit of approximately ten persons dominating square kilometers of terrain.

2. As an armor corps captain while on exchange with the 2nd Royal Tank Regiment, British Army of the Rhine (BAOR), during 1972–74, the author participated in the British Army tank trials of the Swedish S-tank.

3. On average the nations of the G7 spend more than 3 percent of their GDP on R&D whereas their collective defense budgets are less than 3 percent of GDP.

4. Computing performance for the same cost doubles every eighteen months. At this rate computing performance increases 100 fold every decade while the acquisition cost remains constant.

5

The "American Revolution in Military Affairs": A French Perspective

Yves Boyer

Until recently, the issues raised by the Revolution in Military Affairs (RMA) were considered too typically American to be transferred *mutatis mutandis* to France and Europe. The way the debate has been conducted in America, the interests at stake in the U.S. defense establishment and the world military leadership the RMA might lend to the United States are proofs that support this judgment. The phrase "American Revolution in Military Affairs" used by Admiral William Owens, thus, translates well the notion that maybe only the United States has the capabilities to carry out this revolution (Owens 1995–96, 37). The debate surrounding the RMA specifically reflects the U.S. political, administrative, and military system, that is, a system in which one finds the benefits of intellectual debate within and outside officialdom, a tradition of nonconformism, and the capacity to translate rapidly broad policy objectives into specific political, military, and budgetary decisions.

The RMA debate in the United States has so many aspects that it is difficult to grasp its total significance. In order to disentangle this web of issues, a series of questions has to be raised:

- What are the functions of the RMA?
- Is the RMA a response to the radical transformation of the geostrategic environment, as a result of the end of the Cold War and the implosion of the Soviet Union, which requires a redefinition of the role and functions of U.S. armed forces?
- Does the RMA provide a framework for U.S. military policy so as to fill the void left by the disappearance of the Soviet threat?

THE FUNCTIONS OF THE RMA

The advent of an era of revolutionary change in military affairs as a result of technological progress in the realms of battlefield surveillance, reconnaissance, and precision strike was forecast by Soviet, and a few American, analysts well before the Gulf War showed the potential of some of these new technologies. The Gulf War, however, with its mix of traditional weapon systems and military preparation techniques, on the one hand, and advanced information systems, on the other, created a climate favorable to the RMA and in particular to its doctrinal implications. The Gulf War seemed to indicate that military art was on the threshold of a radical transformation; although what struck observers at the time was the scope of the change predicted rather than its pace. Subsequently, the scope of the RMA was likened to the revolution produced by the appearance of nuclear weapons (Libicki 1996b).

As the RMA became the subject of studies, an increasing number of technological, organizational, and conceptual issues were raised. Specific arguments arising from the lessons of the Gulf War blended with a broader questioning about how to maintain, explain, and justify America's military leadership in the post–Cold War era. In the early 1990s the implosion of the Warsaw Pact, the consequent loss of the "enemy," and talks about "peace dividends" could have led to a massive demobilization. Some in U.S. military circles dreaded that the United States would end up in the future with no credible armed forces to speak of, for lack of efforts to understand forthcoming strategic and technological changes; changes that resulted as much from the new geopolitical environment as from an accelerating movement toward the postindustrial age. In that context, failure to adapt raised the specter of a decline in U.S. power. The negative effects on military preparedness of the "peace dividends" discourse had to be countered by the attractive idea of a radical transformation of the U.S. military establishment. In that sense, one can argue that the RMA was instrumentalized as a discourse to help make sense of a period of uncertainty.

The transformation of the U.S. military instrument after the Cold War raised the question of what ought to be emphasized: the short term, that is, the "next military" and force readiness, or long-term military needs stemming from the RMA, namely, the "military after next" (Bracken 1993). Advocates of the RMA argued that the United States had to take advantage of the lull in strategic competition to invest in research and development (R&D) and a major restructuring of its armed forces rather than in short-term contingencies—as tended to be the case with official U.S. planning documents such as the *Bottom-up Review* and the *Quadrennial Defense Review*. The priorities implied by the short- and long-term visions were in stark contrast: to invest in short-term modernization and readiness meant being able to deal with regional conflicts at the expense of a radical transformation of U.S. forces that might guarantee U.S. security well into the twenty-first century; while investing in long-term transformation was to wager that emerging technologies would pay off ultimately, but at the expense of current and near-term force readiness and contingencies. Investing in the long-term option, "the military after next" or the RMA, meant asking such fundamental questions as:

- How can the United States retain its competitive edge, notably in operational concepts, against other nations, and in particular those identified as potential peer competitors?

- How to understand the new nature of such traditional dimensions of military strategy as time, distance, and the scale and tempo of operations?
- How to create new organizational forms capable of sustaining the transformation of the U.S. military system?

Some analysts, like Paul Bracken and Williamson Murray, liked to point to the spirit of intellectual innovation found in the interwar years at the Naval War College and other U.S. military institutions of higher learning as an example to follow; they stressed the importance of independent thinking and of tolerance for the resulting plurality of approaches (Bracken 1993; Murray 1997b). By gradually shifting the RMA debate from technology to the transformation of the U.S. defense establishment, this line of argumentation raises the issue of the organization of the Pentagon, of a possible reform of the delicate bureaucratic equilibrium that has kept it functioning, because without a thorough reform of the Pentagon, the RMA is unlikely to bear fruit. This is the key issue, unless some dramatic upheaval on the international scene brings a new dynamic to the development of the RMA.

THE GEOPOLITICAL CONTEXT

Can one identify geostrategic factors that could explain, from an American perspective, the RMA? Answering this question requires a discussion of two themes: (1) the nature of international society in the forthcoming decades, and (2) the role that armed forces could play in it to promote U.S. interests.

In the face of the uncertainty and complexity of the post–Cold War era, different theoretical approaches are put forward to describe the evolution of the international system and its implications for U.S. foreign policy (Mathews 1989). In the absence of the Soviet threat, which provided a middle- to long-term framework for action, the conduct of foreign policy could become driven by domestic political concerns. Eliot Cohen, for instance, warned against the risks associated with a loss of self-confidence and a refusal to resort to force, and the paralyzing effects of domestic issues on the conduct of foreign policy (Cohen 1990). Many U.S. analysts also emphasize the various factors favoring a proliferation of anarchic situations, clashes between cultures, and the emergence of nontraditional security threats, such as those emanating from nonstate actors or from environmental degradation and pandemics.

In military terms the concerns revolve around the issue of asymmetric conflicts: if the United States with the RMA prepares itself only for conflicts against the armed forces of peer competitors and for conventional warfare, could it become vulnerable to states or nonstate actors that would resort instead to asymmetric strategies to confront the United States? U.S. military leaders are conscious of the necessity of developing armed forces that can also be used at the lower end of the conflict spectrum and in operations other than war, and are less reluctant than before to envisage such operations (Reimer 1996). This opinion is also found among mainstream defense analysts; for instance, Carl Builder, a senior analyst at the RAND corporation and a firm believer in emerging technologies back in the 1980s (Builder 1985), argues that what the United States needs is not a high-tech army, but readily deployable forces that could carry out constabulary duties, which do not require much technological sophistication (Builder 1995). Another well-known military analyst, Ralph Peters, similarly argues that the present and future missions of U.S. armed forces will be more about dealing with unconventional threats, such as foreign criminal organizations, than preparing for an unlikely conventional war (Peters 1995).

Other analysts, like Susan Strange and Edward Luttwak, argue that geostrategy and issues of war and peace have been displaced by geoeconomics and globalization; perhaps a vision close to the perceptions of the Bush and Clinton administrations (Luttwak 1993; Strange 1996, 1997). In the absence of a major threat, the priority is the economy rather than military confrontation. The discourse on the importance of geoeconomics is often accompanied by arguments about the decline of the state. The globalization of the economy makes war and the state obsolete (Strange 1997; van Creveld 1996). In this new world control of flows of information, money, goods, and services becomes more important than control of territory and natural resources (Rosecrance 1996). One could argue, however, that a liberalization of trade will give other nations access to technologies they could use to develop a military potential capable of challenging the United States on a regional basis. In order to prevent such a development the United States would have to keep abreast of technological innovations that have military applications. The RMA would then be an additional guarantee of the capacity of the United States to shape the international environment (Owens 1996).

The product of these multiple assessments gives rise to a series of somewhat contradictory recommendations for U.S. foreign policy; as a result, both advocates and opponents of the RMA can find arguments that suit their views. Among the former group some argue that the United States should adopt a policy designed to prevent the emergence of a peer competitor, without necessarily antagonizing other powers (Haas 1995; Khalilzad 1995). Such a policy of "discriminatory detachment" would rest on the ability of the United States to intervene militarily over long distances thanks to the new power projection capabilities stemming from the RMA. As a result, the United States could become an off-shore balancer in different regional security systems without having to deploy significant forces abroad. This notion is close to Martin Libicki's "virtual" or "vertical" coalitions, whereby the United States would use its formidable reconnaissance and intelligence assets to assist nations around the world in resolving their security problems (Libicki 1996b, 3; 1998, 420–21).

Other analysts, like Charles Maynes, advocate a foreign policy based on a new internationalism (Maynes 1993–94). This policy was also advocated by Madeleine Albright while she was U.S. ambassador at the United Nations. At the time she summed up U.S. foreign policy with the concept of "assertive multilateralism." While a consensus exists on the necessity of a revolution in U.S. security policy, this revolution does not equate necessarily with the RMA. In light of the preceding discussion, it is clear that the necessity, if there is one, to transform U.S. defense through the RMA does not stem from changes on the world scene. On the contrary, for many American analysts the RMA is not a panacea for the pathologies of the world (dis)order in the wake of the Cold War. If the transformation of international society does not provide an obvious rationale for a radical transformation of America's military posture, where else than in the Pentagon can we find the origins of the RMA?

THE RMA AND THE PENTAGON

How and why did the Department of Defense (DOD) give birth to the concept of RMA? In order to provide a relevant answer to this question, one has to identify the channels through which the idea was instilled into the intellectual defense community and the DOD. In a way the debate about the RMA was prepared as early as 1988 by the report of the Commission on Integrated Long-Term Strategy (also known as the Iklé-Wohlstetter Commission) called *Discriminate Deterrence*, which emphasized the potential of new technologies and the transformation of the international system. This report sowed the seeds for the notion of "military technical revolution" (MTR), which became in 1994 the "revolution in military affairs" (RMA) when the agenda was broadened beyond issues of technology (Mazarr, Shaffer, and Ederington 1993; Metz and Kievit 1995).

For the RMA to take roots in the U.S. defense establishment also required the presence of promoters of this idea within the system. In that respect, Andrew Marshall, director of the Office of Net Assessment (ONA), and other analysts like Phil Petersen at the Office of the Secretary of Defense and John Hines at the ONA played a significant role by making U.S. and allied defense establishments aware of the analysis conducted in the Soviet Union on the impact of technological innovations on the art of war. Soviet analysts, including Marshal Ogarkov and Generals Gareev and Vorobeev, had emphasized how new means of conducting reconnnaissance and long-range strikes would transform operational art and tactics with revolutionary consequences for concepts of operation, doctrines, military organizations, and command structures. This set of interactions between technological breakthroughs, doctrinal evolution, and organizational transformation underlined by Soviet analysts was picked up by the ONA and developed into the RMA concept. Andrew Marshall, head of the ONA, shared this analysis with William Perry and Admiral William Owens who became respectively secretary of Defense and vice chairman of the Joint Chiefs of Staff (JCS) in 1994 (Ricks 1994). Perry was held in high esteem within DOD and his position of authority was a tremendous asset for the promotion of the RMA; while Admiral Owens was in a position, notably through the Joint Requirement Oversight Council, to make sure that the equipment developed for, and acquired by, U.S. armed forces reflected the priorities of the RMA. Owens also promoted the RMA within the JCS, where the notion of jointness provided an additional rationale for the JCS to assert its control over the various services, one of the objectives of the Goldwater-Nichols Department of Defense Reorganization Act of 1986. Jointness, that is, the seamless integration of the various services' capabilities, is an essential condition for the transformation of U.S. defense along the lines developed by advocates of the RMA. Finally, the publication in 1996 of *Joint Vision 2010* by the JCS provided an overarching doctrinal framework for what had been until then service-specific doctrines informed by the RMA (CJCS 1996).

With the triumvirate of Perry, Owens, and Marshall, the RMA became official policy within DOD from 1994 to 1996. Actually, the influence of the concept quickly expanded beyond the Pentagon and into the U.S. defense industry. For instance, the acquisition of Grumman by Northrop was influenced by James Roche, top strategist for Northrop and formerly from the ONA, who understood the importance of the RMA and saw in Grumman's expertise in surveillance technology and systems integration key assets for the emerging U.S. defense architecture (Ricks and Harris 1994). That the DOD intends to promote a transformation of the U.S. defense industrial base in order to meet the challenges of the RMA has also been underlined by the nomination of reform-minded individuals like Paul Kaminski and Jacques Gansler as under secretaries of Defense for Acquisition and Technology in recent years.

Some themes are recurring in the U.S. discourse on the RMA and the defense industry. One of these concerns the nature of future technological innovation. During the Cold War military technological innovation came largely from the defense industrial base, while from now on it will come increasingly from the whole national industrial base. In fact, innovation in such a crucial sector as computer technologies comes from a myriad of small and medium businesses with few or no connections to the defense establishment. The postindustrial age thus requires a redefinition of relations between the military and industry commensurate to the one required when the industrial age became reality (Bracken 1994: 6). The military and the DOD will need to tap the resources of thousands of businesses instead of a few large industrial firms. Weapon development and acquisition processes will have be modified accordingly, so that the military are in tune with the postindustrial production network and can exploit the military potential of new technologies. This could go as far as assigning military officers to do liaison with high-tech firms and developing within the services experts able to monitor industries and identify innovations with defense applications (Bracken 1994, 7–8). The interaction between the military and the high-tech industrial sector is not limited to the transfer of technologies. The military could also learn from the way these firms operate: team networking and flatter, less hierarchical, organizational structures could be models for developing jointness and new organizational forms for the armed forces.

While the RMA has had a definite impact on the way projects and ideas are sold in the Pentagon, it has not yet become the source of all decisions, in particular about equipment acquisition, but also in regard to doctrinal development by each armed service. It could not have been otherwise, given the power structure within the Pentagon. The institutional equilibrium that emerged from the reorganization of the U.S. defense establishment after 1945 has remained largely intact; the independence of each armed service in determining spending priorities and the incomplete powers of the chairman of the JCS—in spite of the Goldwater-Nichols Act—are serious obstacles to a full implementation of the RMA. So far, attempts at reform, such as the Commission on Roles and Missions and the Quadrennial Defense Review, have only produced modest results. No matter how deep the RMA takes roots within DOD, however, the U.S. military establishment cannot ignore the new vision of the battlefield offered by the RMA.

OPERATIONAL CONCEPTS

As previously mentioned, the concept of MTR briefly preceded the broader notion of RMA. The earlier concept emphasized a series of technologies that had been embodied before in such operational concepts as NATO's Follow-on Forces Attack and the subsequent U.S. Joint Precision Interdiction, all designed for theater conventional warfare. The Gulf War lent added credence to the notion that new means of reconnaissance and long-range strike were on the verge of transforming the art of war. While not casting their net as wide as Andrew Marshall and the ONA, a number of U.S. analysts consequently forecast a new military strategy based on jointness and the emerging technologies, or for short a Joint Attack Warfare Strategy (JAWS) (Kendall 1992). This new operational thinking emphasizes some key themes: the importance of the information infrastructure that would sustain the new mode of warfare; the deep battle, that is, the necessity of attacking the entire depth of the enemy area from the front lines to the rear; and a three-dimensional vision of the battlespace in order to reflect the increased importance of air and space assets (Galvin 1993).

As a result of these changes, the nature of future conventional warfare will be radically transformed. The exercise of command over mobile forces involved in fluid operations will be facilitated by the digitization of the battlefield. Commanders will get an improved representation of events on the battlefield and will be able to convey their intentions and the necessary information to all participants in an operation; conversely, the success of any operation will depend on the ability of the organization to understand and share in the commander's vision. Although such a representation of future command raises the danger of military micromanagement, namely, the intrusion of high-level commanders in tactical decisions at the expense of local commanders and the overall direction of operations, most analysts expect U.S. armed forces to develop a new command structure that takes into account the greater diffusion of information and decision-making stemming from the integration of information technologies into field units (Cohen 1994, 115, 118; Gumahad 1997). Long-range precision strikes and the nonlinearity of future battles imply also that attacks could be conducted simultaneously through the whole depth of a theater, that is, the close battle would be fought concurrently with strikes in the enemy's rear and defense of one's own rear areas.

The importance of information systems in the new form of warfare makes dominant battlespace knowledge a key concept; in the future armies might well struggle to get an advantage in terms of information instead of fighting for terrain features as they did in the past (Cohen 1994, 113). Precise knowledge of the battlefield, however, will not prove decisive unless it is part of a broader and more complex system architecture that links intelligence, surveillance, and reconnaissance means to intelligence-data processing, battle management, and long-range precision strike systems. This system of systems, according to Admiral Owens, "will give [U.S. armed forces] dominant battlespace knowledge and the ability to take full military advantage of it" (Owens 1995–96, 37). For Martin Libicki the system of systems, which he calls metasystem, could make possible virtual coalitions, whereby the United States "can assist its allies and influence military outcomes all over the world without really showing up" (Libicki 1996b, 3).

In a military context where seeking information is more important than the application of force, the latter should be focused on the enemy's center of gravity. Force should aim at inflicting functional, not just physical, damage. This raises a major difficulty: the necessity of identifying a target system rather than individual targets (Cohen 1994, 119). The infrastructure that sustains the smooth operation of a modern society is an ideal target system, in particular for airpower; consequently "civil society must inevitably become a target" (Cohen 1994, 123). The direct and indirect casualties resulting from the breakdown of infrastructure, however, would be difficult to reconcile with the notion that warfare based on precision strike can cause few, if any, losses to noncombatants.

A final point must also be kept in mind. The knowledge derived from the digitization of the battlefield will not dissipate totally the fog of war and friction. The aim of digitization and of the resulting dominant battlespace knowledge is to create a differential between two opponents in regard to friction; the side that benefits from these information technologies would experience a lower level of friction than the side that would not. The residual friction affecting digitized forces should not, however, be underestimated, particularly since information technologies could produce their own source of friction. A plethora of ambiguous digital bits of information can lead to incomplete or wrong deductions and to errors, as when in 1988 the U.S. cruiser *Vincennes* shot down an Iranian civilian airliner that radar operators had identified as a hostile aircraft (Cohen 1994, 113).

CONCLUSION

The preceding analysis of the American RMA debate leads to a conservative assessment of the short- to middle-term impact of this phenomenon on the organization, budgetary choices, and doctrines of U.S. armed forces. In the absence of a clear and uncontested definition of the RMA, the phenomenon can be interpreted in two ways. The first, the more ambitious, conceives it as an extensive and profound revolution in military art stemming from technological development. The second interpretation is more modest; without denying the current transformation in military art, it emphasizes that the changes are integrated in an evolutionary fashion by the U.S. defense establishment. This second perspective underlines the function the RMA fulfills within the U.S. defense debate: the RMA is an attempt to modify the current power structure and resulting budgetary choices within DOD in an uncertain strategic environment where the role and missions of armed forces are called into question.

This assessment would be only of theoretical interest if we did not consider its implications abroad; and notably in France, where the American RMA is often interpreted in more ominous terms. One school of thought considers the RMA to be a "plot," a "disinformation campaign." The RMA discourse claims that technology offers to the United States, and allies willing to follow in its steps, a new form of military power and new concepts for the use of military force; that the United States is uniquely endowed to attain this higher form of warfare, to implement it; and that nations that do not follow will be relegated to the second rank. For those who are suspicious of U.S. intentions, this discourse reminds them of the

Reagan administration's competitive strategies designed to exhaust the Soviet Union through a series of costly programs designed to counter alleged U.S. strategic and technological innovations—the best example being the Strategic Defense Initiative—only now the strategic bluff is aimed at the Europeans rather than the Soviets.

This thesis is not very convincing for two reasons. First, the U.S. politico-military system is largely decentralized. It would be an error to assume that it has the coherence of, say, the French system when it comes to developing a coherent policy such as the one implied here. Second, an analysis of the RMA debate shows that it serves above all a domestic function; it is designed to influence American actors rather than foreign ones. This domestic function can be broken down into three aspects. First, it serves to preserve the motivation of military cadres and the capacity of U.S. armed forces to innovate in the absence of the threat that was at the basis of defense planning during the Cold War. Second, it justifies new armament programs to the Congress at a time when defense is in competition with other governmental spending priorities. Finally, it serves to prevent a sclerosis in the U.S. military establishment like the one that prevailed in France and Great Britain in the interwar years and that made them vulnerable to other powers, like Nazi Germany, which took advantage of new technologies to challenge the international order.

A second school of thought, in part related to the first, links the RMA to U.S. defense firms, in search of a justification in strategic terms for their latest range of high-tech products. Again, this explanation is not convincing. The U.S. defense equipment budget has decreased by 53 percent in the period 1990–97 to reach about $44 billion, a sum well below the annual $60 billion that General Shalikashvili, then chair of the JCS, estimated necessary to equip the armed forces. In short, the notion that U.S. armed forces driven by defense-industrial interests and the discourse on the RMA are in a "shopping spree" seems far-fetched, when the armed forces are actually struggling to maintain their arsenal and readiness. In fact, a significant theme in the RMA debate is the cleavage between a few advocates of long-term investment in RMA technologies, even at the expense of the size or modernization of current forces, versus a majority of advocates of a more cautious transition that would preserve current forces (Blaker 1997a). Advocates of a "dynamic status quo" want above all to preserve force readiness so that the United States retains a range of options for the use of force across the conflict spectrum, from operations other than war to a regional war like the 1991 Gulf War. Given the constraints on the equipment budget, it is difficult to see how an ambitious policy of full and rapid implementation of the RMA could be adopted; that being said, there is no denying that the United States is engaged in a gradual, but nevertheless radical, transformation of its military power.

If we discard the two previous theses, a third and more moderate interpretation of the RMA can be offered. This is the one adopted here. If we acknowledge the necessity of thinking about the role, functions, and types of armed forces required in an international environment characterized by uncertainty, both in regard to threats and to the scope of technological progress, the RMA debate appears to be needed and helpful. The RMA has not yet attained, however, the status of an overarching project that could replace the Soviet threat to justify organization, equipment, doctrine, and deployments to the Congress and U.S. public opinion.

Many signs over the years have shown that the United States is engaged in a slow, but sustained, process of qualitative transformation of its military structure as a result of developments in computer and related information technologies; but this transformation does not yet originate from a master plan as embodied by the RMA. Instead, a cumulative series of diverse and often small measures are what sustain the confidence of U.S. authorities in their current military supremacy and in the likelihood that it will increase in coming years.

With the benefit of some hindsight, we can conclude that the RMA is both a success and a failure. It is a success because the RMA now informs most debates on the strategic options open to the United States. It is even integrated in the Congress budgetary process, as in 1996 when legislators required DOD to provide a report about the effects of technologies available in 2005 on the structure and doctrines of the armed forces (U.S. House 1996). The RMA has achieved an undeniable marketing effect; as some American analysts have observed, it is now *de rigueur* to refer to the RMA even if only for the purpose of "window dressing." In that sense, the goal of bringing an awareness of RMA issues in the public debate and among policymakers has succeeded. For Europeans, the challenge is not to fall victim to the most futuristic and technologically driven aspects of the RMA as a result of a superficial analysis or of bureaucratic interests, which would translate into an overemphasis on technological considerations in the elaboration of defense policies. The RMA is also a failure, however, because its budgetary and organizational implications cannot be carried out in the power structure that prevails in the U.S. defense establishment, a structure that none of the key actors can, or want to, modify currently.

6

The Labor of Sisyphus: Forecasting the Revolution in Military Affairs During Russia's Time of Troubles

Jacob W. Kipp

INTRODUCTION

This chapter discusses contemporary Russian military forecasters in their attempts to confront Russia's military crisis and to address the shift from quantity to quality in military affairs, that is, the Revolution in Military Affairs (RMA), during this "Time of Troubles" [*Smutnoe vremya*] for Russia. The focus of the study is on the efforts of Russian military forecasters to deal with the complex set of changes now reshaping the international system, Russia itself, its military, and the nature of future armed conflict. This chapter addresses the Russian origins of the RMA concept as developed by military forecasters in the late Soviet period. It also provides intellectual biographies of some of the leaders in contemporary Russian military forecasting, addresses their various views, connections, and objectives, and assesses the current impact of their forecasts on Russian military doctrine, force structure, military art, procurement, and research and development. One of the central features affecting Russian military forecasting is the institutional pluralism of the present epoch. If in the tsarist and Soviet periods a centralized, authoritarian order claimed a monopoly on directing military development, defining its political context and identifying threats, current Russia has no such all-powerful, central institution. President Yeltsin has fostered a government of men and not laws, of personal relations and not enduring institutions. The issue is one of competing visions and weak but evolving institutional relations.

SOVIET MILITARY FORECASTING AND THE REVOLUTION IN MILITARY AFFAIRS

The term Revolution in Military Affairs [*Revolyutsiya v voyennom dele*] is Soviet in origins. In the 1970s it replaced the term "military-technical revolution," which had been used from the late 1950s to define the central role of nuclear weapons and their delivery systems in the military strategy of future war (Sokolovskiy 1962, 235–48). The term "revolution in military affairs" implied a new and distinct relationship in the transformation of military art brought about by the direct application of scientific and technical innovation to military art without a preceding transformation of the mode of production in the economy. Thus, nuclear weapons, computers, and ballistic missile technology emerged in the military sphere without the advent of direct civilian applications for the associated scientific discoveries or technical inventions. In 1973 members of the Military Academy of the General Staff published a collection of essays devoted to "scientific-technical progress and the revolution in military affairs." These authors viewed the RMA as a far wider phenomenon than just the advent of nuclear weapons and ballistic missiles, and depicted it as a direct consequence of the accelerated pace of scientific-technical innovation in the post–World War II era, which was having a profound impact on military art, namely, strategy, operational art, and tactics. They focused their attention on nuclear weapons, their delivery systems, space reconnaissance systems, air and missile defense systems, and automated systems of troop control (Lomov 1973). During the tenure of Marshal Nikolai Ogarkov as chief of the Soviet General Staff (1977–84) the Revolution in Military Affairs assumed even greater import and was extended to the transformation of conventional warfare as well. In 1979 M. M. Kir'yan, writing in the *Soviet Military Encyclopedia*, linked the Revolution in Military Affairs to "fundamental qualitative changes taking place under the influence of scientific-technical progress and the development of the forces of production." The Revolution in Military Affairs was transforming "the means of armed struggle, the organization and training of the armed forces, and the methods of conducting war and military actions" (*Sovetskaya* 1979, 7:82). In 1982 Kir'yan placed the Revolution in Military Affairs in historical context and discussed its impact on all services and branches of the Soviet Armed Forces (Kir'yan 1982). Confronted by the burden of maintaining and modernizing its nuclear and conventional forces in the face of the RMA, a new Soviet leadership chose to seek strategic disengagement and domestic reform. In the end the very process of reform brought about the collapse of the Soviet system.

In this context Russian military forecasting may, at first glance, seems an exotic and even misplaced topic in the post–Cold War era. The Soviet Union has collapsed. Russia, which inherited its mantle and much of its armed forces, is weak, divided, and in a deep, protracted, and complex crisis. One can argue that the costs of the protracted military competition with the United States and its allies were what ultimately broke the Soviet state and contributed to the current crisis. What possibly can these former Soviet forecasters offer in the area of foresight in military affairs? Is there really any need for foresight in military affairs when a technological revolution and social change have handed the West undisputed world leadership? Moreover, has not the end of ideological conflict and Cold-War militarization put an end to the threat of large-scale war, which is the only war the Soviet Union ever really prepared to fight?

Russian forecasters are, in fact, modest in the claims for their methodology and conclusions. Their work, as General of the Army Makhmut A. Gareev, one of their most distinguished practitioners, has asserted, is like the "labor of Sisyphus," that is, the process of perpetually rolling the forecasting stone up the mountain of today's uncertainties only to have it roll back down under the impact of diplomatic, economic, political, social, technological, and military changes. The forecasting effort is never complete and final. Forecasters are engaged in perpetual struggle with the challenge of change, assessing whether the changes in the nature of armed struggle are evolutionary or revolutionary, trying to see how their tendencies will impact military art. The process is always dialectical, implying that the clever mind of a determined potential opponent is seeking to assess the same tendencies and contradictions to gain useable military advantage in future conflict. Forecasts are by their nature incomplete, contradictory, and subject to constant revision. As Gareev points out, "[h]istory knows many sagacious predictions regarding separate aspects of future war, however, to foresee correctly the nature of a new armed conflict in its entirety has practically never been achieved" (Gareev 1995, 5).

Forecasting [*prognozirovanie*], which includes highly sophisticated techniques of operations research and systems analysis, is a basic tool in the exercise of foresight [*predvidenie*]. In both cases analysts use applied mathematics to break complex problems into solvable parts and develop algorithms that solve the parts and provide a probable forecast of the outcome of the problem with optimal effectiveness. The analysts present such outcomes as statistical norms. Soviet analysts defined (military) forecasting as "the determination of future probable findings on possible directions and tendencies of development of the armed forces, military equipment, and military art in one's own country (coalition of countries) as well as in the probable or real enemy, the course and outcome of armed struggle and war as a whole" (*Sovetskaya* 1977, 6:558). Forecasting grew in importance with the application of cybernetic modeling and computers to military affairs in the 1950s. Political and military forecasting and foresight were guided by Marxism-Leninism as a unifying field theory and were viewed as a weapon the skilled commander could wield against his opponent. While Soviet authors freely acknowledged all the difficulties associated with foresight in military affairs, admitting that it was more complex than in other sectors, they still saw foresight as a skill to be used by a commander to achieve victory over his opponent (*Voyennyy* 1983, 585).

Foresight and forecasting over the last two decades have become increasingly important because of the accelerating pace of change in military affairs. As General of the Army I. E. Shavrov and Colonel M. I. Galkin observed in 1977:

The contemporary period of military construction is characterized by the unprecedented intensity of the renewal of the means of war, the appearance of qualitatively new types of weapons and equipment, by searches for such forms and means of strategic, operational and tactical action, which have never been employed by a single army of the world. New means of the conduct of military actions, new ways of perfecting the organizational structure of the armed forces, methods of their combat preparation and raising their combat readiness must be found and theoretically substantiated before they can become the property of military praxis. All this leads to a sharp rise of the role of military science, which has become the most important factor of the combat might of the armed forces, and scientific troop control is the decisive condition for the achievement of victory. (Shavrov and Galkin 1977, 3–4)

The relationship between military science and foresight is explicit. As these authors emphasized, "In its essence, *military science is the science of future war*" (Shavrov and Galkin 1977, 64).

Military forecasters were Soviet Cassandras during the late Brezhnev era. Their warnings regarding the radical implications of an emerging information revolution for the Soviet military and society found only a few sympathetic voices among the military and political leadership. One of these was Marshal N. V. Ogarkov, then chief of the General Staff. Ogarkov began to speak of a new revolution in military affairs associated with the development of advanced conventional weapons and foresaw the appearance of weapons "based upon new physical principles," which would reshape armed conflict in the twenty-first century. In 1982 he warned, "Under these conditions an imperfect restructuring of views and stagnation in the working out and realization of new issues of military construction are fraught with serious consequences" (Ogarkov 1982, 31). Such trends called into question "the most universal historical achievement of developed socialism," namely, "the military-strategic parity" between the United States and the Soviet Union (Kirshin et al. 1985, 127).

To Ogarkov the new challenge demanded a more innovative approach, reflecting the seriousness of the problem, especially in the face of the U.S. defense build-up. Strengthening Soviet defense capabilities was nothing less than "an objective, vital necessity" (Ogarkov 1985, 80). The economic implications of what Ogarkov described as a new arms race into the twenty-first century, when the Soviet economy already was running into serious structural problems, were troubling. Ogarkov's persistent efforts to draw attention to the problem were a major factor in his removal from the post of chief of the General Staff in 1984.

General-Colonel Gareev, then a deputy chief of the General Staff and its chief director of Military Science, associated Ogarkov's revolution with a "leap" in military affairs:

Now we can speak about a turning point in the development of military science and military art. In general, a new qualitative leap in the development of military affairs, connected with the modernization of nuclear weapons and especially the appearance of new types of conventional weapons, is ripening. In connection with this [process] there has arisen the need to rethink the basic military-political and operational-strategic problems of the defense of the socialist Fatherland. (Gareev 1985, 438)

Gareev's call for a military-political response to this technological revolution represented a sharp break with the Brezhnev era and was a harbinger of things to come. Because of the nature of the Soviet system, however, military forecasters focused on military-technical issues, leaving the military-political issues in the hands of the Politburo. Given the on-going war in Afghanistan and the increasing evidence of economic decline and technological stagnation in the face of a renewed arms race with the United States, hard choices had to be made.

The Soviet political leadership during the period of stagnation and the post-Brezhnev interregnum had been slow to respond to this systemic challenge. Their failure to take timely and vigorous actions in a society, supposedly dominated by long-range, rational, central planning, revealed glaring flaws in the edifice of "mature socialism." N. N. Moiseev, former head of the Academy of Sciences Computing Center and a leader in Soviet military simulation work, observed that ideological dogmatism, careerism, and bureaucratic inertia precluded a timely and effective response to this pressing challenge. The command system that had worked during Stalin's industrialization, the Great Patriotic War, and even the nuclear and space challenges, would not meet this new challenge (Moiseev 1988).

The Gorbachev era began with a challenge to the military-technical monopoly that the General Staff and Ministry of Defense sought under "mature socialism." It raised a wide range of questions associated with military-political issues that included disengagement from the Third World, demilitarization of the confrontation in Europe, and withdrawal from Afghanistan. Domestic reform demanded a significant reduction in the national resources devoted to the military. Under perestroyka the prevention of nuclear and global conventional wars became an explicit task for military science and forecasting, even as attention focused on increasing prospects for local wars and conflicts using advanced technologies (Larionov and Kokoshin 1991). The Soviet Union needed a reduction in international tensions to focus on domestic reform. Glasnost managed to push back the element of secrecy, which had given the military and the military-industrial complex a monopoly of knowledge on a wide range of technical issues. Reform called into question, however, the very priority that military requirements had attained since Stalin's industrialization. Moreover, it unleashed a wide range of discontent within the system. With the end of the Soviet state and Communist power, the Russian military had to begin a redefinition of the role of military science and foresight to fit a radically transformed environment.

The Russian military has offered its own definition of military science, emphasizing continuity and change. According to that new definition, military science is:

A system of knowledge about the laws and military-strategic nature of war, the ways of preventing it, structure and training of the armed forces of the country for war, the methods of conducting armed conflict. War as a complex sociopolitical phenomenon involves all spheres of the life of society and is studied by many social, natural, and technical sciences. The basic subject of military science is armed struggle in war. (MORF 1994, 2:130)

The continuity is in the systemic view, the emphasis upon laws, the focus upon armed struggle in war, and the author himself, General Gareev. The changes included the disappearance of the explicit linkage of military science to Marxism-Leninism and the class-struggle theory in defining the threat, the return of Russian military science into the general trends of military science as a whole, and an explicit acknowledgement of the failure of Soviet military science to provide foresight (MORF 1994, 2:130–33). In his discussion of military science in the 1980s, General Gareev, president of the nongovernmental Academy of Military Sciences, identifies military science's failure to provide foresight with the Soviet leadership's inability to comprehend the political consequences of the economic burden imposed by the Cold War: "Military science did not to a full measure foresee the preciousness of participating in the arms race and failed to work out economically more rational ways of military force structuring" (MORF 1994, 2:133).

In his recent work on the changing nature of armed conflict over the next twenty to twenty-five years, General Gareev calls for a restoration of the foresight function of military science and speaks of the exercise of military foresight as the challenge to foresee correctly the nature of new armed conflicts. He calls it a necessary but difficult and frustrating activity, "[n]evertheless this labor of Sisyphus continues" (Gareev 1995, 5, 6). Part of that struggle has been about the definition of military science, its relationship to forecasting, and the impact of existing political, economic, military, and technological trends on the nature of armed conflict. Gareev has noted the fact that various military theorists in periods of profound change in military art have argued over the existence of military science (Gareev 1994, 46). And such a debate is now going on in Russia. Military science occupied an ambiguous position even in the Soviet Union where the State Attestation Commission recognized graduate degrees in this field of study from the Ministry of Defense's institutes and academies, while the Academy of Sciences contained no section or institute devoted to military science as such. Looking back to the period of military reform in the 1920s, which led to the innovations associated with deep operations, mechanization, and mass, industrial mobilization, Gareev sees foresight as a necessary but difficult part of military reform. He concluded, citing Frunze, that military science does exist and should have a critical role in guiding the military-technical aspects of military reform (Gareev 1994, 46).

In defining the specific objective processes that only military science addresses, Gareev includes:

[t]he nature of armed struggle, the methods of preparing and conducting it on the strategic, operational, and tactical scales, the organization and technical equipping of the Armed Forces, the control (leadership) of troops (forces) in peace and war time, troop education and training, the influence of armed struggle on the economy and the economic support of force development, the preparation and combat employment of the Armed Forces, [and] past military experience. Thus, the subject of military science is armed struggle. (Gareev 1994, 47)

Unstated and implicit in this treatment is the continuing role of military doctrine in bringing these military-technical issues into line with the military-political issues. As Andrei Kokoshin, military inspector and head of the President's Security Council, has noted, the key point was to find a way of integrating both under what A. A. Svechin had defined as "the integral commander," a structure that coordinated all aspects of the preparation and conduct of war (Kokoshin 1995, 46–48).

The imperative to imagine future war emerged with the transformation of warfare from the "Age of the Great Captains" to that of mass, industrial war. The advent of nuclear weapons had the ironic consequences of negating the utility of mass, industrial war as an instrument of policy even as it pushed forecasting forward. General-Major (retired) V. V. Larionov observed, regarding the revival of military forecasting under Khrushchev, that it was directly connected to the U.S.-Soviet strategic competition and provided the backdrop to the writing of Marshal Sokolovskiy's *Voyennaya strategiya* (the first edition of which appeared in 1962). Larionov, who was one of the leading authors of that study, asserts that it was directly tied to two distinct policy objectives. Khrushchev wanted to reduce conventional forces and their burden on the national economy and to bluff the United States into accepting strategic nuclear parity with the USSR, when no such parity existed. Khrushchev's claim that missiles could be turned out "like sausages" took an industrial metaphor and applied it to strategic issues of the nuclear age and helped stimulate a strategic arms race. In the end the Soviet military-industrial complex was the chief beneficiary of this arms race in the 1960s and 1970s. Under Brezhnev production of conventional and nuclear weapons continued at great cost to the Soviet economy (Larionov 1996, 170–74). Colonel (retired) Vitaly Shlykov, who headed a research institute within the Main Intelligence Directorate of the General Staff in the 1980s, commented that this bias toward industrial war was what led to an overestimation of Western military-economic potential and large-scale procurement of both conventional and nuclear weapons (Shlykov 1996, 131). Shlykov further described the impact of excessive secrecy in assessing external threats and said that the Soviet Union lost the Cold War not because of a shortage of weapons but due to a shortage of "think tanks" (Shlykov 1996, 132). Speaking of the role of President Reagan's Strategic Defense Initiative (SDI), Shlykov says that the program was not understood. Actually, it was a major driver for all sorts of advanced weapons programs that became part of the Revolution in Military Affairs. Bureaucratic inertia, however, the "armor" bias of the senior leadership of the General Staff, and the interests of the military-industrial complex frustrated a timely response to the U.S. research and development initiatives. Shlykov asserts that Andrei Kokoshin was the figure responsible for mistakenly calling SDI a "bluff" [*blef*] (Shlykov 1996, 137). But Kokoshin emerged as the most prominent civilian defense analyst with support in military circles, a point made by Christopher Bellamy in April 1992, when Kokoshin was about to be appointed first deputy minister of Defense (Bellamy 1992).[1] Bellamy drew a parallel between Kokoshin and the tsarist banker, railroad magnate, and military forecaster, Jan Bloch (also known as Jean de Bloch), and expected him to play an analogous role.

General Larionov, who worked closely with Kokoshin, saw President Reagan's SDI a bit differently than him. It was not simply a bluff. The program of strategic defense was itself unrealistic but masked a program of technological innovations that would create new, advanced, highly accurate conventional weapons and weapons based on new physical principles. This, in turn, would mark another revolution in military affairs or, as some Russian observers have called it, "sixth-generation warfare." The practical harbinger of this revolution was the U.S.-led coalition's campaign during Desert Storm. This is a revolution based on microelectronics, automated systems of troop and weapons control, advanced sensors, and radio-electronic combat (Larionov 1996).

QUANTITY TO QUALITY: THE REVOLUTION IN MILITARY AFFAIRS

Defining the RMA is at once easy—the shift from mass, industrial warfare to information warfare—and difficult—limited combat experience and massive uncertainty about the pace, direction, and content of the socioeconomic, political, and technological changes that will reshape societies, the international system, and militaries. While it is relatively easy to date the manifestation of the RMA in practice, namely, the campaign fought by the U.S.-led coalition during the Gulf War, and note the impact of information warfare on the conduct of that war, it is much more difficult to determine the impact of its salient features over time or define the transformation it will bring to military art.

Russian analysts have noted the priority being given to the technologies seen as critical for automated command and control (Sergievskiy 1993). Their defense leadership has openly acknowledged the need for serious and sustained effort in the area of information warfare. Then First Deputy Minister of Defense Andrei Kokoshin raised the issue of information warfare under the topic, "the nature of future wars and armed conflicts." Kokoshin, Russia's leading expert on foreign defense policies and defense forecasting, put the issue squarely:

Before us very sharply stands the issue of the necessity of working out the theoretical and practical bases of the conduct of information hostilities [*protivoborstvo*], since it has become an integral part of armed struggle. Here we still have a lot of work before us, although some progress has been made over the last two-three years. (Kokoshin 1996, 7)

Under the rubric of long-range armament programs, Kokoshin has noted the need for nuclear modernization and has emphasized those systems associated with the RMA:

[C]reation of forces and means of information warfare (R[adio]-E[electronic] W[arfare], intelligence, communications, means of combat control, means of protecting systems of control from enemy actions); the development of high-accuracy weapons systems of the next generation with different ranges and missions; the development and procurement of non-lethal means of armed struggle; the modernization of the means to support the mobility of formations and units of the Armed Forces; the creation of fundamentally-new systems of personal armament and equipment for the soldier. (Kokoshin 1996, 9)

Without using the term RMA, Kokoshin provides a very clear picture of what he sees as its key directions and capital features.

Russian analysts and military leaders have been speaking of a military-technical revolution, involving weapons based on new physical principles since the early 1980s, but the practical implementation of those capabilities did come as something of a shock. The Gulf War was but a "glimpse" of these capabilities that will continue to reshape warfare in the Information Age. That this glimpse coincides with the end of the Cold War, a general reduction in forces, a radical recasting of the international environment and the transformation of the Russian state and society has made foresight particularly difficult.

The answer becomes clear if we shift the focus from the industrialization of war to the "crisis of control," which industrialization created, and the control revolution, which resolved it (Beniger 1996). James R. Beniger, looking at larger processes leading to the birth of information societies, placed its roots in a crisis of control in industrial economies that began in the late nineteenth century. In the course of resolving that crisis, "a control revolution" gave birth to information societies in the post–World War II era. Beniger does not address the very same crisis of control that affected military art, but its resolution gave rise to an analogous "control revolution" in military affairs (Coakley 1992, 32–40). In this case, however, competitive advantage was not a matter of a single firm or industry's profitability but of military victory against a determined and deadly adversary. The driving force was not efficiency in the market place but combat effectiveness.

The key point of the rise of the information society is the fact that it "has exposed the centrality of information processing, communication, and control to all aspects of human society and social behavior" (Beniger 1996, 436). Soviet society under the hegemonic domination of the Communist Party embraced industrialization and central planning as solutions for peace and war and sought to mobilize in such a fashion as to optimize its strengths for mass, industrial war. As long as the new means of control remained large capital-intensive systems associated with costly mainframe computers, the Soviet solution in peace and war remained viable. As socioeconomic changes in the West moved toward the creation of information societies, the Soviet edifice proved unable to adapt domestically in either the military or the technological sphere. Central planning, vertical control, and mass production could create quantity but it could not guarantee innovation or qualitative breakthroughs. Untested by general war, as a consequence of the advent of nuclear weapons and the balance of terror, the Soviet Union continued an investment in conventional military power that, when tested in Afghanistan, failed to win a local, irregular war. Now Russia finds itself behind in the process of transition to an information society and creating a military based on information technology.

Russia will enter this information era later, just as it did the industrial era and, therefore, has a potential advantage in learning from the mistakes of other societies in charting its own course. Serious difficulties in this transition, however, arise from the fact that it must overcome the legacy of what has been called "industrial feudalism." This legacy makes the problem of selecting a path of development to a postindustrial or information society much more difficult. One author and a leading expert on information systems has identified several alternative paths. One leads to the transformation of Russia into a source of raw materials for the developed world and its own marginalization and decline. A second leads back to industrial capitalism, based on the export of resources and the development of selected high-tech industries, and only later to a "poliform society" and postindustrial, information economy as the basis for an information society. The author proposes bypassing industrial capitalism and making a transition directly to a postcapitalist order and information economy (Tsvylev 1996, 6–7). He dismisses the path through industrial capitalism on the basis of Russia's weakened internal condition. As an example of the internal problems facing Russia in a protracted transition, the author points to the area of public health and environmental protection. The low level of current investment in this area in comparison with the developed countries leads to the conclusion that if the government does not radically increase the share of the state budget—currently 0.1 percent of GDP—now invested in the health of the nation and environmental protection, Russia will "within 10-15 years face an ecological catastrophe... and later a sharp fall in population and worsening of its composition" (Tsvylev 1996, 7). Russia's population declined from 149 million in 1994 to 147 million in 1996. Male life expectancy continues to decline and is now fifty-seven years.

In Russia the creation of an information society is seen as a matter of national necessity, even as the ground that has to be covered is great and strewn with obstacles. As R. I. Tsvylev has stated, failure can carry the gravest consequences:

However, we are speaking not only about our deepening provincialism. The point is that the price of backwardness can prove much greater. One civilization can exploit (delicately and unobtrusively) another: the countries with a traditional economy are quite probable victims of the so-called info-technological colonialism, the carriers of which come from the more highly-developed states. In its threat to the fortunes of our country this type of colonialism surpasses traditional resource colonialism. (Tsvylev 1996, 204)

The United States and much of the West are already on the edge of that society and must deal with the immediate implications of the transition, even in the military area. Its advantages are the very source of threat, to which Russian analysts point when they speak of a Russian "brain drain" to the West and the transformation of the national economy into a supplier of raw materials on the periphery of the world economy. As Russian analysts have pointed out, U.S. attention to concepts and capabilities for the conduct of information warfare has gone hand-in-hand with concern for the vulnerability of the United States itself to information warfare (Pozhidaev 1996).

Like some Western military forecasters, Russian analysts see the RMA as a matter of new means of automated control of weapon systems transforming warfare from a struggle of forces and means into a contest between systems of systems (Owens 1995b, 175–76). The term military systemology [*voyennaya sistemologiya*], a subfield of general systemology, is in wide use among Soviet and Russian military systems analysts to describe very large, dynamic, complex systems (Ryabchuk et al. 1995). In fact, military systemology is not new. In the early 1970s V. V. Druzhinin and D. S. Kontorov published two works directly relating to the application of systems analysis and system-design engineering to issues of decision-making in the areas of automated troop and weapons control (Druzhinin and Kontorov 1972, 21–49; 1976, 37–72). The authors expressly acknowledged the linkage between the use of computer modeling and systems analysis in military affairs by developing "quantitative methods of describing and solving fundamental problems of military practice" (Druzhinin and Kontorov 1976, 5–6). The volume drew upon work done in the area of mathematical modeling in other fields, including production processes (Buslenko 1964). The book included an extensive discussion of "reflexive control [*rekleksivnoe upravlenie*] of the enemy" as a form of psychological warfare and the utility of adaptive control in complex organizations. The models and language used here were those of self-organizing organic systems as opposed to the models and language of Newtonian physics and Clausewitz—*Schwerpunkt* [main effort or *glavnyy udar* in Russian] and center of gravity—to be found in force-on-force models. The combination of advanced automated command-and-control systems and reconnaissance, fire, and strike systems negate traditional correlation of forces methodology by making possible precision fire throughout the depth of enemy dispositions across a military theater.

Russian forecasters have concluded that future war will be dominated by such a struggle of systems of systems. General V. D. Ryabchuk, professor of military science at the Frunze Military Academy, has championed military systemology under similar terms and defines its method as "modeling and the functional-structural analysis of armed conflict as a process of mutual interactions of combat systems of the contending sides" (Ryabchuk et al. 1995, 3). The method of systemology, in fact, stands systems analysis on its head, emphasizing complexity and the need for models based on dynamic, evolving, self-organizing systems and a shift from modeling combat as force-on-force to system versus system (Ryabchuk et al. 1995, 3).

Russian assessments of the Gulf War confirm its importance for the development of military art. The Faculty of the History of Wars and Military Art of the Academy of the General Staff saw the war as a watershed, comparing it with the Franco-Prussian War in terms of impact, "[f]or [its] influence on the development of military art [this war] should be considered a major event in military affairs." The authors called for a serious review of military art and its assumptions:

Now, as never before, it is important to rapidly adopt and energetically introduce into the practice of the Russian Armed Forces all the latest [and] progressive [developments] that have arisen in military affairs under the influence of scientific-technical progress and the appearance of new weapons, to work out and employ more effective methods and means unknown to the enemy, to learn to make original and valid decisions in order to confound the enemy, subject him to our will, [and] achieve victory with the lowest loss of personnel. (*Voyennaya* 1995, 586)

The Gulf War was, in fact, the last war of the industrial age and only the precursor of warfare transformed by the RMA. General Gareev agrees with much of this argument but questions the emphasis upon long-range, precision systems as one-sided. Close battle will still exist but will be fought with radically different systems, as different as an armor force was from the cavalry that it replaced. Tactics will be negated and transformed (Gareev 1998, 105).

RUSSIAN FORECASTERS CONFRONTING THE RMA

For Russia the dilemma posed by information warfare is even greater as it moves from a centrally planned, militarized, command economy, where control of information was power, toward a market one, based on the easy flow of information and takes its first halting steps toward an information society. Russian experts have acknowledged this fact. Indeed, it stands at the heart of the crisis of military science. General-Major Ryabchuk for one has gone so far as to suggest a fundamental recasting of military science as complete as that attempted by the Jewish-Polish banker Jan Bloch in *The Future of War* (first published in 1898). He has made a plea for serious basic research in the field of military science, and called for an eclectic approach, using diverse methods and free of ideological controls, that Marxism-Leninism had imposed on Soviet military science (Ryabchuk 1994).

While the West has made the leap to creating information societies, Russia is trapped in the role of resource provider, an extractive economy, with little prospect of gain for its backward industrial sector from trade with the West (Isaev and Filonik 1996, 5). Russian reformers hold out the hope of achieving an information society as a distant vision. Vladimir Filippovich Shumeyko, a westernizer and chairman of the Federal Council—Russia's upper house of parliament—spoke of the need for presidential vision in defining Russia's future, which Shumeyko saw as a blending of Russian traditions and modernization on the road to the creation of an information society (Shumeyko 1996). In June 1996 General Aleksandr Lebed, then the newly appointed secretary to the Security Council and speaking of that institution's role in the issue of economic security, addressed the goal of transforming Russia into an information society, a process that had only just begun:

It is essential even at this stage to start developing methods and ways of gearing Russia to new production and financial relationships, which are characteristic of the so-called information society and which are based on increasing labor productivity first of all by creating science-intensive technologies and technical systems to control production, marketing, and financial flows. (Lebed 1996)

Within the parameters of military science, several military-technical themes touch upon the RMA and deserve serious attention. As we have noted, the current work on military systemology and the theory of combat systems, as developed by a group of researchers led by General-Major Ryabchuk, proposes to use a model of system versus system warfare in place of the existing force-on-force modeling. The emphasis is upon the synergy of systems and the combat effectiveness of attacking enemy subsystems, especially those relating to automated troop control. Captain First Rank (Russian Navy, retired) Edvard Shevelev, a former professor at the Academy of the General Staff and now a professor with the Department of National Security of the Presidential Academy of State Management, has also stressed the importance of military systemology and the theory of combat systems in training a new generation of national security cadres among Russia's senior bureaucrats (Shevelev 1996, 22–23). The objective is to provide military and civilian leaders with the tools to deal with the RMA. The theory of combat systems is seen as the most important approach available to military science in assessing the impact of the RMA on armed conflict (Shevelev 1996, 24).

A second area that deserves detailed attention is General Gareev's reinterpretation of B. H. Liddell Hart's "indirect approach" strategy but adapted for postindustrial warfare, information warfare, and the application of advanced, precision weapons to local war. His main point is that the RMA is not making the world safe from armed conflict. On the contrary, it carries a grave risk of bringing with it unintended and unexpected consequences that are beyond the ability of those who unleash war to control. Gareev warns against those who see an end to war as a consequence of the RMA:

They think that the revolution in military affairs will bring about and transform itself into a bloodless, global, antimilitary revolution. One can only hail these noble and marvelous hopes, but unfortunately they still are unrealistic: objective political, economic, nationalist contradictions remain, and they cannot always be overcome by peaceful means. Quite often wars flared up even when both sides have tried their best to avoid them. This can not be ignored. (Gareev 1998, 38)

War is still a continuation of politics, and often politics lead to gross miscalculations of means and ends. Gareev rejects the cult of "super weapons," the capabilities of which are often oversold in the struggle for their procurement. He also depicts profound changes, however, in the scope and content of future armed conflicts, which will dictate radical changes in the composition of forces, the nature of military art, and the raising and training of armed forces. Nuclear weapons will remain a powerful deterrent to general war, but significant changes in the international system have raised the risk of local wars. Gareev speaks of the application of advanced military technology to the prevention and management of local wars but warns that such efforts will not always be successful. He sees such conflicts dominated by joint (sea-air-land) operations and warns of the advent of "conventional strategic weapons," based on long-range, precision-strike systems and the need to counter this threat to national command-and-control capabilities.

Finally, there are the concepts of information operations, conflict, and warfare developed by those associated with Rear Admiral (retired) Vladimir Pirumov, former Head of the Directorate of Electronic Warfare of the Main Naval Staff, chairman of the Section on Geopolitics and Security of the Academy of Natural Sciences, and until the spring of 1997, the chairman of the Scientific Council of the President's Security Council. Rear Admiral Pirumov brought to the problem of information security his extensive experience in the field of radio-electronic warfare, which he combined with his analyses of the Falklands War and the Gulf War, and his understanding of the "cardinal changes in the military-political situation in the contemporary world." These provided him with the tools to forecast the capital role that information warfare would play "in future wars, armaments, and military equipment of the twenty-first century" (Pirumov 1996, 1). In this context he developed a broad, working definition of information warfare: "a new form of struggle of two or more sides which consists of the goal-oriented use of special means and methods of influencing the enemy's information resources and also of protecting one's own information resources in order to accomplish assigned objectives" (Pirumov 1996, 2).

Information warfare goes on in peace and war. In peacetime such operations are covert and take the form of intelligence and political-psychological actions directed against an opponent's armed forces and civilian population, and at its control systems for production, science, culture, and so forth. The objective of such operations is to compromise the information security of the population, state, and society of the opponent, while maintaining one's own information security (Pirumov 1996, 9).

With regard to the conduct of information warfare in the course of armed conflicts, Pirumov noted that in wartime such operations take on a more overt character and are focused upon getting and maintaining "information superiority" [*prevoskhodstvo*] over the enemy:

Information warfare in operations (combat actions) is the aggregate of all the coordinated measures and actions of troops conducted according to a single plan in order to gain or maintain an information superiority over the enemy during the preparation or conduct of operations (combat actions). Information superiority assumes that one's own troop and weapon command and control components are informed to a greater degree than are those of the enemy, that they possess more complete, detailed, accurate and timely information than does the enemy, and that the condition and capabilities of one's own command and control system make it possible to actualize this advantage in combat actions of troops (forces). (Pirumov 1996, 2)

As Pirumov stated, information superiority was a direct function of winning the "command of the ether," which had become a precondition for the successful conduct of air operations, fires and strikes, and then ground maneuver (Pirumov 1996, 7). Pirumov describes the impact of information warfare on future armed conflict as revolutionary:

In other words, under the influence of new weapons and new equipments, especially informational, combat has become non-linear, three-dimensional, deep, ground-air-space, electronic-informational. In this the important, even decisive, role of information cooperation and conflict, of automatized control and the disorganization of enemy control is singled out. The progressive growth of the dependence of combat tactics, its results, on the capabilities of information means and systems is one of the most important tendencies of the development of contemporary military affairs. (Pirumov 1996, 15)

Pirumov, unlike his fellow military forecasters, has commented on military-political issues and has suggested a national security concept promoting the retention of Russia's status as a great power in a multipolar world. He sees the current era as one with radically reduced risks of nuclear and global war, but one of heightened prospects for local conflicts. National and religious conflicts, socioeconomic shocks, and border disputes provide sufficient sources for such conflicts. He notes that Russia faces such threats, which have assumed the form of "large-scale terrorism," based on separatist demands and national extremism. In the case of the war in Chechnya, Pirumov asserts that Russia failed dismally in the practice of information war: "we practically were unable to effectively organize the conduct of information combat [*bor'ba*]" (Pirumov 1996, 16).

Pirumov also analyzes the use of information warfare in support of peace operations and conflict resolution, emphasizing the role of political measures in conflict management. He notes that in the case of Chechnya, the Russian government failed to make use of "measures of information combat and non-lethal weapons." Russian forces proved completely ineffective in their efforts to disrupt and disorganize Chechen command and control (Pirumov 1996, 20). Instead, Russian forces relied upon conventional methods and means of warfare, which not only could not defeat the Chechen irregulars but also inflicted significant casualties upon the civilian population and destroyed the very infrastructure upon which a revived economy and public order would depend. In the final analysis such methods inflicted serious damage on the government's own cause. Pirumov argues that the solution to this problem lies in mastering the lessons of the Chechen conflict, the creation of forces and means to conduct such information combat actions, and the working out of the appropriate methods for employing such means. According to him, "[o]nly this can achieve a definite result in such widespread actions against extremism as in Chechnya" (Pirumov 1996, 20).

As noted above, these military forecasters have close institutional ties to the Russian government's defense and security establishment, especially A. A. Kokoshin. Their ideas have influenced the current debate on military reform and Russia's military-technical response to the RMA. Russia's internal crisis and continuing instability, however, have slowed the pace of reform and left military-political issues unresolved. Those close to Kokoshin have emphasized the creation of a new Russian military that will sustain Russia's status as a great power in Eurasia. The nationalist-communist opposition has a different vision of military-political issues. As Alexander Yanov has argued, their view includes undoing

Russia's reforms, reconstituting the Soviet Union or the Russian Empire, and overthrowing the international order that emerged after 1991. As in Weimar Germany, a key part of this ideology is the explanation of defeat as resulting from "the stab-in-the-back" by reformers and democrats (Yanov 1995, 244–57). This political-ideological struggle dominates Russia's Time of Troubles and will in good measure determine whether these military forecasters are Oracles of Delphi or Cassandras (Kipp 1996a).

THE MILITARY IN RUSSIA'S TIME OF TROUBLES

The environment under which Russian military forecasters now operate can be defined by one ancient Russian term, *Smutnoe vremya* [Time of Troubles]. In historical usage the term has come to mean a period of intense and protracted crisis in the state and society testing the dominant institutions, social arrangements, and sovereignty of the state as occurred in Russia in the early twentieth century, and earlier in the late sixteenth and early seventeenth century. By the end of perestroyka, Russian intellectuals talked of a *smuta* as a short, but intense crisis of state, economy, and society.[2] After 1991 and the breakup of the Soviet Union, the onset of economic crisis, ethnic or national conflicts, weak statehood, criminalization and corruption, the *smuta* became deep, protracted, and potentially fatal to Russia's experiment with a market economy, political democracy, and an open society. Critics began to link external threats to internal instability and suggested that only an authoritarian solution could resolve the multiple and interconnected crises. Andrei Sakharov noted a pattern to the "troubles" in Russian history and suggested that authoritarianism had gained ground with the end of each crisis, laying the foundation for a new stable order but carrying within it the seeds of a new crisis. Indeed, he identified Communism and Stalin's revolution from above as such a trouble:

After each trouble Rus', the Muscovite state, [and] Russia settled down for a long time, restoring the broken economic ties, creating new state institutions corresponding to the times and tasks, re-establishing the ruptured foreign policy connections, joining together the regions that had become politically unraveled. At the basis of these processes is the ordinary logic of the nation's self-revival, its self-protection. (Sakharov 1996, 92)

Sakharov noted a wide range of possible solutions to the present troubles, ranging from democratic to neo-Communist.

The role and place of the military in Russia has become a topic of public debate in terms of current conditions, prospects for reform and outcome of the Time of Troubles. Advocates of a democratic and open society have recognized the crisis within the military as a decisive factor in Russia's situation and advocated sweeping military reforms in keeping with Russian interests, economic potential, and sociopolitical stability. They played down external threats and focused upon internal instability and the excessive costs of an unreformed military. Aleksei Arbatov, a Duma member from the reformist Yabloko Party and deputy chairman of the Defense Committee, has outlined such reforms beginning with even greater cuts in manpower, modernization of nuclear forces, and a rearmament program in the first decade of the twenty-first century (Arbatov 1997a, 2–17). Timely reform and effective civilian control of the military were, according to Arbatov, the only way to avoid an explosion within the demoralized military. At the heart of the issue was the development of a military doctrine in keeping with the international environment, the conditions of state finances, and Russia's domestic requirements (Arbatov 1997b).

The first Chechen conflict (1994–96) heightened the already high political disaffection of the officer corps from the government and existing order and made the military into an unknown factor in the current political crisis. In short, immediate requirements would seem to make the RMA irrelevant to Russia's armed forces. Military defeat in the Second Battle of Grozny in August 1996 further underscored the low combat capabilities of Russian units and once more revealed the conflict between regular army units and the troops of the Ministry of Internal Affairs. Rumors of strikes and demonstrations by elements of the military are so frequent that they have become almost normal. Creeping coups, minicoups, and rumors of coups dominate the mass media. Officers of the General Staff have sent open letters to the minister of Defense, warning that, unless the government pays the arrears in salaries owed to the military, he may face open revolt. In short, Russia's multiple armed forces are both highly politicized and in desperate need of reform after a decade of much talk and little action. In June 1997 Colonel-General Lev Rokhlin, the hero of the second assault on Grozny and the chairman of the State Duma's Defense Committee, sent an open letter to Yeltsin as commander in chief, charging that military reform was little more than slogans and that the army was dying. He began the organization for the Movement for the Support of the Army, Military Science, and Defense Industry and managed to generate chapters in sixty-nine of Russia's oblasts and republics. In the fall of 1997, the Movement held its first congress, drawing support from serving soldiers, veterans organizations, cossacks hosts, and a wide range of nationalist and opposition parties, including Zyuganov's and Zhirinovsky's parties. In its opposition to the government's program of manpower reductions and military reform, the Movement has adopted the rhetoric of the nationalist-communist opposition (Radzikhovskiy 1997).

CONCLUSION

Past Russian and Soviet responses to military defeats and periods of intense political and socioeconomic instability suggest that concepts and ideas now being developed will have a profound impact on the Russian military in the first decades of the twenty-first century. In almost every past case, Russia began its response to the challenge of change in a disadvantageous position. In each case the response involved adaptation of "foreign" initiatives, creation of a Russian infrastructure, and the evolution of a distinctly Russian solution. During the previous Times of Troubles, the military emerged as winners, precisely because they were the leading institution in this adaptation to change, even as their structure, size, and costs later became a brake on the further evolution of the system. A key element in that outcome was the perception of immediate threats and the need for military transformation to meet such threats. A capital feature of the position of current reformers within the government, for example, Andrei Kokoshin, and some of the moderate opposition, for example, Aleksei Arbatov, has been the perception that Russia now has a "window of security." The absence of a pressing external threat has given it time to carry out necessary domestic reforms to revive state and society while postponing the acquisition of advanced military technology until such changes generate sufficient resources to fund the effort sometime around 2005. In the meantime investment should be directed toward the maintenance of a research and development capability. The immediate threat to the state is its own instability and the crisis within Russian society. A key element of that internal instability is a large, obsolete, and demoralized mass army, which must be reduced to make way for a smaller, professional, and modern force. Arbatov has pointed to weak civilian control of the military as a factor in delaying necessary reforms and downsizing. The end product of such reforms will be smaller, more professional, armed forces that can defend the interests of Russia as a great continental power.

A unifying theme that connects various strands of the defense debate in Russia is a new attention to geopolitics, and a wide and diverse interpretation of what geopolitics means for Russian defense and security policy. In its most benign form, geopolitics represents simply a pragmatic escape from the ideological assumptions of Marxism-Leninism and a search for a security policy that takes into account Russian vital interests in the various regional security systems in which Russia must operate. Rear Admiral Pirumov provided such a benign definition of geopolitics as "a science concerned with socioeconomic and political processes in their inter-relations, and with the systemic influence of the natural environment on state power" (Pirumov 1994, 200). In its ominous form geopolitics represents nothing less than a revanchist ideology, anti-Western and imperial in form and content. Whichever position comes to dominate Russian security policy, it will address the RMA and seek to modernize Russian forces in a manner in keeping with its threat perceptions, political objectives, and ideological assumptions. Perhaps the most important recent work in this regard is Aleksandr Dugin's *Foundations of Geopolitics: The Geopolitical Future of Russia* (Dugin 1997). In this work Dugin provides an ideological-geopolitical basis for an ongoing conflict between Atlanticism and globalism [*mondializm*] and Russian Eurasianism. In this interpretation a conflict between the United States, as a thalassocracy, and Russia, as a telluocracy, is inevitable. Dugin, a self-styled "conservative revolutionary," rejects both liberal democracy and Communism in favor of a third path. Russia's current reformers are no more than "agents of Western influence" (Dugin 1997, 439–48).[3] Dugin's geopolitics calls for the creation of a sweeping Eurasian alliance from North Africa to the Far East to recast the balance of power against globalism. In military terms this third path rejects the current proposals for military reform in Russia because they would transform the armed forces into those of a regional power. Instead, Dugin proposes to create an army of imperial reach. These forces would emphasize high technology and global systems to challenge the United States. Thus, nuclear weapons, strategic defenses, space assets, naval, missile, and strategic aviation forces get top priority. Ground forces are treated as internal forces and only airborne forces are given serious attention (Dugin 1994, 263–71). While some points in this military program sound very much like those of Russia's current reformers, the context of a renewed global military competition is quite different. For Dugin geopolitics defines the constants for Russian foreign and defense policy, and for its military doctrine the core reality is that "the main 'potential enemy' is namely the Atlantic Bloc" (Dugin 1994, 299).

In the end Russia's response to the RMA will depend less upon the military-technical arguments of military forecasters and more upon the outcome of the Time of Troubles. The outcome of the current crisis will determine whether Russia can become a normal great power, seeking integration into the world economy and international system or will adopt the position of those seeking to restore the empire. Andrei Kokoshin, a leading proponent of military modernization to meet the RMA, has called attention to a sociopsychological vacillation over the nature of Russia and its place in the world. Without the resolution of that struggle, Russia cannot define its national interests or rejoin the community of nations. Kokoshin described Russian national character of the late 1980s and early 1990s as vacillating between "messianism and self-praise and self-destruction, negating all that was valued in our society even things that were of the very highest world standards" (Kokoshin 1995, 249). Kokoshin hopes that this vacillation will give way to sober appreciation of Russian culture and history in all its grandeur and tragic dimensions. His explicit models for such a national recovery are post-war Germany, Japan, and France, that is, states that adjusted to the loss of empire and achieved the status of great powers. That choice will ultimately shape the Russian state and society and define Russian interests and the threats to them. Military-political considerations will shape the military-technical response, just as they did in other times of military transformation and reform.

NOTES

1. Bloch, however, never enjoyed broad support within the Russian War Ministry. His ties and support came out of the Finance Ministry, where he favored reduced defense spending to promote capitalist economic development in Russia (Kipp 1996b).

2. In a discussion with Dr. Andrei Piontkovsky at a round table held at King's College, Cambridge, in January 1991, the author raised the question of whether the Soviet Union had not entered a new "time of troubles" with all its complexity and duration. Dr. Piontkovsky answered that it was a "trouble" [*smuta*] but thought that it would be of short duration.

3. On Dugin's views on the third path as uniting the extreme left and right in an assault on the liberal democratic order in the name of "the Absolute Revolution," see Aleksandr Dugin (1994).

7

The PLA's Revolution in Operational Art: Retrospects and Prospects

Jianxiang Bi

The revolution in military affairs (RMA) sought by the People's Liberation Army (PLA) is designed to build armed forces for the twenty-first century, based on an optimal combination of "innovative operational theories," "reasonable forces structures," and "advanced military technologies." To achieve this strategic objective, the PLA has conducted research on each of those interacting elements (i.e., theories, structures, and technologies), rather than on the RMA as a whole. The PLA's revolution in operational art (ROA) aims to develop an "adversaries-doctrines-surpassing" [*chaoyue duishou*] and "Chinese-tradition-falsifying" [*chaoyue ziwo*] theory in an effort to respond to different policy agendas, threat perceptions, and conventional warfare (Chen 1997; Cheng, J. 1996, 214–15; Zhang, X. 1997). As a result the PLA is determined to produce a cast-iron, comprehensive operational art based on high-tech, combined-services and combined-arms warfare, and limited war operations. This requires a transformation of its traditional operational art based on human resources, ground forces, and total war operations in order to make it more flexible, less dogmatic, and more suitable to contemporary operations while using obsolete weapons.

The contradiction between a "cast-iron" operational framework and "flexible" approaches led senior commanders and military scholars to constantly debate issues related to revolution and tradition, limited and total war, and weapons and soldiers throughout the military modernization period. This contradiction confounded the military's efforts to narrow the gap between the contemporary and the traditional, to make distinctions between limited and total war, or to work out the relationship between technological and human factors. Western scholars were equally frustrated, finding it difficult to understand how the PLA could be victorious in contemporary high-tech limited wars using obsolete weapons and traditional operational art. Their frustrations are reflected in the literature that focuses on China's strategy. Nevertheless, few, if any, scholars have examined the PLA's finely tuned ROA, though it is often indirectly touched upon. The commentaries have continually missed key points, overestimating or underestimating such a revolution. A major reason why the topic is misunderstood is the lack of primary materials, which itself contributes to misinterpretations and misperceptions (Godwin 1992; Johnston 1995–96; Lewis and Xue 1988; Malik 1990; Shambaugh 1996). In fact, the contradictory conclusions arrived at have further mystified the PLA's operational art. This has happened despite a plethora of new and uncensored materials now available in Western university libraries.

This chapter examines the progress made in revolutionizing the PLA's operational art, assesses pertinent conceptual, organizational, and technological issues to explain the mixed results of the revolution, and demonstrates consequential implications for contemporary high-tech limited war operations. The examination starts with the PLA's concepts, so as to highlight the framework in place. It then analyzes the conceptual ROA sparked by early theoretical debates on "seeking truth from facts" and the 1979 Sino-Vietnamese border conflict, the attempt to modernize operational art in the mid-1980s, and the new challenges facing operational art in the early 1990s. Finally, it explores the issues that prevent the PLA from developing a cast-iron, comprehensive operational art compatible with high-tech limited war operations relevant to the twenty-first century.

CONCEPTS

The PLA's concept of operations [*zhanyi*] has roots in the distinct tradition of Mao Zedong's "people's war" [*renmin zhanzheng*]—the Clausewitzian total mobilization of societal resources for war, in which masses of soldiers sought the total destruction of enemy forces with available weapons, to liberate and defend their homeland. People's war has molded Chinese operational art, which is preserved by both commanders and scholars and has become the bible for operations regardless of space, time, and enemy. The concept of *operations*, however, lacks a clear-cut definition. The authoritative military encyclopedia defines it as "the total sum of engagements waged by armed forces according to a central plan in a direction or a region of war within certain time for reaching partial objectives of war or war zone-wide objectives" (Zhongguo 1989, 1236). In contrast, standard military terminology simply characterizes it as "the total sum of engagements fought by rivals on the basis of plans in a direction or space" (Li, Jijun 1994, 149). Some military scholars challenge those vaguely defined concepts, since they fail miserably to reflect operational tradition and realities. For them, operations are "military action conducted by group armies or equivalent troops according to a unified plan within certain time for specific objectives" (Guan 1993a, 7–8; Sun 1990, 58–61). In spite of the conceptual disputes, the concept has four basic elements: (1) operations involving a series of ground engagements as part of war; (2) the basic combat unit is one or several group armies; (3) operational space and time are coordinated in accordance with central planning; and (4) operational objectives are, normally, if not exclusively, designed to annihilate thoroughly, rather than just defeat, large enemy units.

Today the PLA faces difficult questions about this traditional definition. Though a group army or group armies may fight a series of ground engagements,[1] as is often the case with border conflicts, the level of conflicts may never escalate to the operational level. Or one side may be intent on waging combined services and arms operations, while its adversary may be trying to fight guerrilla warfare. Or both sides may use their forces to engage and defeat rivals at or over the border. Chinese military scholars, however, deliberately seem to avoid dealing with those definitional problems.

The concept of *operations* also contains two levels: basic theories and applied theories. Basic theories [*jichu lilun*] or operational science [*zhanyi xue*] focus on a theoretical study of operations that provides universal laws, concepts, principles, and methodology. Basic theories determine applied theories [*yingyong lilun*] or operational art [*zhanyi fa*], which concentrate on specific laws such as the operational nature, characteristics, contents, procedures, and methods—operational art guides any operations, be it combined, land, naval, air, strategic missile or other operations, and operational logistics.

Applied theories, or operational art, originate from military tradition and operational experiences that provide intellectual justifications for the refinement of basic theories. Based on Mao's lessons extracted from people's war operations, they involve four components: initiatives, offense, the three-in-one system, and societal support. First, *initiatives* are designed to fight (and perpetuate the momentum of) operations by emphasizing the creation of opportunities to find the enemy's weak points through the exploitation of strategic, operational, and tactical environments. Second, *offense* aims at striking the identified weak points through a series of rapid and unexpected concentrations of superior forces, encirclement, outflanking, and close, night combat in waves to break the enemy's spirit, will, and cohesion, and to physically destroy his large units one by one. Third, the *three-in-one system*—the fighting styles—is directed at engaging in combined operations through mobile, positional, and guerrilla warfare; waged by regular forces, local troops, and militias; and by ground, navy, and air forces so as to maneuver the main forces to where they can deliver a devastating blow against the enemy. Fourth and last, *societal support* under unified command of the party, the government, and the military is essential to secure operational logistical supplies. Also central to applied theories or operational art is flexibility. To make them flexible enough to encompass various applications, applied theories are designed to fit operational environments, rather than operational environments being truncated or distorted in order to fit them. As primary criteria for judging, guiding, and fighting operations, they serve as a bridge linking war and engagements.

At the theoretical levels of war and engagements are the sciences of strategy and tactics, which deal respectively with the laws governing war situations as a whole and engagements. Chinese strategy, operational art, and tactics are always multifaceted in the sense that the three levels may be affected in different ways by political, economic, social, military, and technological considerations and may therefore be incongruent with the logical order of strategy, operational art, and tactics. The essence at each level is total mobilization for total victory. In the Chinese phrase it is "to pit the weak against the strong," namely, to fight human resources–

oriented operations to compensate for deficiencies of technology and logistics, or to exchange human resources and territory for time.

Regardless of whether it is total or limited war, human factors—intellectual, physical, and psychological—are decisive. This theme persists throughout operations and is the "cast-iron" framework of operational art. On the other hand, the four components are always skillfully combined, since operations are complex military activities; tractable in some respects and intractable in others. The successes and the failures of historical operations suggest a dialectical tractability-intractability pattern; keeping operational art open is the most rational way to fight successful operations. Despite valuable experiences, however, the relevance of traditional land operational art to contemporary combined services and arms operations seems limited as a result of the RMA. To meet new demands in a fast-paced world, the PLA needs a new "cast-iron" comprehensive operational art designed to explain, guide, and fight combined services and arms operations.

CONCEPTUAL REVOLUTION

A theoretical debate on criteria for judging truth was launched by reformers in the late 1970s, in order to "emancipate the mind" [*jiefang sixiang*], to "break dogmatic spiritual shackles" [*dape jiaotiao zhuyi jingshen jiasue*], and to restore the tradition of "seeking truth from facts" [*shishi qiushi*]. Much emphasis was placed on the issue of whether Mao's thought was still valid as a guide for modernization. Reformers adopted a pragmatic approach to Mao's thought. On the one hand, they vigorously criticized "two whatevers" policies (praising whatever policies Mao formulated and carrying out whatever instructions Mao issued), denounced Mao's personality cult, and attacked some of his policies in order to remove "the whatevers faction" from power. On the other hand, they tried to draw a theoretical demarcation between Mao's mistakes, which apparently "derived from lack of practical experiences in political and economic reconstruction" and "divorced theory from practice," and Mao's wisdom, which underlay party, state, and military legitimacy and infallibility—and thus also the reformers'—since without it, the reformers' claim to control the party, the state, and the military might itself appear illegitimate. With this new perspective on Mao's thought, crafted to ensure the reformers' legitimacy, "seeking truth from facts" became the fundamental criterion for judging truth.

This debate triggered the PLA's attempt to develop the new operational concept of "killing chickens by using a heavy sword" [*shaji yong niudao*], according to which the PLA brings overwhelming superior forces and firepower against a weak neighbor's invasion—in order to fight a short battle and to force a quick resolution. The attempt provided the momentum for the ROA centering on the questions of reassessing "military thought in the 1930s," "operational experiences in the 1940s," and "training methods in the 1950s, 1960s, and 1970s." In fighting against political opponents or in distancing themselves from the "two whatevers faction," senior generals strove to revolutionize Mao's operational art so as to shore up support for reforms. The revolution aimed neither to preserve all operational principles Mao proposed nor to abolish established military thought, combat experiences, and training methods; but rather to consolidate the political power of senior ranks within the PLA. This politically motivated revolution, however, overlapped with the 1979 Sino-Vietnamese border conflict, a Chinese "people's limited war" against Vietnam, designed to teach it "lessons" for maintaining southern border order, while sustaining the Khmer Rouge regime in Cambodia. The conflict was a test of Chinese operational art, not only in that it exposed anomalies in Mao's operational art, but also in that it showed the necessity to theorize changes in war and operations in order to plan future war and operations against a possible foreign (then presumed Soviet) invasion.

Initiatives

Traditional initiatives centered on the creation of combat environments favorable to the strategically defensive PLA, through calculations, manipulations, and dispositions designed to identify the enemy's weak points. In the 1979 conflict, however, the strategically offensive PLA tried to explore Vietnamese strong points in order to launch a broad frontal, preemptive strike to gain a quick resolution. This changed focus deeply frustrated the PLA, since it was hard to identify where the Vietnamese strong points were along the border.

Vietnam relied on army-civilian joint defense, which involved "frontal linear defense" and "area-oriented defense" with regular armies, local troops, and militias sustained by mass societal support along wide border areas with limited depth, while attempting to organize counterattacks against the invaders. As Vietnam had limited troops for deployment along the border and limited mobile troops for a rapid response (its best troops were actively engaged in Cambodia), its border defense created large undefended gaps. To remedy this weakness, it gave priority to "people's war," in which regular forces, local troops, and militias coordinated with one another to strengthen border defense through positional or guerrilla counterattacks in the jungle. This Vietnamese operational art partly reflected its rich experiences in the Vietnam War, wherein the United States had favored conventional division-level operations, while Vietnam responded with infusions of its own regulars to create large-scale guerrilla operations. The war became a highly fragmented struggle, with few large battles, and no decisive ones until the end. Thousands of small unit actions took place every day across Vietnam. The war had no fronts. Because American professional soldiers had been trained, equipped, and organized to fight regular war with special emphasis on modern weapons, mechanical mobility, and concentration of firepower, they expected to search and destroy the enemy in large-unit combat. The United States failed to prepare for and failed to win against guerrilla warfare (Osgood 1979, 40–43; Rosen 1982, 106–9). Army-civilian joint guerrilla warfare was the essence of Vietnamese operational art.

Like American soldiers, Chinese soldiers did not fully prepare for guerrilla warfare, either. They severely underestimated Vietnamese soldiers, and American experiences in Vietnam. As a result, they sought American-style large-unit offensive operations to quickly destroy Vietnamese defense forces. This error, according to senior commanders, sprang from old mindsets and arrogance. Some, if not all, commanders assumed to know the relevant factors and military maxims very well, so they downplayed factors favorable to the Vietnamese defense (e.g., solid fortifications and mastery of guerrilla warfare and infantry weaponry). Chinese soldiers, on the other hand, were poorly trained, less experienced, and unfamiliar with operations against guerrilla warfare, partly because of the Cultural Revolution. Lack of serious war and operational planning was also reflected in the fact that some soldiers were simply massed from construction sites or farm fields; and that higher command issued combat orders, restructured combat units, and distributed weapons as troops proceeded to the front. Some commanders did not even know their soldiers, and vice versa. Poor preparations contributed directly to the inability to handle Vietnamese "hit and run" tactics at the very beginning of the conflict. And apparently, operational commanders never did extract proper or useful lessons from their naive underestimation of Vietnamese troops. As soon as the conflict ended, they once again reiterated that they understood Vietnamese approaches to war operations; and that it was easy to deal with them (Zhou 1995, 246, 255). In fact, the PLA's failure to use guerrilla warfare against (Vietnam's) guerrilla warfare severely thwarted its initiatives to create favorable combat conditions, so as to teach Vietnam the promised "lesson."

Offense

Traditional offense stressed the concentration of superior forces to encircle and outflank the enemy and then to fight close, night combat in waves to destroy him in one single blow. Operations in Vietnam in 1979, however, witnessed changes in operational objectives, from the traditional annihilation of large units, to the occupation of key targets along the border with small units and strong ground firepower. The changes raised essential questions about how to manage offense under contemporary conditions.

In offensive operations the PLA followed its tradition of concentrating superior forces, firepower, and logistical supplies across services and arms, since this method had repeatedly proved to be the most efficient way to fight a strong enemy with obsolete weapons in total or limited war. Yet the operations in Vietnam appeared to contradict this tradition. The PLA, now armed with relatively advanced weapons, faced relatively weak Vietnamese regular units, local troops, and militias. In order to destroy the large units in one short blow, Chinese commanders tried to "use a heavy sword," but felt embarrassed not knowing how many troops would constitute a sufficiently heavy, sharp sword to destroy the enemy.

According to traditional doctrine, the extent to which Chinese forces could be concentrated was determined mainly by the size of operations in which they would be involved. Large-unit operations in the jungle would waste resources; but small-unit operations could not easily achieve the objectives, because Vietnamese regular and local troops took advantage of fortifications and terrain favorable to them, while militias harassed Chinese rears and flanks. To calculate how many troops would be used in combat, it was argued, the PLA must account for factors such as troops responsible for covering command posts, rears, and transportation lines, as well as for searching and destroying dispersed enemy soldiers and militias. But however superior their numbers, combat troops still proved insufficient. The difficulties in estimating enemy forces and in deploying troops were compounded by further difficulties in identifying the enemy. In combat it was hard to make distinctions between militias (sometimes local troops) and civilians, since none of them wore "uniforms." "They" constantly struck Chinese troops, however, and threatened rears and flanks. Operations were further complicated by poor combat environments. The weather in the mountainous jungle was extremely hot and humid. Roads were too narrow to deploy large numbers of tanks, artillery, and armored vehicles. To avoid these problems troops must, senior commanders thought, conduct a quick campaign by concentrating superior forces. In fact, the efforts to eliminate guerrillas by waging small-unit combat often led to dispersing, rather than concentrating troops (Long 1992, 211–14; Zhu 1996, 85–89). Despite the waste of resources, commanders managed to mass more troops and firepower than required, organized them into several echelons, which alternately struck key targets, while small units destroyed dispersed Vietnamese soldiers and guerrillas.

Such operations required encircling and outflanking Vietnamese troops in order to assault their rear, while sustaining a frontal main attack. The mountainous jungle provided cover, but it also created difficulties for the movement of mechanized troops. Despite such difficulties, some PLA units successfully carried out operational encirclements as deep as seventy kilometers behind the Vietnamese defense lines along with support units; but others often lost their way as a result of the absence of advanced location systems and communication equipment. Even worse, once they were deep behind enemy lines, they could neither transport wounded soldiers to safety nor supply troops with ammunitions, because of lack of a reliable logistical system.

More important, night, close combat was a fundamental principle for fighting a strong enemy, equipped with advanced weapons, but in Vietnam, the PLA appeared to be unable to fight its favorite combat, since Vietnamese troops were used to it. During the night they were always on high alert against any possible strikes. Conversely, long-range firepower by daylight often reduced Vietnamese initiatives. Regardless of great efforts made to destroy Vietnamese main forces, the planned large-unit operations had to revert to small-unit guerrilla warfare, with occasional surges of regular military action, in which Vietnamese troops harassed Chinese formations and inflicted heavy casualties on them.

Three-in-One System

The traditional three-in-one system opposed flexible fighting styles against the enemy's regular warfare. In 1979, in contrast, the PLA waged regular warfare against Vietnamese guerrilla warfare. According to the high command, this conflict was a limited war aimed at destroying Vietnamese regular troops who defended strategic points and vital communication lines. The PLA quickly found, however, that once Vietnamese defenses "collapsed" (sometimes fortifications were simply abandoned), enemy troops dispersed in the jungle and fought small-unit actions. Such tactics forced Chinese regulars, local troops, and militias to reorganize into small combat units to search and destroy them, while securing logistical supplies, transportation lines, and rear areas. Such dispersed small-unit combat severely restrained them from waging combined arms operations.

Combined arms operations refer to coordination among infantry, artillery, and tanks. In theory, artillery and tanks provide fire support for infantry, but in operations they often failed to achieve close cooperation with the infantry. Some artillery commanders did not know how to take advantage of the terrain, or how to deploy in combat formations, or how to perform combat tasks. Although their technical skills were considered "fine" according to their own standards, their tactical and operational skills were poor because they misinterpreted their mission as mainly providing fire support for infantry soldiers under combined operations command. Such misinterpretation convinced them that they had no operational art, or tactics, or autonomy to sustain infantry operations. It led to friendly fire on infantry troops (Song, C. 1984, 250–52). Tank crews, like artillery troops, had no sense of combined arms operations. Without proper coordination, advanced communication equipment, and combined training, tanks and infantry troops were often disconnected in operations. Tank crews conducted their own battles without infantry support, while infantry troops launched their own assaults on Vietnamese troops without artillery and tank support (Huang 1984, 260–61). Those problems stood in sharp contrast to experiences in previous wars, in which the PLA fought infantry operations in waves without or with little combined arms support, and showed the necessity of adapting the traditional three-in-one system to contemporary operations on foreign soil.

Societal Support

Traditional societal support focused on securing logistical supplies provided by the masses and organized by the unified command of the party, the government, and the military. In the 1979 conflict the PLA experienced poor societal support for operations, though more than 320,000 militiamen were directly involved in combat missions (Zhu 1996, 85). In the war zone most local residents on either side of the border were members of national minorities, who shared culture, language, and religion. Because of the close ties, they were reluctant to become involved in operations against their friends or family members across the border. The PLA had to help local party organizations and governments "reeducate" the masses to provide traditional logistical support. Yet poor societal support, exacerbated by the severe geographic environment, undermined logistical supplies. The PLA tried to maintain a ratio of about 1.76:1 between forces and logistical support personnel, but failed to provide sufficient ammunitions, fuel, food, and water (Zhang, Z. 1984, 529). All supplies needed for combat depended exclusively on soldiers, who carried their own ammunition, food, and water, or on militias, who carried supplies for soldiers, so that operations again fell within the old-style one-week offensive pattern used during the Korean War. Shortcomings in logistics arose, to some extent, from mismanagement or lack of a powerful command system—hundreds (sometimes thousands) of trucks and tanks were regularly jammed in a narrow jungle road for several days. The PLA had to assign 21 percent of combat soldiers to protect those jammed roads or transportation lines (Zhou

1984, 569). Despite these problems, militias and civilian laborers made great contributions to the operations in Vietnam. They carried out tasks such as carrying and supplying combat materials for units at the regiment level and below, transporting wounded soldiers to the rear, and repairing or safeguarding roads and transportation lines with soldiers. The PLA realized that, without full Chinese societal support, it could not conduct successful human resources–oriented operations on foreign soil.

Assessment

The most important lesson the PLA learned or relearned from those human resources–oriented, infantry-centered operations was the lack of a unified operational art compatible with contemporary border conflicts, along with issues such as poor adaptability, poor training, and the inability to properly handle weapons. Traditional operational art was merely a set of "cast-iron" principles that stressed a flexible application to operations. Without a comprehensive operational art, commanders mechanically followed these principles, essentially to avoid political, rather than military, setbacks. In fact, political pressures narrowed initiatives to adapt the principles skillfully to combat. Su Yu, deputy minister of Defense, argued that Mao's operational principles were still "valid," though some were "invalid." The methods of operations fighting varied in different wars or in different stages of a war, in different times and places, with different enemies or with different weapons. It was necessary to adapt the traditional operational art and tactics to contemporary war and operations, and to study and master the latest tactics developed along with new technology and equipment. Contemporary war and military operations required this generation of soldiers to refine theories for guiding war, operations, and engagements (Su 1984, 24). Even though Su questioned the relevance of Mao's operational art under contemporary conditions, commanders still conducted training on the basis of what Mao said, rather than on the basis of combat conditions. Li Desheng, commander of Shenyang Military Region, was critical of these old mindset commanders. Mao's military thought, he contended, was a science. Yet his theory, based on particular cases, is not universal truth, and cannot guide all training and combat (Li 1984, 339–40).

To replace Mao's "flexible" (operational) dogma, senior commanders sustained the concept of a flexible operational art, but accepted his "cast-iron" framework centering on initiatives, offense, the three-in-one system, and societal support as the fundamentals with only slightly different interpretations. According to them, the conduct of future war, operations, and engagements against foreign invasion must be based on their own combat model. In the words of Song Shilun, president of the Academy of Military Science (AMS), when war against foreign invasion broke out, "we will not accept any rule to define limits or boundaries for operations such as limited time, areas, and means. If the enemy launches an aerial attack, we will wage a land attack; if he attacks us from the east, we will respond from the west" (Song, S. 1984, 56). Unlike the traditional strategy of "luring the enemy in deep to conduct mobile warfare," the PLA would mainly fight "positional operations around borders" against foreign invasion. During the operations, the rational concentration of superior forces and firepower for combat in waves was the surest way to annihilate him totally, but "soldiers must be well organized, equipped, and trained" (Zhang, C. 1984, 125). Clearly, senior commanders were critical of Mao's "flexible dogma," in the name of the ROA so as to make it consistent with ongoing political reform. Thus, the formulation of unified operational art allowed senior commanders to show loyalty to political reform, but also to preserve the people's war tradition. The significance of this politically motivated ROA in the late 1970s was the conceptual change, designed to restore a set of more flexible operational principles to provide a rational guide for operations against potential foreign invasion. Nevertheless, in the end, the PLA simply used Mao's strategic thought of human resources–oriented total war to revolutionize his operational art in hopes of making it consistent with contemporary limited war operations. The revolution remained incomplete, since the PLA never explored or found a solution for swiftly killing weak "chickens" by employing "a heavy sword" in future border or offshore conflicts.

THE SEARCH FOR A UNIFIED OPERATIONAL ART

In 1985 China finally abandoned its long-time assumption of fighting "an early war, major war, and nuclear war" on the basis of Deng Xiaoping's assessment of the international strategic environment. Instead of the old mindset, a new assumption focused on preparing for local, limited war or low-intensity conflict on China's periphery. To make the PLA congruent with the new strategic assessment, Beijing dramatically demobilized one million troops (some were simply transferred to armed police units), restructured services and arms, and upgraded weapons and equipment. The PLA became leaner, more combat efficient, and relatively modernized. Those changes, however, required a new operational art consistent with contemporary local, limited war along the borders. Major military threats to national security, according to the PLA, were from the Soviet Union, who then had more than one million troops along the Sino-Soviet-Mongolian borders. This perception implied that the regions neighboring the Soviet Union, namely, Northeast, North, and Northwest China, could become battlefields during a potential Soviet limited invasion.

To minimize the military utility of Soviet nuclear weapons, Gao Rui, vice president of the AMS, asserted that a revolution in technology would undermine the dominant position of nuclear weapons as a principal combat means (Gao 1988, 5). They would be undependable, whereas conventional weapons would be decisive in future limited war. His comments apparently echoed Marshal Nikolai Ogarkov's RMA—the revolution relegated nuclear arms to the role of final deterrent and focused instead on the modernization of conventional forces and on the development of new conventional and exotic weaponry that might acquire a nuclear-type efficacy without the nuclear weapon's albatross of loss of control and purpose. On the other hand, to maximize the political utility of the splendid Chinese tradition in contemporary war conditions, Yang Yi and Yin Pelun also claimed that an opponent who had advanced conventional weapons and contemporary operational art without adequate ideas about how to fight against people's war would not prevail in local limited war (Yang and Yin 1988, 36–43). While some military scholars downplayed the decisive roles of Soviet nuclear technology, advanced conventional weapons, and contemporary operational art, the PLA's dilemma then appeared to be its inability to systematize, theorize, and carry out operational art and experiences to make them compatible with contemporary local, limited war, partly because of domestic politics, and partly because of the lack of sufficient means to launch effective operations—due in part to inferiority in technology. Li Jijun, vice president of the AMS, also accused "conservatives" of having blind faith in tradition. For him, operational practice desperately needed further development, yet no attempt was made to update traditional operational art in order to develop a new operational art. In the contemporary world, there was never a poorly organized and equipped army that could defeat the enemy by simply following traditional operational art or imitating enemy operational art (Li, Jijun 1994, 149–57). Yet the consensus was to consider as a rational alternative for executing future antiaggression operations the incorporation of Soviet deep-operation concepts into Chinese operational tradition. The ROA was to develop a unified operational art of "total deep, three-dimensional, multidirectional operations" [*quan zongshen, liti, duofangwei zhan*] to defeat a superpower invasion.

Initiatives

Like Soviet deep operations, the PLA's deep operations emphasized initiatives to create favorable combat environments. Along with operational nuclear weapons, tank forces suitable for rapid advances through regions subjected to weapons of mass destruction could be employed on the main axes of land operations and in offensive operations in conjunction with rocket troops, aviation, and airborne landings to seize or strike key objectives in the enemy's deep rear, making possible the rapid achievement of the most immediate operational objectives (Vigor 1988, 143–44; Wang 1989; Yao 1988). Those changes implied a series of shifts: from infantry and artillery coordination to combined services and arms operations, from linear battles to air/land battles, and from a focus on the front to a focus on front and rear operations simultaneously. Local, limited war became air/land, multidirectional, deep operations. To make it suitable to such a war, unified operational art was designed to deliver a devastating blow against the enemy's deep rear through calculations, manipulations, and dispositions, while strengthening a well-established frontal defensive line or conducting frontal attacks.

In response to any Soviet attempts at deep operations, the PLA's calculations centered on "attacks on vital points," "three-dimensional operations with focus," "survivability," and "the balance between firepower mobility and forces mobility." "The vital points," it was believed, were weak and susceptible nodules, namely, command posts, command, control, communications, and intelligence (C^3I) systems, weapon control systems, and electronic warfare troops. These soft targets had complicated structures, a unified system, and high vulnerability. The damage of one part would likely lead to the collapse of the whole system, reduce the effectiveness of harder facilities, put the enemy in a less favorable position, and make him powerless. "Three-dimensional operations with focus" meant that, in deep operations, the front was still the focus, while in three-dimensional operations, land operations were the focus. Due to increased firepower, "survivability" would be a priority for all commanders to avoid or reduce casualties. The balance between firepower mobility and forces mobility was essential to produce comprehensive combat effectiveness (Huang, Li, and Xiao 1988). Even though it stressed attacks on enemy rear targets, the PLA's traditional operational art favored linear battles, frontal strikes, and forces mobility. A major barrier to preventing the PLA from waging deep, three-dimensional operations was the shortage of technology, which forced it to employ forces mobility to adjust firepower mobility. In contemporary combat, however, infantry soldiers never caught up with firepower mobility. Poor forces mobility in fact neutralized the effectiveness of firepower. Obviously, the PLA tried to identify Soviet weak points, while avoiding Soviet attacks on its own weak points.

Manipulations were regarded as a way to paralyze the enemy's comprehensive offense and defense. Despite superiority in the technology necessary to wage deep, three-dimensional operations, the presumed enemy had his own weakness inherent in war waged on Chinese land. He was unfamiliar with the terrain; his field offense and defense would create undefended space open to deep penetration; and his vulnerable combat systems could be paralyzed by striking weapons, C^3I, and logistical systems, and the relatively undefended rear. Meanwhile, the PLA's capability to conduct deep operations would gradually be improved. Recently re-equipped, relatively advanced, long-range neutralizing artillery could reach the enemy's deep rear; new tanks and armored vehicles substantially increased mobility, defense, and firepower; and new air defense guns and missiles formed a fire network at high, medium, low, and ultra-low altitudes. As a consequence, further strengthened land/air mobility, assault capabilities, and three-dimensional combat effectiveness could eventually produce decisive, disarming effects. With rich experiences in operations on home land, the PLA had a solid foundation for fighting deep offensive operations against an invader's weak points (Meng 1988). But the PLA understood that there remained huge technological gaps between China and the Soviet Union. A superpower's smart bomb could destroy a tank, whereas, to destroy the same target, Chinese artillery fired perhaps as many as 180 shells; its advanced helicopter gunships and combat aircraft might strike targets with missiles while remaining beyond the effective range of Chinese air defenses; and its forces could fight deep, three-dimensional operations, whereas the Chinese heavily depended on linear, mass infantry operations with limited air or naval cover. The fundamental weakness inherent in Chinese "short arms, slow legs" required the PLA to create opportunities to strike swiftly and force the enemy to reverse his way of fighting.

Thus, it was postulated, skillful dispositions might facilitate the crushing of a Soviet offensive. They involved comprehensive defensive means such as constructing positions or fortifications in strategic areas and directions, deploying troops in echelon formations, coordinating air/land firepower, and placing obstacles in deep rears to defend key points, to control linear areas, and to deny the airspace. The measures reinforced "a deep, focused, multidirectional, three-dimensional defensive system," which would foster resistance against Soviet attacks and prevent rapid breakthroughs by centering on space, time, and strength. As traditional firepower waves were replaced by contemporary persistent shock firepower, the resistance against such firepower on the deep, three-dimensional battlefield became an issue of life and death. To curb the air/land firepower assault and reduce casualties caused by conventional, nuclear, chemical, and biological weapons, it was recommended that combat units should take advantage of the terrain to construct solid positions, while launching counterattacks to change passive defense into active defense—with "deep surprise attacks inside and outside defensive positions." In deep surprise attacks inside positions, soldiers should adopt traditional ambush, block action, surprise attacks, and counterattacks to annihilate the enemy, while in attacks outside defensive positions soldiers should prevent enemy movements by waging mine warfare or carrying out blocking actions or long-range fires against mobile troops, command posts, control centers, and logistical support bases, thus disrupting enemy attack formations, or at least delaying their attacks. To achieve the objectives, operational emphasis must be placed on the skillful management of relations between "frontal and rear defense," "holding positions and waging surprise attacks outside positions," "resistance against land strikes and resistance against air strikes," and "independently holding positions and emphasizing mutual support."

Deep defensive operations contained two interdependent elements: frontal and rear defense. Frontal defense was the center of the defensive system, because Soviet assaults on deep rear targets were simply directed to support frontal attacks. As long as they could hold positions, defensive units should concentrate on cutting off Soviet attack channels and crushing their breakthroughs. Although the Soviet Union might employ its airborne troops to penetrate, outflank, and strike the PLA's deep rear, firm control over frontal positions would eventually stabilize combat lines. The focus on the front and the rear would secure comprehensive defense. "Holding positions and waging surprise attacks outside positions" were designed to take advantage of defensive strength to disrupt the enemy's coordination, to reduce his combat effectiveness, and to strike his reserves and soft targets. Defensive units should block frontal attacks, preventing the frontal enemy from joining those who had penetrated, while organizing mobile firepower and troops to destroy the latter. To maximize resistance on the ground, "resistance against the enemy's air strikes" was essential. The Soviet main assault forces were mechanized infantry troops. Their deep multiroutes, multidirectional operations might pierce the PLA's defensive system and race into its rear creating isolated, surrounded positions. The combat units holding those isolated positions would need strong willpower to fight independent combat, and have a strengthened sense of mutual support in the effort to hold key positions.

The comparative study of operational strengths and weaknesses was designed to avoid the Soviet main strength, and to minimize frontal engagements as much as possible, while selecting the vulnerable points that were to be disrupted. The most vulnerable targets, according to the PLA, were soft and hard targets in the deep rear. Swift strikes against them would give the PLA a breathing space. But the absence of technological means to collect information, along with the prospect of Soviet preemptive strikes and rapid breakthroughs, implied that the PLA would not in fact be able to determine the exact locations of the soft and hard targets. For the strictly military purpose of deep operations fighting, Chinese initiatives became meaningless.

Offense

A dominant feature of PLA's deep operations at the time was to launch Soviet-style deep, multidimensional, preemptive strikes or counterstrikes. Senior commanders and military scholars held that deep operations were merely the extension of traditional operational principles such as encircling and outflanking to strike the enemy's weak rear points (Yang and Yin 1988, 48–49). As the annihilation of the enemy one by one required combat units to strike from different directions and at different places, the deployment of troops in multidirectional, echelon formations might reduce time and distance gaps between assaults and deprive the enemy of breathing spells. Thus, small combat-unit operations were an effective way to wage surprise attacks against his rear command posts or logistical centers, to ambush him in movement, and to strike his rear-deployed artillery. As soon as they achieved expected objectives, small combat units should quickly withdraw or disperse from the battlefield. To avoid heavy losses, Li insisted, targets must be "selected," "small," and "isolated" (Li, Jijun 1994, 159–60).

In contrast to traditional encircling, outflanking, and close combat, deep operations gave priority to striking the (Soviet) rear with the intent to facilitate a strategic transition from defense to offense. This approach to offense persisted throughout the PLA's deep operations developing period. In real operations it would not be easy to strike such targets. The Soviet Union would move its mechanized second echelon troops into the salient quickly so that they might take up defensive positions along the exposed flanks. The employment of precision munitions would further strengthen the protection of the flanks. Prior study of the terrain and adequate combat intelligence would also help identify where counterstrikes were likely to be delivered and allow the preparations necessary to thwart them. Equally important, the lessons learned from the Sino-Vietnamese border conflict showed that the PLA had no chances to organize large-scale counterattacks over difficult terrain and against enemy defensive measures. In 1979 those difficulties seriously undermined China's offensive against Vietnam and would continue to challenge Chinese counteroffensives against a Soviet invasion.

Three-in-One System

Unlike Soviet deep operations, which are dependent on combined-arms mobile forces under long-range air/land firepower cover, the PLA's deep operations rested on combined mobile, positional, and guerrilla warfare, in which regulars, local troops, and militias cooperated to strike the enemy's rear and front under limited firepower cover offered by ground, naval, and air forces. In fact, PLA's deep operations remained infantry-centered warfare. Central to Chinese deep operations was a unified command designed to reduce command layers, to control operations, and to increase rapid responses. Such command was based on a flexible combination of "centralized command for large battles" and "decentralized command for small battles," in an effort to maximize the combat-initiative potential of all commanders. Under these commands, combined military and civilian resources provided strong professional, technical, and logistical support to (hopefully) ensure operational successes.

In those missions, combined regular, local, and militias forces took advantage of night and terrain to penetrate deep into the Soviet rear. Once there, they would swiftly assault vital points such as roads, bridges, and tunnels. The missions might be reinforced by utilizing the air force for "limited air blockade." As the enemy had strong land and air mobility, the PLA acknowledged that the reliance on land encirclement, associated with "limited air blockade," might not result in the total destruction of the encircled enemy. In fact, deficiencies in coordinating air/land firepower might weaken prospects of Chinese offensive combat effectiveness.

Despite changes in weapons, the three-in-one system was also anticipated to improve Chinese defense. The establishment of multi-echelon and combined troops might facilitate the countering of Soviet deep operations; small combined units would harass the movement of their forces; and the organizing of mobile, three-dimensional, multi-laid, and area-oriented firepower would likely reduce enemy firepower. The new interpretation of the three-in-one system convinced the PLA that combined deep operations must focus on selected key targets in order to account for variability in a main defense direction, enabling change in defense directions according to Soviet main attacks (Zhang 1988). Such operations required exceptional C^3I to link small units maneuvering on the battlefield. The absence of powerful C^3I, however, reduced the potential effectiveness of the PLA's deep operations.

Societal Support

The cornerstone of the PLA's deep operations was societal support that sharply contrasted with Soviet professional logistical support. In essence, China's strategy was defensive. This defensive nature provided a foundation for and justified the mobilization of masses. The guidelines for logistical support under local, limited war conditions were "one logistics system for all the services" [*sanjun yiti*], "the compatibility of military logistics with civilian supply" [*junmin jianrong*], and "the integration of logistics for peace and war" [*pingzhan jiehe*]. *Sanjun yiti* aimed at facilitating supplies across services and arms, while reducing administrative layers. This logistical system was sustained by a larger military-civilian network of logistics: the PLA stockpiled only weapons and key spare parts, while the civilian auxiliary provided other war and operational materials, and masses undertook noncombat missions such as the construction of field positions and barriers to block or slow Soviet mechanized units (Xu 1988, 260-62). This logistical network for war and peace was under the joint command of the party, the government, and the military. Societal support of this kind would, it was hoped, ensure logistical supplies for deep operations.

Once again, the ROA not only served to show political support for Deng's strategic transformation, but also reflected the real desire to incorporate Soviet deep operations into the PLA's traditional operational art. The old belief in the total mobilization of masses, nurtured by ideology and history, clearly encouraged the PLA to follow the traditional way of operations. But such operational tradition never explained how to wage successful deep operations without sufficient air/ground firepower, reliable C^3I, and secure logistical support. The lack of those capabilities made its deep operations less than ideal. The only possible solution appeared to be to fight human resources–oriented total war operations against a Soviet limited invasion.

NEW CHALLENGES

In the 1990s the clash of Chinese and American (Western) cultures became a dominant issue of reforms. To preserve its traditional socialist values, China rejected the American concepts of individual liberty, human rights, and democracy, and portrayed them as well as a series of contentious issues in its relations with the United States as threats to its national interest. Deep concerns over these threats, together with the successful campaign against Iraq waged by the U.S.-led coalition in 1991, shaped the ROA, contributing to the PLA's serious study of the air/land battle doctrine, in order to understand the American way of fighting under high-tech conditions. Even though the United States is not an immediate enemy, the PLA insists, the doctrine does raise questions about the effectiveness of Chinese "total deep, three-dimensional, multidirectional operations" under high-tech limited war conditions. As a result, it then became the measure that the PLA employs to determine its combat effectiveness.

To win high-tech limited war, the consensus among senior commanders and military scholars is in favor of "conducting comprehensive resistance, winning through protracted operations" [*zhengti kangji, chijiu zhisheng*]. This new "old idea"—people's war under high-tech conditions—was deemed the best weapon to curb American-style high-tech limited war. For the PLA, the most vulnerable point of high-tech limited war lies in its "limits." To reduce high costs, at the very beginning of the war, a superpower may take all necessary means, including strategic weapons, and strike strategic targets in order to achieve his limited strategic objectives in the shortest possible time. Chinese deep operations must center on this vital point, through both the expansion of the operational space and time and the reinforcement of army-civilian resistance, if they are to gain the final victory in high-tech limited war.

Initiatives

The PLA's initiatives in high-tech limited war are designed to identify weaknesses inherent in the U.S. air/land battle doctrine, but high-tech limited war ironically challenges this traditional approach. High-tech limited war stresses "synchronized operations" under a joint and unified command responding to missions that come from a supreme political authority. It aims neither to destroy the enemy, nor to occupy his territory, but to devastate specific political, economic, and military targets. The essence is to fight combined services and arms operations linking close, rear, and deep battles into an operational whole by relying on firepower and attrition to keep combat losses as low as possible, while inflicting heavy casualties on the enemy. The objective is to collapse the enemy's will and avoid, if at all possible, the use of nuclear weapons (Dai 1993, 50; Freedman and Karsh 1991, 40–41; Jacobsen 1990, 347; Kipp 1987, 143–46, 154–55). The challenge perplexed senior PLA commanders and military scholars. Some argued the enemy was "invisible," "untouchable," and "indestructible," as a result of means of delivering firepower from long distances or high altitudes, or from under the protection of composite armor, so that it was impossible for an army equipped with obsolete weapons to conduct such a war; but others asserted human factors would remain decisive in high-tech limited war, since "soldiers control high-tech weapons, high-tech weapons do not control soldiers." As Deng stated, "there is no such thing that computers can replace field commanders" (Li, Jihong 1994, 65). Despite the controversy over weapons and soldiers, both sides emphasized initiatives to assess strengths, to identify weaknesses, and to create opportunities to strike the enemy, rather than to conduct decisive operations in the sense of "confronting the tough with toughness." According to calculations, the air/land battle doctrine was not suitable to "urban warfare," "jungle and irregular warfare," and "offshore warfare." Other anomalies in the U.S. doctrine suggested that the PLA might defeat the enemy by manipulations, devoted to confusing the enemy by "creating false targets," "hiding troops and equipment," and "taking advantage of environments." A combination of these elements would eventually lead to an expansion of operational space and time so as to turn high-tech limited war into total war (Liu 1995, 10–13).

Those objectives required the PLA to keep dispositions with an emphasis on the interplay of "exterior-interior," "offensive-defensive," and "positional-mobile combat." "Exterior-interior" operations aimed to resist enemy frontal attacks and to prevent penetrations and airborne assaults into the deep rear, while striking enemy rear echelons, reserves, and other targets. "Offensive and defensive" operations were devoted to assaulting the enemy's deep rear—since offense is the best defense—while strengthening positional defense at key points. In other words, only through swift attacks on the enemy's deep rear could the PLA enlarge operational space and time and generate initiatives to conduct comprehensive operations.

High-tech limited war requires limits. These limits would, senior commanders and military scholars assumed, create "safe havens for the civilians and the military," which would facilitate the conduct of attacks or counterattacks on the enemy's poorly defended deep rear. If the PLA accepted the limits set by the enemy and restrained its defense and offense within limited combat areas against the strikes of enemy high-tech weapons, it would surely be beaten on the battlefield. To shift the center of gravity, it must open up a second battlefield to smash the enemy's offensive. The solution was to fight a "people's limited war," rather than a limited war within the enemy's framework (Hu 1994). The premise for conducting such war was to understand the enemy. The traditional way to know him depended on infantry soldiers and mobilized masses to collect information, but this did not fit the requirements of high-tech limited war. Instead, the PLA now intended to utilize both advanced means such as "satellite and electronic, air, and radar reconnaissance" and "mobilized masses to collect information." This combination of "contemporary" and "traditional" approaches would compensate for inferiority in gathering information (Zhang 1994). Even if it got all the information it needed, however, Liu Jingsong, commander of Lanzhou Military Region, acknowledged, the PLA still lacked a "unified intelligence unit" under regional, combined-operations command to collect, store, and disseminate information, because a regional, combined-operations command was a coordination center, not a command center (Liu 1992, 16). Thus, such intelligence about the enemy might not lead to his destruction. Conversely, the revolution in military technology might in fact make him indestructible, in that he might fight long-range, low-observable, digitized operations through the employment of cruise missiles, stealthy aircraft, and an array of sensors and data-fusion technologies to strike targets. The operations would then become "cleaner" by reducing the casualties and collateral damage normally associated with traditional combat. But, due to its operational tradition, the PLA does not seem to have taken those scenarios seriously.

Offense

The focus of the U.S. air/land battle doctrine on the center of gravity weakens Chinese traditional offense designed to destroy large enemy units one by one. The PLA became worried about the growing mismatch between high-tech and traditional operational objectives. Unable to determine where the enemy would strike, the PLA could not afford the deployment of huge troop numbers along borders or in rear areas to protect presumed key targets or launch counterattacks. The dispersal of resources along overextended borders or in vast rear areas would only contribute to losing the initiative. Moreover, operational limits severely constrained the PLA's mobility, decreasing the chances to translate defense into offense, but increasing the opportunities for the enemy to wage shorter, more decisive battles. Thus, instead of passive defense, it was thought that mobile counterattacks might be a rational solution, requiring the deployment of limited troop numbers "in possible foreign invasion directions" or "at hot spots along the border and in the rear." The main operational forces would be located "at appropriate places of strategic, operational depth to launch flexible counterattacks." The bottom line was to make sure that the enemy did not penetrate deeply into China.

Deep operations were deemed an effective way to smash high-tech limited war. According to the PLA's own statistics, in the Gulf War, the coalition forces' deep, incessant air bombing destroyed "twenty-six Iraqi rear commanding posts," "75 percent of communication centers," "44 percent of airfields," and severed logistical supply lines that connected the front with the rear (Zhang, M. 1997, 22–23). The figures indicated that secured deep defense was the foundation for waging strikes against the enemy's deep rear. But the effectiveness of counterattacks relied on the quality of weapons and soldiers, not on their numbers. The change further generated concerns about the traditional approach to the concentration of superior forces. The operational concentration of superior forces was normally adjusted "within a group army," in the sense of giving priority to a main combat direction or main assault by increasing the numbers of infantry troops and weapons. Forces in the main assault direction were strengthened, while forces at other places or directions were weakened; comprehensive combat effectiveness was reduced. As the concentration of forces rarely involved other group armies, it was hard to achieve operational superiority. Moreover, high-tech war required the concentration of not only forces, but also firepower and technology. Thus, it became necessary to build "reinforced group armies," by "transferring crack troops and advanced weapons across the PLA" in order to narrow technological gaps between the PLA and the enemy. Such forces could be used to destroy the enemy's hardware and to smash his software (Qiu 1994, 775–76).

An immediate question emerging from the concentration of superior forces was how to balance the relationship between concentration and dispersion. If forces were overconcentrated in operations, they would become targets for the enemy's powerful firepower, so human waves were no longer the benchmark of combat effectiveness. Conversely, "combined, decentralized, and autonomous combat units at the regiment or division level" might fight successful close, night combat in the enemy's deep rear. But technological innovations substantially increased operational transparency. Night no longer sheltered masses of soldiers armed with obsolete weapons. This change questioned traditional night combat (Deng 1994). The worst nightmare then was an offensive battle with the joint action of several autonomous combat units: how could these units be informed without reliable C^3I? how could they be massed without sufficient air cover? and how could they be deployed to the designated battlefield without efficient force projection capabilities? Traditional offense did not offer any solutions to these new issues.

Three-in-One System

The U.S. air/land battle doctrine undermines the effectiveness of the PLA's traditional three-in-one system. In high-tech war, the enemy uses precision missiles and the air force to sustain independent, massive, incessant raids, sending only small numbers of infantry soldiers or none at all into combat in order to force a quick resolution. War would be on a smaller scale, quicker, and more decisive. In contrast, China had vast territory, rich resources, and strong masses of soldiers armed with obsolete weapons, it might be unable to employ such strengths to execute traditional warfare. Despite this sharp contrast, the PLA maintained that regular armies, equipped with relatively advanced weapons, were the main force; that local troops became secondary; and that militias were complementary to them. An optimal combination of them could still create a comprehensive force able to win high-tech limited war. Such armed forces must have a balanced and focused development. The air force, with special attention to early warning, and command-and-communication systems; fighters capable of rapid reaction; aircraft with night, all-weather, ultra-low flying capabilities; long-range air transport assets; inflight refueling capabilities; and air defense systems, would be "the focus of the services"; while electronic troops, using various means of electronic warfare and countermeasures, would be "the center of the arms." Among combat troops, "high-tech intensive forces such as rapid response ground forces, naval mobile special forces, and long-range air striking forces would be operational crack forces" (Guan 1993b, 40). In operations the special and rapid-response mobile forces were expected to be closely associated with local troops and militias. Senior commanders and military scholars, however, were increasingly cautious about the functions of militias, because they would be unlikely to fight traditional guerrilla warfare. Their main responsibility might be the securing of logistical support.

Without strong air power, the PLA maintained that it was very hard to smash the enemy's air/land battles or to conduct large-scale ground operations—making deep operations meaningless. To make matters worse, China's ineffective air force, designed to provide firepower support or cover for ground operations, is often dispersed and in fact assigned to infantry troops to protect frontal combat lines (Dai 1995, 79–81). The poor quality of Chinese aircraft, along with the inadequacy of their weaponry to fight independent operations, led the air force to seek "local air superiority" [*jubu zhikong quan*], rather than "operational air superiority" to ensure ground forces' mobility, massing, and logistical supply lines (Ball 1993–94, 86; Shambaugh 1996, 293–96; Zhang, Honghai 1993, 149). Despite these fatal weaknesses, antiquated aircraft were still expected to play a key role in air operations. The logical solution was a high-low (quality) mix of Soviet state-of-the-art Su-27 fighters and indigenous versions of Soviet MiG-17, 19, and 21 or Il-28 and Tu-16 aircraft. Poor capabilities to penetrate enemy air defenses, together with limited access to accurate and timely information about enemy deployment and movement, might discourage the Chinese air force from conducting "limited deep strikes" [*youxian zongshen daji*] (Hu 1993, 161). Seeking easy targets, the PLA held that enemy airborne warning and control platforms and inflight refueling tankers might be ideal ones, since they were not equipped with weapons. Their destruction would likely paralyze the enemy's command, bombing, and air strikes. The PLA clearly understands that, without a strong air force, it is impossible to win high-tech limited war.

High-tech limited war called for a unified command and control of services and arms in operations in order to combine two separate ground and air operations into one. Due to the absence of advanced, reliable C³I, combat units had to adopt some backward but practical methods such as "secret signals," "light," and "sound" to ensure effective communication between air and ground forces; or the air force would send "liaison groups to division-level units" for coordination. Sometimes, these methods did not work as a result of poor understanding between different units and they occasionally led to friendly fire incidents (Zhao 1992). Moreover, emphasis on a unified command and control has created another problem, namely, the focus of operational training is exclusively on command procedures, while training data, essential to quantitative analysis, computer simulation, and digital warfare, are lost (Feng and Feng 1997).

Societal Support

American-style high-tech limited war raises serious questions about Chinese traditional societal support for ensuring logistical supplies, but "people's war" remains an essential part of the PLA's operational art. As Jiang Zemin argues, "in accordance with characteristics of limited war under contemporary technology, especially high-tech conditions, the PLA should thoroughly study and actively search for laws for guiding contemporary people's war and develop operational art to beat the enemy with obsolete weapons" (Li, Jihong 1994, 64). The rapid development of military technology did not fundamentally change the Chinese perception of people's war; it only added (some) new meanings. Accordingly, the focus of people's war under high-tech limited war conditions was on "comprehensive national strength." To sustain war, the PLA needed not only "small combined military forces" to assume combat duties, but also "large combined societal forces" responsible for logistical and combat support. The expected high consumption rates of arms, ammunitions, fuel, food, and water required the PLA to constitute an enlarged logistical support system to ensure continued operations. The establishment of a chain of command, composed of the party, the government, the military, and police from the war zone to the district or county level, would reduce the red tape related to military and civilian "feuding hierarchies" [*tiaotiao*] and "territorial units" [*kuaikuai*], and strengthen ties among soldiers, party organizations, governments, militias, and civilians. Under this command, a civilian logistical network would provide operational support such as transportation, medical support, communications, and maintenance (Xiong 1996, 683–87). On the other hand, the PLA was determined to restructure logistical command and forces to make them consistent with high-tech limited war operations. To strengthen logistical capabilities, the PLA readjusted "the internal structures of regional logistical command to give top priority to rapid response logistical support within hot spot areas"; "the ratio of logistical forces between war zones or within a war zone to give top priority to a focused war zone and an important direction"; and "the ratio of service and arm logistical forces to give top priority to the navy, the air force and the second artillery (strategic forces)." Senior commanders and military scholars further recommended "establishing organizationally distinct and high priority rapid support brigades and mobile supply centers to ensure rapid response combat troops operations," "to build high-tech oriented logistical reserves," and "to improve mobility, C³I, and survivability of logistical troops" (Cheng, M. 1996, 19–20). The PLA gradually moved, though it lacked funds to implement the recommendations, in the direction of establishing professional logistical troops. For the PLA the combination of civilian and military networks and professionalized logistics would facilitate the fighting and winning of high-tech limited war.

The ROA itself has recurrently become concerned about the future ramifications of American political, ideological, and economic threats to China's national security. The intensive study of the air/land battle doctrine showed the PLA's determination to crush high-tech limited war by "conducting comprehensive resistance, winning through protracted operations." This principle aimed at prolonging operational space and time to wear the enemy down, through human resources–oriented deep operations. Future operations might, however, involve little or no direct force-on-force contact, thanks to mutually supportive changes in concepts, organizations, and technology so that the PLA's traditional ways of fighting might become irrelevant and even useless; while technological inferiority, insufficient force projection capabilities, and poor coordination between ground and air forces might further jeopardize its ability to manage deep operations under high-tech conditions. The poor combination of old and new concepts in fact continues to undermine the PLA's efforts to develop, test, and refine an operational art compatible with high-tech limited war operations. The unbridgeable abyss between aspirations and resources remains.

CONCLUSION

The ROA has not yet fundamentally transformed the basic structure of the PLA's operational art, with its special emphasis on initiatives, offense, the three-in-one system, and societal support; and which is always deceptive, offensive, infantry-oriented, and society-centered. The inability to develop a cast-iron, comprehensive operational art comparable to Soviet deep operations and the American air/land battle doctrine to fight combined services and arms operations derives from traditional perceptions, forces structures, and technological inferiority.

First, the traditional perceptions of human resources–oriented, ground-centered, total war operations cast a dark shadow over high-tech-oriented, combined services and arms, limited war operations. The irreconcilable contradictions between combat assessment standards, value criteria for judging operations, and relations among strategy, operational art, and tactics apparently are barriers to any formulation of a cast-iron, comprehensive operational art, unless China admits the bankruptcy of people's war under contemporary conditions. The ROA, however, would then become a political and ideological, rather than operational, issue that would go far beyond the soldiers' capability.

Second, the armed forces structures, like their civilian counterparts—"feuding hierarchies" and "territorial units"—jeopardize service and arms interests in developing a joint, unified, and comprehensive operational art, since the air force, the navy, and the second artillery are largely independent of the military regions (war zones) and vice versa. As a result, the armed forces structures contribute to divergent service and arm operational arts focused on fighting independent operations. No matter what efforts the PLA makes to reunify the "family," namely, organizing symbolic interservice, interarm, and transregional war games at the group army level once a year, or once every couple of years, conflicts of operational arts and command structures between vertical hierarchies and horizontal regions substantially weaken the quality of "combined services and arms operations."

Third, the embarrassment of technological inferiority continues to lead the PLA in the direction of building skills-oriented armed forces. In the meantime, however, the PLA still believes that it can beat stealthy technology, precision weapons, and information systems with available obsolete weapons and poorly educated soldiers. Yet even though such euphoric, and highly premature claims may, to some extent, help improve combat skills, skillful soldiers remain significantly short of countermeasures against "invisible," "untouchable," and "indestructible" technologies.

The PLA faces a critical dilemma. It lacks the political, institutional, and technological resources to implement the ROA. Without such a thorough revolution, however, its glorious tradition may not solve the operational issues that it will face during the twenty-first century.

NOTE

The author wishes to thank June Teufel Dreyer, Thierry Gongora, Fen O. Hampson, Carl G. Jacobsen, Michael Ying-mao Kau, Jack Masson, Michelle Peng, and Harald von Riekhoff for their helpful comments.

1. In Chinese terminology, engagements [*zhandou*] normally refer to tactical activities at the division level or below. Operations consist of several engagements between the group army level and the war zone (theater) level. War [*zhanzheng*] involves several operations above the war zone level. Operations in this chapter are military actions between the group army and division levels, since China perceives operations in future border or offshore conflicts as unlikely above the group army level. Such a perception suggests that future conflicts will be carefully maintained at the group army level or below.

8

RMA or New Operational Art?: A View from France

François Géré

TWO CAVEATS BY WAY OF INTRODUCTION

First, strategic creativity in the United States is such that every few years the world learns that a major change in military affairs has occurred. In 1982 there was the introduction of AirLand Battle with the new edition of the FM 100–5 doctrinal document, then AirLand Battle 2000 in 1984; in 1993 there was a short-lived counter-proliferation initiative; but, already, the Revolution in Military Affairs (RMA) was in the offing, its advocates discreetly announcing its existence. No one will believe that strategy and operational art are transformed each three or four years. Does the phenomenon, which in the early 1990s became known as the RMA, correspond to a technological tsunami whose original impulse dates from a generation ago and which is now sweeping in its path military strategy? It is true that all major weapon systems when reaching maturity appear to be revolutionary and suggestive of a break in established trends. In fact, the operational beginning of a major weapon system is what strikes the mind. This moment must be accompanied by enough cheers to warrant the acquisition of the new weapon by armed forces at home and abroad. Thus, we must avoid overestimating a phenemenon that benefits from high visibility in part because of the vacuum created by the disappearence of a major player, the Soviet Union.

The second caveat concerns the origins of the phrase Revolution in Military Affairs, which have become obscured by growing popularity, second- and third-hand information substituting for reality. The phrase was coined by the Soviets in the early 1960s to characterize the changes brought to their defense concepts, military organizations, and doctrines by the massive introduction of nuclear weapons and missiles (Laurent and Ernould 1989, 11). In the United States, however, the Soviet origins of the RMA are dated back to Marshal Ogarkov and other Soviet military theorists who looked at conventional military developments in the United

States in the first half of the 1980s and foresaw the emergence of strike-reconnaissance complexes. The RMA also carries under a new label the arguments of analysts who estimated that emerging technologies were transforming conventional warfare in the 1980s (de Rose, ESECS, and Boyer 1985; ESECS 1983).

This chapter treats the subject of the RMA through two approaches. First, it circumscribes the phenomenon by distinguishing between its cultural and operational dimensions. This will allow us to refer to a New Operational Art (NOA), distinct from the vague notion of RMA, and to draw differences between the RMA and information warfare. Second, it assesses how France takes into account the RMA in relation to its own objectives and needs. What do we need, and for what purposes? What are the challenges we face and precautions we must take in relation to the RMA/NOA?

THE CULTURAL DIMENSION

Warfare in the Information Age or Information Warfare?

The notion that we live in an Information Age has been popularized in France by the writings of Alvin and Heidi Toffler. According to their argument agrarian economies have given way to industrial ones, which are now giving way in some countries to an Information Age driven by an accelerating pace of technological innovation. Power now stems from information. This descriptive account tends to be popular because its evolutionary character is simple to understand and familiar to lay persons. The negative aspects of this transformation, assuming that the Tofflers's prediction is corrrect, are overshadowed by the optimism of the pioneers. Nevertheless, one will have to take stock of the negative aspects of this change of society. In France the RMA is perceived by young staff officers as part and parcel of this broader society-wide cultural transformation. The Information Age is seen as originating from the United States; and the Internet as a means to reinforce the globalization of values and ways of life. Rightly or wrongly, this transformation is often perceived as an intrusion.

According to the evolutionary account put forward by the Tofflers, each stage of societal evolution has a corresponding strategic mode or form of warfare (Toffler and Toffler 1993). Thus, the advent of the Information Age should bring a new and superior form of warfare that will allow information-based societies to outclass industrial and agrarian societies militarily. Of course, this nice theoretical scheme remains to be proven. In spite of the technological gap separating the United States from North Vietnam, the former did not prevail over the latter during the Vietnam War. Technology does not subsume everything, nor does it provide a panacea. An erratic political commitment in Vietnam wreaked havoc with the advanced quantitative management of McNamara's whiz kids. Without a clearly defined political goal, military superiority is of no use, and sustaining a few casualties will be enough to deter from further action as in the case of the U.S. intervention in Somalia in 1993. Despite the prediction about the cultural obsolescence of war, many military officers consider that war remains a feature of human societies, even in the Information Age. Furthermore, the art of war has constant features in spite of the upheavals caused by technical innovations; this argument made notably by General Gordon Sullivan (Sullivan and Dubik 1993) is received favorably in France.

RMA and Information Warfare

A second set of questions concerning the RMA revolves around the impact of information technologies on operational art. In order to comprehend the RMA, one must understand its relation to information warfare. In that respect we are confronted by two broad and fuzzy concepts. Our American colleague Martin Libicki (cf., chapter 3) has shown how information warfare includes diverse and quite autonomous dimensions. The first studies on the subject conducted at the *Fondation pour les Études de Défense* led to a debate about how to translate the term (Fiorini n.d.). A literal translation of information warfare into *guerre de l'information* was found wanting; *guerre médiatique* (media warfare) and *guerre informatique* (computer warfare) were no better at capturing the meaning of the American concept. Perhaps the following definition better captures the distinction between the RMA and information warfare (IW).

RMA = $C^4I+SR+LRPW$; where C^4I stands for command, control, communications, computer applications, and intelligence; SR for surveillance and reconnaissance; and LRPW for long-range precision weapons.

IW = $C^2W/EW/IntelW/EcoW/CW/PsyW/HW/CyW$; where C^2W stands for command-and-control warfare; EW for electronic warfare; IntelW for intelligence warfare; EcoW for economic warfare; CW for communication warfare; PsyW for psychological warfare; HW for hacker warfare; and CyW for cyberwarfare.

Far from being a holistic concept, the notion of New Operational Art (NOA) refers to a subset of Information Warfare (IW) that corresponds to electronic or electronic and computer warfare, including intelligence gathering and communication systems, but not necessarily the information content of these systems. Although electronic and computer technologies play a key role in the RMA, the latter cannot be reduced to the former. The RMA also corresponds to a new NOA stemming from a strategic culture that is not narrowly American. The question, then, is: do we face a revolution and what is its extent?

Revolution and Levels of Strategic Rupture

There is a quasi-official definition of the RMA in the United States found in annual reports of the secretary of Defense:

[A]n RMA occurs when the incorporation of new technologies into military systems combines with innovative operational concepts and organizational adaptations to fundamentally alter the conduct of military operations... the change is considered revolutionary rather than evolutionary because new technologies, when combined with new methods of warfare, have proved far more powerful than the old and dramatically altered scope and application of military power. (Cohen 1997)

In spite of regular references and support for the concept, the RMA is rather briefly treated in the official publications of the U.S. DOD. As a result the RMA discourse can also be rationalized as an effort to counter cuts in the defense budget, to maintain or increase U.S. military-technological lead, and to promote more interactions between military and civilian R&D programs.

The RMA concept also corresponds to the system-of-systems notion put forward by Admiral Owens—vice chairman of the Joint Chiefs of Staff in 1994–96. According to this notion, the successful integration of the various command, control, communications, computer applications, and intelligence (C^4I) systems, intelligence, surveillance, and reconnaisance (ISR) systems, and long-range precision weapon systems acquired by, or under development for, U.S. armed services would produce dominant battlespace knowledge and devastating conventional fire (Owens 1995a). What is interesting in Admiral Owens's work is the idea of pushing the RMA to its limits: dissipating the fog of war, making the battlespace so transparent that reserves are no longer required to meet unexpected enemy actions, and that fire, rather than mass, is concentrated to achieve results. Through jointness, that is, a better pooling of resources and cooperation between services, revolutionary results could be achieved.

Utlimately, however, Dr. Andrew Marshall and the Office of Net Assessment (ONA) were largely responsible for the intellectual development of the RMA concept within the Pentagon (Blaker 1997b, 5–6). The function of Marshall's office is to conduct long-term prospective analysis in order to insure that the United States maintains its military superiority against any opponent; this prospective-analysis function has gained in importance with the end of the Cold War and the ensuing strategic uncertainty. Essentially, Marshall and the ONA came to the conclusion that military superiority could be derived from the efficient exploitation of technological developments and that nuclear weapons could be made redundant by high technologies. Therefore, one of the objectives of the RMA is to insure that the United States remains without peer, that it cannot be "equalized" by the deterrent value of nuclear weapons, or by another nation catching-up technologically. Strategically, by negating the equalizing value of nuclear weapons, the RMA makes inequalities of power decisive once again.

At the operational level the RMA corresponds to a rupture in operational art. Can we develop this notion further? First, as General Beaufre pointed out, past ruptures in operational art—from Napoleonic warfare to the blitzkrieg—had a pattern: the moment of uncertainty is followed by adaptation, then a build-up phase, and finally the reassertion of initial superiority as innovations stiffen into dogma (Beaufre 1972). Second, and most importantly, ruptures in operational art fail when, beyond tactical successes, they confront the strategic capacities of certain states, witness the German blitzkrieg when it met the capacities of the Soviet Union and the United States.

In consequence one has to be more specific in characterizing the RMA. It is a profound technological transformation with the potential to create a new operational art, but it is not a strategic rupture. A strategic rupture occurs when, for a given geopolitical area, an actor with capabilities equal or superior to those of the other actors present in the area appears or disappears. It can also occur as a result of the development of a new strategic function, or the overdevelopment of an existing one that leads to its dominance over other strategic functions. For instance, during World War II, U.S. logistics got the better of German operational art.

The new operational art tends to be characterized as revolutionary because its technological maturation occurs simultaneously with a dramatic strategic rupture: the end of the Cold War, the implosion of the Soviet Union. As a result, a power now has a nearly absolute superiority in logistics, communications, and firepower. The true strategic rupture is the strategic superiority now enjoyed by the United States, the RMA being an attempt to translate this superiority in the realities of military operations and combat. As a result, it reinforces U.S. supremacy and accentuates the political rupture with the previous period. Finally, the RMA corresponds also to a new operational art that (1) seeks to achieve superiority over the opponent's command system, and (2) attempts to evade through technological superiority close fighting with enemy forces and the attending risk of losses to friendly forces.

THE OPERATIONAL DIMENSION

NOA and Asymmetric Conflicts

In recent years both the U.S. and French armies have laid emphasis in their publications on asymmetric conflicts. Again, like the RMA, this concept is rather ambiguous, but it tends to be understood as conflicts involving opponents that are at different technological levels. The strategic objective of the United States in this regard is to prevent another power from achieving a symmetry of resources, technologies, and operational art with the United States; to maintain a favorable asymmetry in terms of technology and operational art with industrial-age middle powers like Iraq; and to avoid extreme asymmetric conflicts like the intervention in Somalia in 1992–94.

The RMA and the Maneuver of Forces: Decapitating Strikes

To destroy or disable the enemy's command structure is a basic strategem as old as the art of war. The RMA makes us think that it is now a practical military option through precision strike, electromagnetic impulses, or information warfare, however, the complexity of the system required to implement such a strategy creates a double vulnerability. First, at the internal level, such surgical strikes require personnel and technologies that work flawlessly; human errors and technical failures become unacceptable. Second, at the external level, the integrated system-of-systems required for such strikes becomes itself a target of choice for an opponent's decapitating strike. Conversely, a less sophisticated, but flexible, opponent could counteract decapitating strikes by restructuring its forces into a network of relatively autonomous units.

Toward a Clean Battle

The NOA also corresponds to how high-tech societies would like to conceive battle, that is, less chaotic, unpredictable, and bloody. Through perfect knowledge of the enemy's means and intentions and the ability to act or react faster than him—while he is kept in the dark as to one's own forces and plans—one can achieve such a decisive advantage that the resort to arms becomes theoretically superfluous; only confirming through a highly lopsided military confrontation what was already evident. This ideal might be said to have informed all great strategists from Sun Tzu to Napoleon.

If information defeats the enemy and firepower clears the ground, then one could envisage only two types of combat troops in the future: the scouts who work forward and infiltrate behind enemy lines and the rear troops who operate the surveillance and reconnaissance platforms and long-range precision weapons. The importance of the scouting function will require more special forces. Such a development will involve more than an increase in the number of elite troops, it also requires a qualitative transformation. Special forces will serve an intelligence-gathering function for possible strikes by long-range weapon systems and will carry out fewer strikes by themselves. This future vision stems from a trend already identified in military doctrines since the end of the 1970s, that is, lower force-to-space ratios that translate in a more porous front and a nonlinear battle zone. As a result, it is more feasible to penetrate behind enemy lines in order to gather intelligence and strike.

With such a strategy we hope to resolve one of the oldest problems associated with combat, namely, the losses suffered when in close contact with enemy forces; but I am not sure that we will ever elude the necessity of close combat and the price of blood. The low casualty rate suffered by the Coalition in the Gulf War of 1991 was a godsend unlikely to be repeated. The differences in French and U.S. attitudes toward [friendly] military casualties in the post–Cold War era remain significant (Friedman 1995). In France the objective of a no-dead (in French, *zéro mort*) war is seen as the central parameter of military planning in the United States since the early 1990s. As a consequence, many French conclude that U.S. armed forces are increasingly incapable of action; whereas, in France, a sense of sacrifice remains, as well as the will to expose soldiers to the risks inherent to their profession.

This perception oversimplifies the issue. It emerges from various interviews I conducted with U.S. military leaders that the concern for casualties reflects a broader concern for preserving the human capital essential to a high-quality volunteer force. A neglectful use of such volunteer forces would represent a squandering of precious resources and would jeopardize the recruitment and retention of high-quality personnel. This situation creates difficulties, but it does not prevent military action. In the case of the United States, however, there is an additional problem, one of political will in regard to the resort to military force, in a country that is traditionally reluctant to use force and applies it only in a massive and brutal way. Finally, Americans have always tried technological fixes to their problems and as a way to prevent losses in combat.

It is probably illusory to think that France could adopt a totally different approach in the future. As the French army becomes more professionalized, it will become a capital to be preserved. The spirit of sacrifice will appear as a symbol of a past age that contradicts efficiency. If armies want to attract quality personnel, they must guarantee its protection and preservation. Contact with the enemy will become the exception rather than the rule. The NOA calls for a certain revolution in the minds of young officers in the ground forces. A certain French tradition will be challenged.

WHAT CHALLENGES LIE AHEAD FOR THE FRENCH ARMED FORCES?

The challenges that the French armed forces and defense establishment will face in the years ahead can be put into three categories: the assessment of the American RMA, the strategic implications in terms of deterrence and defense policy, and the competition for the technical-industrial base. In turn, each category can be subdivided between challenges that are likely to be tackled with success and those that will pose serious problems.

Assessing the American RMA

The first challenge consists in knowing and correctly assessing the American RMA: its nature, scope, and goals. Unfortunately, much of this process of researching, thinking, and debating the RMA is conducted by military institutions of higher learning and various branches of the French defense ministry, such as the *Délégation générale pour l'armement* [Directorate for Armament] and the *Délégation aux affaires stratégiques* [Directorate for Strategic Affairs]. Outside of this inner circle, there is little awareness about the RMA in France; though in September 1996 Seth Cropsey, a former U.S. defense official under the Reagan and Bush administrations, gave a lecture on the subject for French parliamentarians (Cropsey 1997). The problem is not one of lack of quality information, but rather one of circulation. Nevertheless, among the few publications available in French that address emerging military technologies and the RMA, one should mention a collection of essays edited by General Alain Baer and published by the *Centre de recherche et d'études sur les stratégies et technologies* (CREST) in 1993; an article by Andrew Krepinevich, a well-known American analyst of the RMA; as well as a summary of a study conducted by Laurent Murawiec for the French Ministry of Defense (Baer 1993; Krepinevich 1994a; Murawiec 1998). The reflection on the RMA in France has been slow to start, but it is catching up as the implications of this revolution dawn upon French decision makers.

Nuclear Deterrence and the NOA

Because of its revolutionary potential, the NOA is sometimes perceived as rendering nuclear weapons obsolete. A strategic air campaign conducted with cruise missiles and other stand-off weapons might be able to achieve results on a national economy or command structure comparable to the use of strategic nuclear weapons, while concentrated use of smart submunitions could achieve result comparable to a tactical nuclear weapon against modern armies; in both cases without the ecological risks and opprobrium associated with nuclear weapons. This notion has a certain appeal from a U.S. perspective, because it magnifies U.S. technological prowess and minimizes the fact that nuclear weapons remain a great equalizer of military power, and therefore a constraint to the full exercise of U.S. military predominance. Sounding the death knell of nuclear weaponry would be premature given their continuing massive destructive potential and deterrent value. In fact, there has never been in the history of wafare an instance of a destructive weapon being made obsolete by a more modern weapon with less destructive potential. The United States is certaintly conscious of this fact, and this explains why it remains committed to the maintenance of its nuclear arsenal and the possibility of resorting to it not just in retaliation for a nuclear strike.

The relationship between the NOA and nuclear weapons is complex. In fact it might even be said to be counterproductive because as the superiority of the NOA becomes confirmed, more nations that are unable to afford its equipment or practice its art will rely on nuclear weapons for deterrence and war-fighting purposes. This last hypothesis should concern us all since an operational use of nuclear weapons has serious implications. The other aspect of the relationship between the NOA and nuclear weapons is their interaction at the strategic level. Would it be possible to disarm a nuclear state with a preemptive strike with precision weapons? Conversely, could we improve a nuclear arsenal with some of the detection, reconnaissance, and targeting technologies part of the NOA? These questions would require a detailed study that cannot be conducted here, but that will certainly inform some of the reflections on the future of French nuclear forces.

The NOA and the New Parameters of French Strategy

France has rediscovered the strategy and complexities of prolonged large-scale operations and the fact that these operations are likely to take place in the context of coalitions. During the Gulf War of 1991, France found that it was not up to the standards of NATO countries in terms of command system for large operations abroad (Palmer 1995). A reform of the planning and command structures was carried out under the leadership of Admiral Lanxade in 1992–96; its implementation being pursued into the late 1990s.

The fact that French defense planning increasingly considers military operations within a coalition raises the question of which coalition: NATO, the European Union (EU), or ad hoc coalitions? There is no doubt that the French decision to join NATO integrated military structures progressively reflects both political realism and an understanding of some of the implications of the RMA. To the extent that NATO is willing to adapt itself to the new conditions of security, France is also willing to adapt itself to NATO. At the heart of this parallel process of adaptation lies the issue of command and control of operational forces such as a combined joint task force (CJTF). Given the significance of C4ISR systems in the RMA, their introduction in NATO forces will only exacerbate the struggle within the Alliance for the control over the chain of command. As network control becomes key to operational success, control over the network becomes essential. In such a context reliance upon another nation or international organization might lead to an irreversible and unacceptable level of dependence. Whether in the context of the EU, of the Eurocorps, or of NATO's CJTFs, the issues of creating and controlling information and command systems in a multinational framework become fundamental in a military world where control over information becomes more important than troops on the ground. The NOA, therefore, implies a hierarchy of powers within any coalition on the basis of the ability to develop and field C⁴ISR systems.

The French and European Defense Industrial Base

The last significant challenge created by the RMA/NOA concerns French, and European, defense industries. At the commercial level, in the ceaseless competition for foreign markets, the RMA gives an additional marketing edge to U.S. defense manufacturers with the promises of weapons with greater performances and interoperability with U.S. forces. More fundamentally, the RMA requires a reform of the whole defense-industrial base so that defense production can benefit from the leading-edge information technologies that are developed by civilian industries. The relationship between military and civilian production therefore has to be reformed to create complementarities between the two sectors. On this matter the old attitudes of wait-and-see and of ad hoc cooperative ventures will not do. It is difficult to talk of force modernization and high-tech research and development informed by the RMA when the French defense industrial base falls behind its U.S. counterpart in terms of the transformations required to implement the RMA. Some sense of urgency has, however, emerged since 1998 as reflected in privatizations and mergers between defense firms in France and across Western Europe.

TAILORING THE NOA TO ONE'S GOALS AND NEEDS

A deep technological transformation such as the RMA is rarely limited to a single state; its structural determinants usually affect all states that share the level of development where the transformation occurs. Its outcomes will vary, however, according to the military-industrial policies adopted by these states. The transformation will therefore assume different forms and serve different applications according to the specific needs of each state. France has accumulated a significant experience in mastering military-technological transformation with its nuclear program during the Cold War; but it has had little similar experience in the field of conventional armament. France, therefore, has to relearn what advanced weapon development means. The decision to proceed along the technological path opened by the RMA will depend upon the government's intention and its representation of the rank France should maintain or achieve internationally. There is a lot at stake: we can misread trends and end up with military forces that are not adapted to the future reality, or we can overestimate our transformative ability and develop incomplete forces. This problem is somewhat simplified when one faces a clear menace, or has clear agressive intentions of one's own. For a peaceful nation in an era of prolonged peace, however, these choices become very difficult. One has to keep a high degree of flexibility in the face of evolutions that cannot be predicted.

One of the most relevant elements of the post–Cold War defense debate is the issue of finding a substitute to the absence of an enemy (Joxe 1996). Does the RMA provide a meaning to defense planning in an era of prolonged peace? France no longer has a designated enemy; neither does the United States. Conflicts are once again regional in scope and conventional in nature; though the latter feature is slightly altered by the possible resort to weapons of mass destruction. In that context, whether in France or in the United States, the RMA appears as a convenient theme to justify continued defense outlays. The United States, however, is also in a unique situation in regard to the RMA: it can use it to maintain its military-technological lead and to consolidate a position in the international system comparable to Great Britain in the nineteenth century. France has never enjoyed a comparable position, that is, of being a dominant power in the international system while not being threatened along its borders. In short, the RMA cannot be conceived and developed in France, or in Europe, like it is in the United States.

It makes good sense for a developed nation like France to explore some of the technological implications of the RMA, in particular in the fields of information gathering and communication. We have shown in the past, with such programs as *Eurêka*, created in response to the Strategic Defense Initiative, that we can follow the United States on some crucial technologies, but to do this now would require that we define the requirements for a NOA that would meet the needs of Europeans for the next twenty years. Once this is done, then it is possible to harness Europe's defense industries for the production of a range of systems that would not be a pale imitation of the U.S. RMA.

France has no requirement for RMA-forces that would give it the ability to fight with the United States in a war with China in 2030 or beyond; that is, in a hypothetical conflict at the high-end of the conflict spectrum in a region where France has no essential strategic interests. As developed in the United States, the RMA aims at fighting and winning a high-intensity symmetric conflict. In fact, such conflicts might never happen; would-be opponents being deterred by the capabilities that the United States would have developed to fight them. France, and European nations, having no such requirements to deal with security concerns in Europe or in the periphery of Europe, would rather seek an RMA able to deal with low-intensity conflicts, humanitarian interventions, or peacekeeping and peacemaking operations. The experience of Bosnia has shown that some of the technologies associated with the RMA, like unmanned aerial vehicles and satellites, can contribute to peace operations. The challenge, therefore, is to find practical applications for the NOA in conformity with national goals, and to suggest solutions for those missions that are pursued through European partnerships.

9

Force Projection: One-and-a-Half Cheers for the RMA

Glenn C. Buchan

The issue I want to address is whether the so-called "Revolution in Military Affairs" (RMA) offers the countries best positioned to take advantage of it—presumably the United States and its traditional industrialized allies—the prospect of a real sea change in their ability to deal with both major regional conflicts and the spectrum of lesser operations that military establishments are increasingly called upon to handle. As the title suggests, I basically argue that the United States in particular really has little choice but to pursue many of the technological options frequently associated with the RMA because in the current environment they probably offer the best practical solutions to many military problems that matter. The net effect, however, may or may not prove to be revolutionary, and in the end, it may not matter one way or the other whether it is or not. Thus, on balance, pursuing the RMA as it is generally defined is probably a good idea for the United States and its allies, but it is unlikely to be the panacea that its most zealous advocates suggest. That probably makes me a "friendly skeptic," and my general line of reasoning is similar to that of Colin Gray (1995), although we may part company on some relatively minor points.

The main points I will try to make are the following:

- There is not a single RMA going on. Rather, there is an "options menu" that different countries will be able to choose from and "mix and match" to suit their particular needs. Who wins in the end is an issue that remains in doubt.
- Those who are likely to be most vulnerable are countries that are just beginning to move toward more "information-based" warfare but have not yet mastered its technology or tactics. Those who might stand to benefit most are regional powers that can selectively adopt some of the new technologies, combine them with "old" technologies (e.g., nuclear weapons) on a modest scale, and develop effective operational tactics and military-political strategies.

- Exploiting the information-related technologies that are at the heart of the currently postulated RMA offers the United States and most of its allies one of the few options for increasing the overall effectiveness of their military forces at a time when both defense budgets and force structures are shrinking. That said, this approach may not work, at least not completely, and is unlikely to be cheap.
- Even if the technological part of the RMA "works" and even proves to be truly "revolutionary," it will be a slow-motion revolution, giving potential adversaries plenty of time to contemplate counters.
- Organizational and operational adaptability is the real key to the RMA. The prize is likely to go to whoever is swiftest at adapting its systems procurement and operational strategy and tactics to the new technologies. Conversely, failure to adapt successfully can render the technology impotent. *There appear to be a lot more likely losers than potential winners in this competition.*
- The potential impact of the RMA is likely to be greatest—and most easily understood—on major conflicts. There may be more room, however, for creative— if not necessarily decisive—tactical applications in lesser operations.

WHAT, IF ANYTHING, IS THE REVOLUTION IN MILITARY AFFAIRS?

At the risk of overworking heavily plowed ground[1] (and even plagiarizing myself [Buchan 1995a, 1995b]), I want to review briefly the RMA concept as it has evolved in public discussions over the last few years. Indeed, both the concept and the acronym have proven to be remarkably durable by the standards of these things, generating a good deal of "chaff," and—fortunately—some "wheat."

Coined by Andrew Marshall, long-time director of the Office of Net Assessment in the U.S. Department of Defense, the phrase "Revolution in Military Affairs" connotes a drastic change in military affairs resulting from a combination of technological change and operational and organizational innovation. Marshall's hypothesis that a new revolution in military affairs may be in progress or just around the corner is based on the proposition that a number of critical technologies are maturing about now that, if taken together and applied properly, might change the way wars are fought, and whoever is quickest to recognize and exploit such a revolutionary potential could radically alter the military equation in world politics. If the United States fails to exploit the RMA, others might, thereby improving their military position considerably, perhaps at the expense of U.S. interests. Accordingly, most of the attention concerning a possible RMA has focused on how the United States might best exploit it, particularly in view of the internal and external pressures already extant to reshape the U.S. military establishment in fundamental ways.

RMAs have come in various forms over the centuries. The major elements of this one are technological.[2] The central theme that connects them is their reliance on information, in keeping with the trendy Toffleresque hypotheses about information-based warfare (Toffler and Toffler 1993). The details of the postulated elements of the RMA have evolved somewhat over the years, partly because the ideas have become more refined and partly as the result of petty bickering among the military services over turf and budgets. The discussion has focused mainly on the following areas, described in various ways over the course of the debate:

- Precision strike and delivery,
- "Information warfare,"
- "Dominant maneuver," and
- Space (systems and/or operations).

They all tend to be mutually reinforcing.

Precision Strike and Delivery

Precision strike is the ability to bring the right kind of firepower to bear at exactly the right time and place to destroy virtually any kind of critical target. The concept is a logical extension of the precision part of the 1991 Gulf War's air campaign and traces its antecedents at least as far back as the use of laser-guided bombs in Vietnam. With more types of precision-guided weapons in current inventories and in the works, more advanced guidance and navigation schemes available, and critical supporting technologies maturing rapidly, large inventories of very accurate weapons should be within the reach of major industrial powers and any other countries with the wherewithal to purchase them in the relatively near future. Equally critical are the intelligence collection, communications, data processing, and command and control systems necessary for large-scale, timely use of precision-guided weapons. Improvement in sensor technology, computer hardware and software, and large-scale communications technology might make possible precision strike on a scale that would quantitatively and qualitatively change the nature of warfare. This "revolution" has been a long time coming—decades, in fact—since analysts first predicted its imminent arrival. Whether its time has finally come and who the main beneficiaries will be is now the issue. Adding "precision delivery" to the menu simply acknowledges the importance of delivering things other than munitions (e.g., humanitarian relief supplies) accurately.

"Information Warfare"

Information warfare is a most unfortunate term (Buchan 1995b) that nevertheless captures the idea that information technologies and the effective use of information are central to any contemporary military revolution. The new technologies make it possible to gather, process, and move vast amounts of information very quickly. In traditional military operations they may make it possible for military commanders to know virtually everything about their enemies as well as their own forces and be able to continuously replan and redirect forces in near real time. How much of this "situational awareness" and real-time command and control is really worth buying remains an issue,[3] but the idea of being able to do better in this arena is central to the RMA. Many other associated types of military operations—for example, psychological operations—are likely to be enhanced by new information technologies as well.

Dependence on information technologies could create vulnerabilities, however, vulnerabilities that a competent adversary might be able to exploit. Protecting one's own information-related operations while attacking an enemy's is likely to be even more fundamental to military success if the newest RMA comes to pass than it has always been in wartime. Another feature of both reliance on information technologies and attacks on enemy information infrastructure is the geographic expansion of the "battlefield," thus forcing military commanders to think more globally.

The other major element of information warfare is the potential vulnerability of high-tech civilian societies—for example, banking and other financial systems, telecommunications networks, anything that depends on computers—to electronic attack. The idea of this kind of "information warfare" has now become so commonplace that it is already part of the conventional wisdom and the cultural folkways of the times. Indeed, the prospects could lead to an expanded definition of national security and new forms of weapons to employ against adversaries.

"Dominant Maneuver"

"Dominant maneuver" has a certain U.S. Army connotation to it, which partly reflects the continuing bureaucratic wars, but the concept is broader than that. The idea is simple enough. Detailed knowledge of an enemy and an ability to concentrate forces and/or firepower against an enemy's weak points could result in dominance on the battlefield. Dominant maneuver is a product of effective use of information coupled with appropriate weapons and forces. While born in the context of land maneuver forces and indirect-fire weapons, the concept could apply as well to air forces and even sea-based land attack forces or, optimally, integrated joint forces.

Space (Systems and/or Operations)

Space is sometimes mentioned as a separate element of a new military revolution even though it does not quite fit with the others. Unlike the three functional/mission-oriented areas, space is a place, one that is deeply involved in all of the key functional areas of the RMA. While space systems have long been important to U.S. national security, trying to integrate them into routine military operations has been a source of perennial frustration.

Space both offers unique opportunities and requires special skills and capabilities to be exploited fully. By their very nature space capabilities offer even modest nations global capability to communicate and collect information. Moreover, with the burgeoning commercial markets for satellite communications, navigation, and remote sensing, the "buy-in" price for even small countries (or, for that matter, nonstate actors) to take advantage of some of the opportunities that space can offer is likely to be greatly reduced. For example, acquiring photographs of virtually anywhere on earth should be easy and relatively inexpensive for just about any nation-state or reasonably well-financed private group. While real-time, or extremely high-resolution, photographs may not be available to everyone, that level of quality should not be necessary for many operations. Similarly, using Global Positioning System (GPS) guidance to enhance the accuracy of weapons or to help forces navigate should be within the reach of virtually any nation or group. The same applies to global communications, although space is only one of the environments for doing that in the modern world. Even minor powers with nuclear weapons and some space launch capability might be able to launch crude nuclear antisatellite weapons that might disable large numbers of U.S. and allied satellites. (This possibility has been a favorite topic in war games for several years, particularly since the United States is generally much more dependent on space support than its enemies.)

It is easy to overstate the degree to which this capability is readily accessible to minor players. For example, the resources, knowledge, experience, and infrastructure needed to support a space program of the scale of the U.S. program are beyond the capabilities of most countries (including, perhaps, the United States itself!). Some types of missions—sophisticated antisatellite capability, strategic defense, massive intelligence collection—are likely to remain too challenging for most countries for the foreseeable future. Similarly, attacking ground targets at global ranges from space may remain the stuff of science fiction for minor players, for the near future, but cannot be ruled out entirely. Even a limited capability could go a long way, however, if applied cleverly, and after all, that is the very essence of the notion of an RMA. Space may provide the quickest method for those who want to achieve "global reach."

Even more aggressive uses of space for direct attack and defense could eventually become more practical than they have been in the past. If so, that could provide a basis for countries to consider radically restructuring their future military forces.

SHOULD WE CARE?

In an important sense, it probably should not matter too much whether a particular set of technical and operational innovations are "revolutionary" or not: good ideas should be of interest however they are labeled. Thus, perhaps we are addressing the wrong question. The fundamental issue, after all, is how a nation defines its security needs, what specific tasks it needs to accomplish to meet those needs, and what the best means are for accomplishing those tasks. That is a never-ending analytical process. On the other hand, the very premise of the RMA is that if it is truly revolutionary, it could have a major impact on basic things that matter in the world. If the postulated RMA were to come about, the nature of war could change quite dramatically. The structure of military forces, the concepts of fighting, the relative emphasis in R&D and weapons development, and even definitions of what constitutes "war" could be quite different. For example, the critical importance of exploiting information (and perhaps denying information to others) could result in a vastly greater emphasis on information-related technologies and systems instead of the traditional emphasis on "shooters," a trend that might be inevitable in any case. Traditional reliance on large ground, sea, and air forces might change as well. The sort of massed force approach that has always been at the core of combat might no longer be practical. Moreover, the broad access of many nations to space-based surveillance, communications, and navigation support may tend to "level the playing field," at least to a degree.

That might rule out some classes of military strategies such as the famous U.S. "left hook" in the Gulf War designed to outflank the Iraqi troops in the Kuwaiti theater of operations and which remained undetected by the Iraqis until it was too late to counter. Also, some of the tools of the next RMA—for example, "information warfare" techniques—may be well within the means of less-developed countries (and nonstate actors) that could not otherwise challenge the United States or other major powers militarily.

Thus, the question is interesting. In answering it, however, one must notice that the potential impact on large-scale campaigns and lesser operations is likely to be quite different, so I will address each in turn.

Regional Conflicts, Some Revolutionary Prospects, but How Real?

It is in major regional conflicts where the RMA is likely to have the most pronounced effects, revolutionary or not. Such conflicts have always been the focus of U.S. planning and have traditionally driven major force structure decisions, although they no longer represent the universally stressing cases that they once did. Since the end of the Cold War, major conflicts in Southwest Asia and Korea have been the U.S. conflicts *du jour* for planning purposes. These conflicts, while they differ in detail, tend to share common characteristics that are relatively well-defined and understood. That, in turn, leads to common tasks that generally have to be performed to prosecute these campaigns successfully. Examples include:

- halting conventional invasions, typically made up of armor, infantry, and/or naval forces;
- defending a country against destructive attacks carried out by aircraft, ballistic or cruise missiles;
- holding territory or preventing an enemy from doing the same;
- destroying or disrupting an enemy's military command and control system and its political leadership and control mechanisms; and
- destroying key elements of an enemy's society infrastructure.

Most major campaigns involve some combination of these tasks, although their relative importance and difficulty can vary considerably depending on the details of each particular situation.

Many of the technologies and operational concepts associated with the RMA address problems that are directly applicable to coping with major conflicts. For example, an ability to locate, identify, and destroy various kinds of targets effectively is critical to accomplishing many of these tasks. Central to the vision of the current RMA is the ability to do just that. The promise of improved intelligence-gathering and precision-strike technology is to be able to destroy most kinds of targets effectively and efficiently.

If fully successful, such a capability could have dramatic implications. For example, an ability to locate and destroy advancing enemy armor *en masse* could make armored invasions impossible and might even appear formidable enough to deter enemies from even trying in the first place. Extending that capability to include other traditional invasion forces, for example, surface naval forces, could make the idea of invading one's neighbors extremely unattractive. *The effect of an RMA that prevented invasions would be revolutionary indeed.* Interestingly, this particular set of technological changes seems to favor defenders rather than aggressors.

There are several other interesting things about this particular example. First, political communities have been launching and trying to halt invasions for millennia. The effectiveness of one side or the other has been variously determined by mass, tactics, and technology in some combination; however, the search for solutions has gone on almost literally forever. Even the current search for precision-guided antiarmor weapons and appropriate surveillance systems has been going on for several decades. If this effort finally comes to fruition, it will have been a very *slow* revolution. However, that is acceptable. Even though the process has clearly been evolutionary—indeed, glacial—the *effect* could still be revolutionary. Of course, potential adversaries have a lot more time to think about counters. That is very different from the nuclear revolution, for example, which occurred almost literally overnight. Nations then spent years—even decades—trying to understand its implications. Second, as Gray (1995, 16–17) points out, the main effect of the new technologies is to increase the *efficiency*, rather than the effectiveness of forces. In the case of halting armored invasions, of course, there are other alternatives, as the historical track record demonstrates clearly. Those alternatives, however, which generally involve a substantial amount of brute force, may not be practical for the United States or most of its allies in the foreseeable future. Practical constraints, particularly budgetary pressures, have already limited the number of platforms (e.g., aircraft, ships, tanks) and the manpower that U.S. forces will have available for some years to come. That means getting the maximum mileage out of the forces available, which in turn means relying on better weapons and more effective use of information. Those are about the only levers available to increase the effectiveness of U.S. forces. Ironically, that approach really may not save much money. It may also be difficult to implement (as will be argued later in this chapter). The alternative of larger forces is simply not in the cards, however. Moreover, the fact that most potential theaters of major conflict are far away from the United States makes moving and massing forces all that much harder.

Also, this notion of efficiency should not obscure the fact that the overall effect is massive effective firepower. That fact comes through consistently in both analyses and war games. The dominating factor in future large-scale conflicts will be massive, overwhelmingly effective firepower, presuming that the new technologies work and are employed correctly. That swamps all other factors in the balance equation. In effect, we are substituting a large number of effective machines for a mass of manpower and a larger number of less-effective machines. And, numbers matter! While future forces of aircraft, ships, tanks, etc., may be small by the standards of earlier times, they will still be sizable in an absolute sense.

There are other even more radical possibilities for conducting future regional campaigns that might or might not ever prove technically practical. Some include (1) a defensive theory of air and land power that will halt invasions and protect against air and missile attacks without violating a country's territory and (2) a combined offensive-defensive theory that accomplishes the same objectives, but includes selective attacks on an enemy's territory. Both would require dramatic technical strides to be effective. The first would require substantial doctrinal and operational changes. The effects of either would be revolutionary, although most of the individual elements are evolutionary. They would change the nature of future war in fundamental ways.

Thus, if all of the schemes envisioned in the RMA were to work, the fact of major conflict could change radically. That doesn't mean the game would end, just that it would change fundamentally, *but that is important.* It is a reason why we should care. We should also be concerned lest others take advantage of these ideas, adapt them to their own needs, and pose problems for us in the future. Interestingly, one of the reasons that some of these ideas may prove effective in major conflicts is that we understand the problems—the military tasks that need to be accomplished—so well. That said, however, the future politics of the world could make these problems much less important, at least for the United States and most of its traditional allies. Ironically, we might "solve" these problems at the very time when they are least relevant to U.S. national interests.

Low-Intensity Conflict and Lesser Operations

Large-scale conflict has never been the only function of the military or the only external security concern of major powers, but in the post–Cold War world, lower-scale military operations have become both much more common and a more important part of foreign policy. Thus, the possibility that the RMA might be effective in these arenas is certainly an interesting one to explore.

The problem with characterizing low-intensity conflicts and lesser operations is that they represent such a diverse set of possibilities, as Table 9.1 suggests. The possible problems to be solved are enormously diverse, as are the tasks that need to be performed to deal with them. Some are relatively straightforward. Others are extremely complex. In general though, there are some characteristics other than sheer scale that tend to differentiate these operations from large-scale conflicts:

- the political context, which is obviously critically important in any military operation, is paramount in this class of operations, which imposes additional constraints and sensitivities;
- technology may play an important role in some classes of lesser operations, but it is less likely to be as decisive as in major campaigns;
- for many classes of lesser operations, there may be no useful analog to the overwhelming firepower advantage that the RMA might provide in major campaigns; and
- taken together, lesser operations instead of major conflicts might prove the stressing cases for information systems.

In short, however, the current RMA may not have as much relative impact on low-intensity conflicts and lesser operations as on major conflicts. First, some of the technical problems in demanding types of operation are probably still too hard to solve. Second, there are usually more fundamental problems in such conflicts and operations that the RMA really does not address.

Table 9.1

Some Generic Types of Low-Intensity Conflicts and Lesser Operations

TYPE OF OPERATION	CHARACTERISTICS
Moderate-Scale Direct Action (e.g., interventions in Grenada, Panama, and Haiti)	• Substantial force and some combat • Limited military objectives, but might have broad political objectives such as toppling a government • Short-time commitment for the bulk of U.S. forces
Raid • Punitive (e.g., air strikes in Libya or in southern Iraq) or • Preemptive (e.g., Israeli raid on Iraqi nuclear reactor, 1981)	• Limited forces involved • Use of force • Risks of "collateral damage" and of political fallouts (potentially high cost for failure)
Rescue Mission • Hostages/prisoners (e.g., Entebbe raid, 1976; U.S. embassy in Iran, 1980) • Combat search and rescue (e.g., downed F-16 pilot, Bosnia 1995) or • Protection/evacuation of noncombatants (e.g., Liberia 1996)	• Intelligence/information vital • Tight timetables • Short duration • Rescuers likely to be outgunned • In- and exfiltration likely to be difficult • Delicate political dimensions • Logistics may be difficult • Likelihood of violence
Disaster Relief (e.g., international assistance after earthquake in Armenia, 1988; or hurricane in Central America, 1998)	• Little or no likelihood of violence • Information vital for efficient intervention • Challenging logistics
Humanitarian Assistance (e.g., Rwanda, Somalia) • With "mission creep" (e.g., later stages of intervention in Somalia)	• Potential for violent opposition • Intelligence/information vital • Timeliness matters • Potential for large-scale operation • Complex politics • Challenging logistics • Mission creep can create a challenging mixture of humanitarian assistance, raid, and hostage rescue operations.
Peacekeeping (e.g., early UN intervention in Bosnia)	• Combination of complex politics and difficult military problems • Potential use of force, in particular for self-defense • Intelligence implicitly backed by force can provide powerful negotiating leverage
Peacemaking (e.g., NATO intervention in Bosnia)	• Stronger form of peacekeeping • Proactive enforcement of peace • Heavier element of coercive military force
Insurgency Support (e.g., U.S. support for Kurds in northern Iraq, and for Afghan resistance during Soviet occupation	• Long-term commitment • Political aspects are central • Intelligence/information is vital

Table 9.1 (continued)

TYPE OF OPERATION	CHARACTERISTICS
Counterinsurgency	• Same factors as insurgency support except for the availability of superior forces
Nation-building (e.g., support to civilian authorities in Haiti)	• Combination of features of counterinsurgency, peacemaking, and peacekeeping operations
Counterterrorism	• Intelligence critical and hard to collect • Measured use of force • Legal and political constraints • Timeliness often critical • Shares many features with raid, hostage-rescue, and counterinsurgency operations
Counternarcotics and Interdiction of Contraband	• Similar to counterterrorism • Both an "offensive" and "defensive" components
Critical Mission within a Military Campaign (e.g., SCUD-hunting during the 1991 Gulf War)	• Timeliness often important • Intelligence vital • Limited available forces • Political dimensions often important • Often takes on a momentum and logic of its own

Adapted from Buchan et al. (1999).

Thus, the new technologies are not likely to have as decisive an effect on strategy in this area as they might where major campaigns are concerned. In fact, future opponents of powers that benefit from the RMA may try to move the competition into this arena rather than confront these powers directly in large-scale conflicts where their technical prowess might prove decisive. That, of course, has been why "weaker" forces have so frequently opted for guerrilla warfare or other unconventional approaches over the centuries when a traditional approach would have guaranteed defeat.

That is not to say, however, that the new information-based technologies and other tools of the RMA might not be useful in low-intensity conflicts. Indeed, in Bosnia, for example, NATO's ability to locate Serbian surface-to-air missiles and to collect intelligence on Serbian military positions in general was an important factor in face-to-face negotiations between NATO and Bosnian Serbs, including those that led to the release of the Canadian hostages that the Serbs were holding.[4] Similarly, anecdotes about U.S. soldiers using laser rangefinders to intimidate and deter snipers in peacekeeping operations in Somalia and elsewhere suggest the kind of creative applications that clever operators on the scene may find for new technology in low-intensity conflicts.

That example actually suggests another major difference between major conflicts and lesser operations in terms of the impact that the current RMA might have. In the case of major campaigns, the greatest impact is likely to be at the level of strategy. It could require adaptive behavior by the largest organizations—entire military services, for example—which could be extraordinarily challenging. By contrast, in lesser operations, the major impact is likely to be much lower, mainly at the tactical and operational levels. Organizational adaptation at that level is likely to be much easier, which could be very important in implementing an RMA. All that is required is giving bright, motivated people the flexibility necessary to do their jobs.

In sum, then, we ought to care about the information-based technologies and operational concepts if they prove useful for solving important problems regardless of whether or not they turn out to be part of a "revolution in military affairs." In addition to improving our own capability, we need to be concerned about others exploiting these technologies and "doing unto others." The current RMA might actually prove to be revolutionary, although it is unlikely to be a panacea even at that. It is less likely to revolutionize low-intensity conflict or lesser operations, but it could open up some creative tactical options.

WILL IT WORK?

Military revolutions have occurred periodically over the centuries, and when they have, they have frequently changed history and sometimes reshaped the face of the world in fundamental ways. Moreover these revolutions have frequently been unexpected—sea changes that sometimes resulted from a confluence of apparently innocuous factors. Revolutions are delicate things, and success is never a foregone conclusion. In this particular case, the RMA is primarily driven by technology, but there are other critical factors as well.

While the new technologies and systems offer considerable promise, they are in different states of maturity. Some may not work as advertised. Moreover, some of the elements of the postulated RMA require massive infrastructures to implement. They also require organizational adaptation to exploit effectively on the battlefield. Finally, potential opponents may develop counters or implement RMAs of their own.

Implementing the RMA

There are at least three kinds of problems to be solved in regard to the implementation of the RMA: implementing the technology effectively, adapting operational art and tactics to accommodate the new technology, and forcing organizations to adapt to the new technologies. There are several reasons why new technology has sometimes fizzled, or at least not had the expected impact, in the military arena:

- *The technology is too immature.* It either does not work well enough or is too easy or cheap to counter. (The ground-implanted sensors placed along the Ho Chi Minh Trail to counter infiltration in Vietnam are examples. Only recently has this technology matured to the point where it might prove useful. More recently, dealing with cheap countermeasures has been a perennial problem for sensors on smart weapons and surveillance systems.)

- *The technology is too expensive.* "Smart" weapons have historically been affected by this factor. Developing affordable, effective antiarmor submunitions remains a challenge. "Cheap" cruise missiles remain elusive. Stealthy aircraft are proving expensive to maintain.
- *The technology may be applied improperly.* Organizations may not adapt rapidly enough to new technology either operationally or strategically.
- *The technology may be solving the wrong problem.*
- *It may not be possible to introduce new technology rapidly enough or on a large enough scale to be decisive if time is relatively short.* (The German V-2 rocket in World War II is one of many examples.)

Cost is always an issue and is even more important in times of fiscal austerity. There has always been a natural tension between the promise of a new technology and the opportunity costs that the initial R&D investment typically entails. The dramatic cost reductions in information-related technologies in recent years are one of the most attractive features of the "information revolution." However, sensor systems and platforms, for example, tend to be relatively expensive, and increasingly have to compete directly with other classes of systems for scarce dollars. That competition is even more challenging since the organizational preferences of the services have traditionally favored "shooters" (specifically, platforms) over sensor systems, or even weapons. Even worse, sensor systems require considerable support to exploit the information they collect, and that support can be both expensive and technically challenging. For example, recent RAND analysis has shown that effectively exploiting the data from an optimal set of surveillance systems for a major theater conflict could require at least a thousand-fold improvement in automatic target recognition technology! Prudent planners are likely to be cautious about proceeding down such a challenging path.

Problems of scale and time are intertwined with investment decisions and overall strategy. The much-analyzed cases of the German "wonder weapons"— the V-1, the V-2, and jet aircraft—illustrate the familiar problem of potentially effective weapons introduced too late and on too small a scale to have much effect on an ongoing conflict, unlike, for example, the Allied development of radar. The United States has had a scale problem with its development and deployment of conventional cruise missiles, in spite of their successful use in the Gulf War and in more recent operations. Deploying them and being able to support them in large enough numbers to be decisive in a major conflict remain problems even now. Fortunately, unlike the Germans in World War II, the United States so far has had the luxury of pursuing these programs during a time of relative peace. Still, a major change in the way the United States fights wars could take some time to implement, even in an era of dynamic technological change. Thus, the "slow revolution" might still be acceptable, although it could be overtaken by events.

All of this suggests that timing is quite critical in introducing and exploiting new technology and that a side that moves too early can miss the mark. Interestingly, that is not necessarily "counter-revolutionary." Indeed, Andrew Marshall, the "father" of the current notion about a potential revolution in military affairs, likes to use the example of the German blitzkrieg to demonstrate that a military revolution can occur when one side effectively exploits relatively mature technology by developing new operational concepts. Thus, a "revolution" could happen very quickly if it comes about by clever exploitation of existing technology. Alternatively, if operational concepts evolve relatively steadily, a mature-technology warmaker might be able to crush "new entries" and really dominate them because of its greater experience with the technology.

Even the best technology cannot be decisive militarily if it is used improperly or applied to largely irrelevant problems. For example, when laser-guided bombs were introduced in the Vietnam War, they certainly increased the effectiveness of U.S. bombing against point targets. That had very little effect on the overall progress of the war, however, mainly because technology was being asked to solve the wrong problem. It just solved the wrong problem more efficiently.

That is why tactical innovation and organizational adaptation are so critical. Failure to handle this part of the problem could cause the RMA to be stillborn. Conversely, as noted above, in a competition involving mature technologies, revolutionary change could occur very rapidly, and the winner could be whoever solves the operational and organizational problems first. History abounds with examples of successful tactical innovation and organizational adaptation that allowed the "weak" to defeat the "strong." The combination of technological innovation—even very simple technological improvements or the clever use of existing technology—and operational innovation has proven particularly powerful historically, sometimes winning decisively for the innovators, sometimes changing the nature of warfare permanently. The converse is also true. There are probably more examples of failure than success. The process is decidedly Darwinian!

The U.S. experience to date is not very encouraging. For example, in the aftermath of the Gulf War while the United States was extolling the virtues of its precision-guided weapons, the U.S. Air Force was eliminating the job category of "targeteer"—the persons responsible for doing all the detailed work of evaluating targets, selecting aimpoints, choosing appropriate weapons, and translating intelligence materials into an appropriate form for the weapons to use—leaving one to wonder how it actually expected to be able to use precision-guided weapons effectively in the future. Similarly, developing the intelligence support necessary to operate smart, stealthy weapons has proven institutionally challenging. After some serious initial missteps, the U.S. Department of Defense has made institutional changes to try to deal with this problem (Hura and McLeod 1993a, 1993b, 1995). How successful their efforts are remains to be seen. Coping organizationally with "information warfare" has been challenging as well. It has brought out all of the worst bureaucratic instincts in the players (Buchan 1995b) and has resulted in some near disasters. The fact that we have, so far, avoided total disasters is only mildly reassuring.

A final example is the U.S. track record in using satellites effectively to support military operations. One might think that Americans would be really good at this considering how long we have been in the satellite business, however, the historical record has been spotty at best. Many of the details are still shrouded in secrecy. The Gulf War experience was instructive in this regard. In some cases, the exploitation of satellite resources worked very well, usually between organizations that dealt informally on the basis of "handshakes" and mutual support. In other cases, however, the "ships passed in the night" and users who might have benefited from the information that space systems could have provided could not "plug in" effectively. These problems have long been recognized, which makes the fact that they have not been solved adequately all the more frustrating. It also should set off alarm bells about the organizational problems of implementing the RMA.

The Gulf War experience suggests that some high-technology systems were not nearly as effective as they could have been because bureaucracies could not adapt quickly enough. On the other hand, where people had the flexibility to be innovative—for example, Air Force staff officers bringing personal computers and software into the field and "making them work"—things went better than anyone had a right to expect.

Thus, organizational adaptation has already proved to be a problem for the United States in taking the first steps toward implementing the RMA. Even with visionary leadership—Admiral William Owens as vice chairman of the Joint Chiefs of Staff—committed to the RMA, institutionalizing the process of making the requisite system trade-offs and acquisition choices remained challenging. In fact, Richard Szafranski is almost certainly right in his conclusion that the U.S. military is unlikely to change its system sufficiently to revolutionize its combat power (Szafranski 1996).

Nor has the track record on innovations in tactics and operational art been particularly reassuring. That is a matter of concern because innovative use of operational concepts, especially when coupled with new or cleverly applied technology, can not only be decisive in particular conflicts, but also sometimes change the way in which wars are fought. Similarly, failure to recognize these possibilities can be a prescription for failure, even of a "superior" force. Thus, studying and understanding the interplay between military operational art and changing technology is essential to exploring the prospective implications of future military revolutions. For example, the battles within the U.S. defense community in recent years on how to use heavy bombers effectively in the post–Cold War era suggest how hard it is for old habits to die. RAND analysis suggested that one of the most effective ways to use heavy bombers in large-scale conventional wars, if the bombers were armed with suitable weapons, was to attack invading armored forces (Buchan 1994; Buchan and Frelinger 1994; Buchan, Frelinger, and Herbert 1992). That was the kind of tactical problem that the United States and its allies faced for decades in Europe and worried considerably about during the early stages of the Gulf War. Using bombers that way, however, as opposed to making deep strikes against "strategic targets" in the enemy's rear area, ran strongly counter to the Air Force's operational culture. Eventually, the U.S. Air Force's Air Combat Command, strongly encouraged by Defense Department civilian officials, changed its position on this, at least to a degree, but it was a considerable struggle. The so-called "halt phase" of operations has gained much more prominence in discussions of strategy and tactics, and bombers are now routinely considered as candidates for performing this mission. That kind of technical, doctrinal, and bureaucratic battle is likely to be repeated over and over again as military establishments try to cope with this generation of technological change. It will be interesting to see whether recent organizational initiatives such as the Air Force's new Battle Lab concept improve the situation.

On balance, then, making the RMA work will require overcoming formidable obstacles:

- the technology may not work as well as expected;
- it is not likely to be cheap;
- development is likely to be slow; and
- organizational adaptation and operational innovation are critical to the success of the RMA, and the track record of the recent past in this regard is not encouraging.

Still, there is no fundamental reason why it cannot be made to work, and all the alternatives appear to be worse.

What Could Potential Adversaries Do?

There are three main questions to consider: What kind of adversaries are likely to be most vulnerable to the RMA? What are the most effective counters? What might others do to pursue RMAs of their own?

The answers to these questions will depend on the particular situation of individual countries: what they aspire to in the world; who their actual or potential enemies are; what their own industrial, technical, military, and economic capabilities are; and how clever and rich they are. In the first place, many military-political situations are likely to be relatively unaffected by this RMA. Situations such as interventions in Somalia and Rwanda, perhaps even in Haiti, and—to a lesser degree—in Bosnia, come to mind. The major elements of the RMA are likely to be of limited value in most of these situations, although there is at least anecdotal evidence that people used new technology in clever ways to help at the margin.

Perhaps the most vulnerable countries are those with relatively large, somewhat modern, traditional military establishments. Countries such as Iraq, North Korea, and perhaps Iran might fall into this category. Were they to try to engage in large-scale Gulf War–like operations, they could be very vulnerable to a United States–like enemy. In fact, most vulnerable of all are countries that are in the initial stages of converting to a more information-based military, but that do not yet have enough experience with it to operate effectively against a skilled enemy. The Serbian Republic in Bosnia might be a modest example. Its forces used a rudimentary, centralized command and control system that was extraordinarily easy for the United States to exploit. That is, they were just modern enough to be vulnerable to modern opponents more accustomed to exploiting the key technologies. Similarly, countries that were just beginning to develop "high-tech" economies, but had not yet become fully conversant with all of the subtleties of modern computer and information-related technologies, could be most vulnerable to "information warfare" techniques. Interestingly, then, the conventional wisdom that military establishments like that of the United States are most vulnerable to information-based warfare is probably wrong. It is the middle-level powers that make the best targets. Lower-tier powers may be only slightly affected.

On the other hand, against technical peers or even countries one rung above or below on the technology ladder, traditional factors like numbers could matter a lot. Fighting the United States, for example, entails risks for any military power because the United States can bring massive firepower to bear if it has time to prepare adequately. Ironically, the main reason the RMA is so important to the United States is that it may be the only way to compensate for the reductions in forces mandated by defense budget cuts. Others—China, for example—might be able to compensate by sheer numbers, particularly if augmented by modern, if not necessarily revolutionary, military forces. Thus, the RMA may allow the United States to fight a large military power by increasing the efficiency of its large, but constrained, military forces. A large enough opponent might find the most effective counter to be sheer numbers, particularly if it could distribute the "value" of its forces (e.g., relying on infantry rather than armor, which makes a more attractive target for high-tech weapons). In general, peer competitors are likely to be only modestly vulnerable to an RMA-like approach. They will presumably have discovered its weaknesses and will have compensated to a degree by adding robustness to their forces and abandoning outdated operational concepts. Thus, a battle against a peer is likely to turn into a modern variant of a traditional attrition-oriented campaign.

The issue of counters is interesting as well. For example, recent RAND analysis suggests that some old-fashioned approaches, some with new wrinkles, are likely to be the most effective ways to counter forces using the RMA-based approach we are discussing. Examples of particularly effective counters include: physical attacks on critical facilities such as command posts and key communications nodes; jamming of GPS navigation satellites; jamming of communications links, particularly the commercial communications systems on which the military increasingly depend; and a mix of concealment and deception schemes to defeat sensors on which precision attack and situational awareness rely. Interestingly, we found these familiar counters to be much more of a threat than the "trendier" information warfare-related counters such as computer "hacking." We found that protecting against and recovering from hacking attacks was not particularly difficult or expensive. The counters that did seem to matter were all relatively easy and cheap to implement, well within the reach of virtually any potential enemy. The enemy does, of course, have to have the tactical insight to know that these things are important. Also, we found that if the United States conducts its operations and structures its forces properly, these counters should only be nuisances rather than serious problems.

That leaves perhaps the most interesting question: How might others adapt the RMA to their own purposes? It is in this area where a rich set of possibilities exists because other nations, having different security needs and indigenous capabilities, may choose different paths. Thus, we are no longer talking about "the RMA" as defined in the current discussions in the West. Rather, we need to consider a range of options for "mixing and matching" various combinations of old and new technologies, operational concepts, and strategic options to produce custom-tailored grand strategies.

First, a small number of advanced industrial countries might choose to develop at least the broad version of the RMA as we have defined it so far. For example, if the United States pursues this course successfully, it may be both sensible and attractive for its traditional allies to follow suit and perhaps even lead in some areas. That is particularly true if coalition warfare is indeed the wave of the future.

It is also conceivable, but somewhat improbable because of the costs and risks involved, that some aspiring global powers could take the radical step of "starting from a clean sheet of paper" to structure their military forces, and that could lead them to choose radically different types of forces from those traditionally acquired by major military powers. For example, some space advocates argue that a country such as India, say, which has some relatively modern technical capabilities, might be better off investing in a space force (e.g., armed transatmospheric vehicles, perhaps armed satellites) than in a traditional navy and air force for projecting power. (See Snead [1995], for example, for a description of the kinds of scenarios that could emerge as a result.) In principle, that could give a country such as India both regional and worldwide strike capabilities far beyond what it could achieve with ships and aircraft at what advocates assert would be an acceptable cost. In addition to the technical and operational problems that such a country would have to solve in order to develop a space force, however, most such aspiring powers already have navies and air forces with their own histories, traditions, and political constituencies that might be hard to overcome. Still, in considering possibilities for revolutionary change, perhaps one should not be too cavalier in dismissing such radical restructuring.

For most of the rest of the world, though, the options are likely to be more modest. There is no reason, however, that other countries have to go through the same evolutionary process that the United States and others have. For example, the burgeoning commercial market in critical technologies such as computer hardware and software, microelectronics, communications, navigation and guidance, remote sensing, and space launch may allow rising nations to "skip a few steps" in the technical evolutionary process. Moreover, with the growing international market in advanced weaponry now unfettered by any constraints of Cold War ideology, any nation (or, in some cases, nonstate actors) with money can acquire almost any kind of weapon system that money can buy. Thus, the entry barriers into the competition are not what they once were and newcomers might easily get a "leg up." Indeed, with careful mixing and matching of emerging and established technologies, a clear set of strategic and tactical goals, and a flexible organizational and tactical approach, some new players could actually benefit more from some form of RMA than the major powers.

Still, one should not get too carried away with the spread-of-the-RMA notion. All countries have budgetary problems that will constrain their ambitions in expanding their military capabilities to some degree. Not all will feel the need to do so. Even those with the technical capability to exploit the new technologies may lack the large-scale systems integration skill and experience necessary to exploit the new technologies fully. However, they could still develop many of the capabilities we have been discussing on at least a limited scale, and that might be sufficient to meet their needs.

Below is a list of some of the paths that different nations might choose to follow in enhancing their military capabilities (Buchan 1995a):

- There will be a significant class of nations for which (and against which) the RMA will have little impact. These states will tend to fight in rather primitive ways that do not lend themselves to either exploitation or threats from the new high-tech approach to warfare. Nations such as Somalia are likely to fall into this class.
- A broad class of countries will be able to take some advantage of the new information-related technologies, particularly communications, computers,

navigation aids, and reconnaissance systems. The dominance of commercial systems in some technical areas will expand this "club" considerably.

- Some will choose to substitute "cheap" manpower for expensive machines. Others may try to enhance the capabilities of their manpower-intensive units, such as special operations forces, and try to use them creatively.
- Computer "hacking" could become virtually universal. As a weapon it *might be most effectively used by nonstate actors* (e.g., terrorists, criminals), which are likely to be harder to identify and punish than nations that practice "information warfare."
- The most cost-effective way for regional powers with at least moderate technical capability to exploit the RMA is likely to be developing counters to some of the superpower systems (e.g., jamming GPS and satellite communications). Also, if their interests are mainly regional, they can probably employ simpler, cheaper technologies (e.g., fiber optic landlines and direct line-of-sight terrestrial relays for communications) to meet their own military needs, while minimizing their own vulnerabilities.
- Regional military powers may become effective "niche competitors" by selecting particular elements of the new RMA technology. This approach might not require new operational concepts to be fully effective. For example, many nations may choose to acquire at least a modest capability for conventional precision strike. Such nations may, at the very least, be able to raise the cost to global powers of intervening regionally.
- The nature of information-related technologies may provide even the smallest national (as well as nonstate) actors with some measure of "global reach" if they choose to use it.
- It is possible, but unlikely, that developing regional powers will be able or *feel the need* to exploit the RMA to the extent that the United States might.
- Nuclear weapons could be "technological equalizers" for a regional power trying to engage a technically superior major power.
- Perhaps the most attractive—and frightening—prospect of all about developing powers would be combining nuclear weapons and modest information technologies (e.g., crude GPS fixes for weapons guidance and commercial-level satellite photography for targeting). Such a combination could be a potent threat even to superpowers.

Unlike in some past technology-driven military revolutions, this time around it does not look like only the "big boys" can play. There could well be many entrants in the competition, at least at some level, and that will affect the way the United States and others conduct their affairs in the international arena. The most important thing to understand is that, even if one accepts the RMA discourse relatively uncritically, *there is no such thing as "the RMA!"* Rather, there is a variety of maturing technologies, which—when matched with suitable operational concepts— may change the face of future warfare. Successful competitors will adopt the pieces of this "revolution" that most effectively meet their needs, leading to a nuanced, differentiated set of military approaches with some common threads.

WHAT DOES IT ALL MEAN: PANACEA, PIG-IN-THE-POKE, OR SOMETHING IN BETWEEN?

On balance, the RMA is likely to be neither a panacea nor a complete failure. Many of the concepts and the applications of technology are sound and worth pursuing regardless of whether they are "revolutionary" or not. In fact, in times of shrinking defense budgets and military force structures, the United States and others may have little choice but to try to exploit information technologies to increase the effectiveness of their military forces.

Still, the possibility that some combination of successful technologies could lead to a dramatic change in the way wars are fought is sufficiently important that prudent planners need to keep a constant weather eye on such possibilities. Some of the current technologies, if implemented properly, might have a revolutionary effect on major campaigns. For example, it has appeared likely for some years now that a combination of advanced sensors and weapons could be fielded that would defeat large-scale invasions, particularly armored invasions, with high confidence and at an acceptable cost. If so, that could lead to a world where large-scale invasions might simply not work. *That would be a revolutionary outcome.* It would not end the game, of course, but it would change it in fundamental ways, and that is important.

Effects of the RMA on lower-level conflicts and operations are likely to be less revolutionary, but there may be more room for creativity at this level than in the more routinized large-scale campaigns. Some of these sorts of operations may actually represent the most stressing cases for information-based technologies and systems.

Successful implementation of the RMA is by no means assured. The technologies may not work as well as expected. Even if they do, the pace of incorporating new technology and weapon systems into military forces has traditionally been glacial, thus leading to a "slow motion" revolution at best. Even if the technology works properly, successful implementation of the RMA will require organizational adaptation and operational innovation to be fully effective. That is really the critical part of the RMA, and few organizations or nations have shown much consistent talent for that. *Whoever does will be the big winner!*

This RMA, if there is one, is likely to come in different forms as different countries try to adapt it to their own particular needs. It is unlikely that potential future U.S. adversaries will follow the same path as the United States in implementing the RMA. Some of the likely options that others might pursue include developing a modest precision strike capability, exploiting commercial technologies and the international arms trade, developing a range of counters to reduce the effectiveness of high-tech U.S. systems, and/or combining modest information technologies and nuclear weapons. Others may opt to rely on manpower in lieu of expensive machines. Some of these approaches could pose formidable threats to the interests of the United States even if its own RMA proves successful. Indeed, selective adoption of emerging technologies coupled with clever tactical application may actually offer more to "have not" nations than the full-blown RMA might offer to "have" nations such as the United States.

NOTES

1. The literature on the RMA is already vast. On definitional and conceptual issues, see, for example, Bartlett et al. (1996); Bunker (1996); McKitrick et al. (1994); and Owens (1994).

2. Others have pointed out, quite correctly, that RMAs need not be technological. For example, Sullivan (1996) points out that RMAs can be ideological. Bunker (1996) makes the same point more broadly in examining competing theories of warfare.

3. Perfect information about an enemy is neither necessary nor sufficient to ensure military victory. As Sullivan has pointed out, historical examples abound of one side knowing virtually every relevant "fact" about its enemy and still losing either because it interpreted the facts incorrectly or the knowledge simply did not matter (Sullivan 1996). Similarly, in the "fog of war," adversaries carry on with insufficient information and still manage to win or lose based on other factors (DiNardo and Hugues 1995).

4. I am indebted to Major-General Michael V. Hayden, immediate past director of the Joint Command and Control Warfare Center and commander of the Air Intelligence Agency, for sharing these experiences and insights that he gained firsthand in Bosnia.

10

The Military-Industrial Correlates of the RMA: The Evolution of Agile Manufacturing

Andrew Latham

INTRODUCTION

Since the late 1980s the U.S. arms industry has been characterized by far-reaching changes in technology, technique, and organizational structure. Shaped by the material requirements of the so-called military-technical revolution, as well as by the discourses of *flexibility* and *leanness*, during the 1990s postfordist production practices began to displace the essentially fordist manufacturing techniques that had long been considered best practice in the American arms industry.[1] As a result, a new arms production paradigm—now commonly referred to as *agile manufacturing*—has coalesced in American military-industrial circles. This new paradigm is still in embryonic form, of course, and it is likely to evolve in ways that cannot be precisely predetermined. Even at this juncture, however, there is a clear sense that arms production is being reconstituted around a radically new industrial vision involving the use of computer-driven flexible machine tools, lean production processes, and rapidly reconfigurable virtual enterprises to undertake low-rate/low-volume production of increasingly knowledge-intensive, high-technology weapons. As it evolves and diffuses through the U.S. armaments industry, this new paradigm is profoundly transforming the nature and logic of armaments production. Indeed, so profound are these changes that the transition to agile arms production can be said to constitute nothing less than a "quiet revolution," marking the end of one era in America's military-industrial history and the beginning of another.

This chapter seeks to illuminate this process of military-industrial transformation. It argues that two powerful motive forces can be identified behind this phenomenon. The first is practical, deriving from both the need to field the kind of increasingly knowledge-intensive weapons deemed necessary to American military superiority in the early twenty-first century and the need to contain costs.

The second is cultural, having to do with the influence that the ideals of information warfare, cyberwar, and postfordist production have gained over the collective imagination of America's managerial, military, and military-industrial elites. At one level the effects of these two forces are difficult to disentangle as the prevailing understanding of the nature of the material requirement for victory in war is powerfully shaped by an ideal that emphasizes the importance of dominant battlespace knowledge and precision (Dunn 1992, ch. 4; Johnson and Libicki 1995). Indeed, it is important to recognize that neither material nor cultural forces have absolute primacy in the shaping of contemporary U.S. military-industrial policy; both are playing a prominent role in reshaping patterns of military (product and process) innovation. Nevertheless, it is crucial to our understanding of the development and diffusion of the agile manufacturing paradigm to develop some sense of the way in which these forces are acting and interacting to transform arms production during the contemporary period. Thus, this chapter attempts to illuminate this process of military-industrial transition by tracing the diffusion of agile production techniques through the crucially important U.S. military aerospace industry. Recognizing that the terrain explored is far too complex to be mapped properly within the limits of this chapter, my goal is not to provide a comprehensive account of the evolution of the American military aerospace industry during the current era. Rather, it is to chart the way in which a key subsector of the arms industry is experiencing the crossing of America's third military-industrial divide.[2] Although it would be preferable to discuss the motive forces driving this transition separately, the way in which these forces interact with one another means that an integrated sketch is all that is possible.

This chapter proceeds in three parts. In the first section I discuss the effects of the Revolution in Military Affairs on the military-industrial environment in the United States. I then examine the state's response to this phenomenon, focusing on both the U.S. government's articulation of a new vision of arms production—agile manufacturing—and on its efforts to encourage the realization of this new vision through a number of key policy initiatives. In the third section I look at the efforts of the U.S. military aerospace industry to implement agile manufacturing. The chapter concludes with some general observations regarding the nature of the U.S. arms industry's transition to a new production paradigm.

THE TRIGGERING EFFECTS OF THE REVOLUTION IN MILITARY AFFAIRS

Although the conventional wisdom states that military industrial restructuring is driven primarily by the contraction in the global arms market associated with the end of the Cold War, there are other forces at work reshaping the arms industry. One of these is the so-called Revolution in Military Affairs (RMA) that is currently transforming the ideas, instruments, and institutions of warfare in the United States.[3] At the battlefield or war-fighting level, the RMA involves the use of microelectronics, precision munitions, stealth technology, near real-time sensing capabilities, and ever more advanced C^3I to generate quantum increases in visibility (the ability to grasp the battlefield), lethality (the ability to destroy or incapacitate the enemy on the battlefield), agility (the ability to respond to developments on the battlefield), and concealability (the ability to prevent an enemy from observing one's forces on the battlefield). In one sense, of course, this revolution can be interpreted as the natural outcome of a process that began during World War II. This is so not only because technology has increasingly dominated weapons development and production throughout the entire period since 1945, but because, as Mary Kaldor (1981) argues, technological innovation during that era was largely a matter of exaggerating and improving the performance characteristics of the weapon systems that had proven decisive during the war. But there is something clearly revolutionary about recent changes in military technology and technique. At a very general level, this is probably due to the fact that, as Soviet military theorists predicted in the 1970s, incremental changes in the means and methods of combat have exerted a progressively more profound effect on the character of warfare, and are now culminating in a *qualitative* transformation in the nature of warfighting (*Soviet Military Encyclopedia* 1979, 7:80–82). On another level, however, the emerging mode of warfare is increasingly viewed as revolutionary because military technologies are more and more frequently breaking out of technological trajectories established during World War II as the search for radically new combinations of generic technologies becomes a primary determinant of the structure of military demand. Whatever the case, there is now a general consensus that the mode of warfare has evolved beyond Industrialized Total Warfare, and that the "Military After Next" will be organized around instruments, ideas, and institutions radically different from those that dominated World War II (Bracken 1993).

The Dynamics of Military Technology in the Late Modern Era

During the era of Industrialized Total Warfare, the means of destruction were essentially electro-mechanical in nature, reflecting the then-prevailing level of technological development. The instruments of warfare included enabling technologies such as steel, steam, and the internal combustion engine, as well as dedicated military technologies such as rifles, artillery, and tanks. With the application of the technologies of the Information Revolution to military purposes, however, these instruments of warfare are increasingly being supplemented (and supplanted) by revolutionary advances in electronics, artificial intelligence and computing, C^3I systems, and advanced materials. As in the civil sector, these technologies are exerting truly revolutionary effects. Indeed, they have already begun to transform the battlefield by vastly increasing single-shot kill ratios, providing near real-time command and control, and creating an ever more transparent battlespace (Libicki 1996a). As these knowledge-intensive military technologies continue to evolve, some argue that, in the not too distant future, the fundamental technical bases of warfare will be transformed, and that "aircraft carriers, tanks, fighters and bombers will cease to have a primary role in the postmodern theatre of war" (Stix 1995, 94). In this scenario the battlefield of the twenty-first century will be dominated, not by massed troops and armor, but by "networks of intelligent mines and unpiloted drones that can perform reconnaissance and launch or plant weapons. Highly dispersed special forces may scout for targets and evaluate battle damage. Remotely fired missiles may become the main instruments for destroying enemy targets" (Stix 1995, 92).

For the moment, of course, such scenarios remain the stuff of science fiction; warfare today continues to be dominated by "baroque" versions of the military technologies that achieved preeminence during World War II. Indeed, many of today's most advanced weapon systems are the culmination of a long process of more or less linear "trend innovation," which Kaldor (1981, 4) describes as "perpetual improvements to weapons that fall within the established traditions of the armed services and the armourers." But the constant, continuing press of technological innovation is increasingly yielding a plethora of military technologies that break out of existing technological trajectories, either as a result of the development of radically new technologies or as previously discrete generic technologies are dynamically recombined in novel ways.

Simply stated, then, the onset of the RMA has given rise to a new "great desideratum" in American military circles: knowledge-intensive weaponry. This ideal has come to exercise enormous influence within the American military, generating a dynamics of perpetual innovation that is increasingly forcing arms producers to seek an enhanced capacity to upgrade existing weapon systems, to develop radically new weapons technologies (by combining generic technologies in new and innovative ways), and to reduce "lab-to-field" cycles so that new technologies are not obsolete before they are deployed. It is also accelerating the pace of technological innovation. Military innovation, of course, has always been an important element of interstate rivalry, and the phenomenon of perpetual innovation can be traced back at least to the "invention of invention" in the nineteenth century (van Creveld 1989, ch. 15). What distinguishes both the emerging mode of warfare and its military-industrial correlates is that as we enter the twenty-first century the capacity to develop, produce, and field ever more innovative and knowledge-intensive weaponry is becoming *the* primary determinant of military power and victory in war. This differs from the preceding era, during which the capacity for technological innovation, while important, was less decisive than the capacity for social and economic mobilization.

The Effects of the RMA on the Military-Industrial Environment

After World War II market conditions in the civil sector were such that manufacturers were able to organize production around specialized machine tools and rigid, mechanically guided production lines employing relatively unskilled labor. This system was sustained by an interlocking framework of state, market, and institutional control systems that stabilized and standardized demand, unleashing the full productive potential of the fordist paradigm. This fusion of the fordist production paradigm with an appropriate regulatory framework generated unprecedented economic growth during the post-1945 era. Indeed, so great was the economic expansion initiated by this growth model that the period is often referred to as the "golden age of capitalism."

In the arms sector, on the other hand, conditions could scarcely have been more different. Where commercial firms serviced a market that encouraged the standardization of products and parts, the pursuit of economies of scale, the mechanization of the manufacturing process, and the lowering of product prices, arms manufacturers had to produce for a monopsonist state that demanded relatively small numbers of specialized, increasingly "baroque," performance-maximising weapons (Kaldor 1981). Cold War rivalry and the system of perpetual military innovation it fostered worked against the implementation of commercial-style fordism in several ways. First, it blocked the kind of standardization of demand that allowed the widespread use of specialized production machinery in the civil sector. The emphasis in U.S. strategic thought on technological superiority meant that designs had to be updated in order to incorporate the latest technological advances. This worked against the kind of dedicated mechanization increasingly common in the commercial sector. Second, perpetual innovation and the pursuit of technological superiority worked against product simplification, giving rise to increasingly complex (baroque) technologies that were not particularly amenable to fordist production practices. Finally, in the aftermath of World War II, levels of demand dropped dramatically, and never again reached levels that could be called "mass." While the military often procured large quantities of specific types of weapons, demand never reached the mass proportions that were common in the civil sector.[4] This precluded making the kinds of investment in advanced, dedicated machinery that had enabled commercial firms to continually increase productivity through the 1960s. It also encouraged the development and diffusion of flexible manufacturing systems, as well as an increased dependence on skilled labor (Gansler 1980). As the Cold War progressed and the tendency toward baroque technology intensified, these differences in the regulatory and cultural context were exacerbated, widening the breach between commercial and military variants of fordism, though never severing the material and cultural links connecting them.

Against this backdrop the onset of the RMA triggered the terminal decline of military-fordism. By the late 1970s the disjuncture between patterns of military demand and the logic of the prevailing arms production paradigm had begun to manifest itself as a growing inability to produce affordable high-technology weapon systems (Gansler 1989, 170–71). At first these tensions between the military-fordist production paradigm and the technical demands of the prevailing mode of warfare had been problematic, but manageable. During the late 1980s, however, the quantum leap in knowledge-intensity and technological density of warfare associated with the RMA, coupled with the reduction in military spending associated with the end of the Cold War, intensified these tensions to the point where they reached crisis proportions. Indeed, even before the end of the Cold War, it was clear to many in both industry and government that changes in the technical bases of warfare coupled with the transformation of the global security environment had signaled the terminal decline of the existing arms production paradigm (U.S. Department of Commerce 1989).

From the point of view of the state, the exhaustion of the military-fordist paradigm manifested itself first and foremost in terms of a radical inability of U.S. arms producers to undertake the kind of low-rate/low-volume production of technologically dense goods required by knowledge-intensive warfare. Under military-fordism there was a clear correlation between rate/volume of production and unit costs: the more units produced, and the more rapidly they were manufactured, the lower were individual unit prices. Conversely, shorter production runs tended to result in higher unit prices as the cost of development and tooling were amortized over fewer units of output. This was not terribly problematic during World War II, when levels of demand were roughly comparable to those prevailing in the commercial marketplace. Following the war, however, sharp reductions in the levels of absolute demand, coupled with the rising technological density and complexity of weaponry, began to drive costs upward. Almost invariably, this meant that with each successive generation of weapons fewer and fewer units could be purchased.[5] As a result unit prices were driven up still further, setting off the escalatory spiral that subsequently came to be known as "structural disarmament." Primarily as a result of the RMA, by the late 1980s this situation had become much worse, and it was generally acknowledged in U.S. military-industrial circles that the tendency toward structural disarmament, which was rooted in the very nature of military-fordism, had reached crisis proportions (Callaghan 1988, 57).

The onset of the RMA, then, created an unbridgeable gap between the nature of military demand on the one hand and the logic and best practices of military-fordism on the other. This initiated a crisis in U.S. military-industrial circles as government fears of structural disarmament converged with industry fears of declining profits and bankruptcy to initiate a period of profound intellectual ferment and practical experimentation related to arms manufacturing. Out of this process a new set of military-industrial desiderata emerged during the late 1980s and early 1990s, key elements of which include:

- *Cost-efficient low-rate/low-volume production.* A key part of the military's vision of the arms industry of the future is a capacity to produce limited numbers of knowledge-intensive weaponry at affordable costs (with costs defined not only in terms of initial purchase prices, but overall life-cycle expenses as well).
- *A capacity for rapid technology realization and insertion.* As the RMA accelerates the arms industry of the future must be able to develop and insert advanced technologies rapidly. This involves not simply developing and producing new platforms in a timely fashion, but also a capacity for quickly inserting leading-edge subsystems into ongoing production programs.
- *A capacity for rapid prototyping.* In a military-technical environment where not every new technology can be put into quantity production, technology demonstrators, technology integration demonstrators, production retrofit demonstrators, and operational prototypes are viewed as playing an increasingly important role in U.S. acquisition strategy. In such an environment the capacity to develop rapidly and cost-efficiently and produce prototypes will be crucially important to maintaining a technological edge.
- *A capacity to draw on the broader civil technology and industrial base.* As the commercial sector has taken the lead in technological dynamism, there has been a recognition that continued American military-technical superiority requires the creation of a unified national technology and industrial base (U.S. Congress [OTA] 1994).

For arms firms, then, the RMA and the associated quantum leap in the knowledge-intensity of weaponry have initiated a clear rupture with the industrial best practices of the post-War era. Whereas during the Cold War the tensions between military demand and the logic of the arms production paradigm were manageable (if only at great expense), since the onset of the RMA (and the end of the Cold War) they have reached crisis proportions. This has generated pressures to adapt manufacturing processes, business practices, and intra- and interfirm relations in order to enhance flexibility and innovative capacity, the goal being affordable low-rate/low-volume production of knowledge-intensive weaponry. In recent years this process has culminated in the adoption by arms producers of those postfordist manufacturing practices that are widely perceived to underpin the technological vitality of the global electronics and automobile industries.

THE PENTAGON AND THE EVOLUTION OF AGILE MANUFACTURING

Pressured by the demands of an accelerating military-technical revolution to restructure and modernize, and inspired by the successful application of postfordist production techniques in the U.S. automotive and electronics sectors, over the last decade or so American arms producers have simultaneously undertaken innovations in product technologies, development and manufacturing processes, and corporate/ managerial structure. As a result the (essentially fordist) production paradigm around which U.S. arms manufacturing has been organized since World War II has entered into a period of terminal decline, and the defining features of a new arms production paradigm are now becoming visible across the American military-industrial landscape.

Conditioned to a significant degree by the example of the Japanese and American automobile industries, this emerging paradigm is based on four principles. The first is the pursuit of flexibility, which involves efforts to adopt new technologies and techniques in order to decouple rate and volume of production from unit cost. The second is the pursuit of accelerated technological innovation through the adoption of a variety of practices intended to shorten design-to-field times and encourage the dynamic recombination of previously discrete technologies in new and innovative ways. The third organizing principle is the pursuit of "leanness" through the relentless elimination of waste and inefficiency at every stage of the production cycle. The final principle is "agility," defined as the ability to create electronically integrated virtual enterprises (comprising civil and military firms) quickly and painlessly to respond effectively to constantly evolving demand patterns. This new paradigm can be conceptualized as *agile manufacturing*—a term that has been advanced in various military-industrial circles to refer to the adaptation of postfordist production techniques to the military-industrial environment of the early twentieth-first century. Since the early 1990s agile manufacturing has become *the* paradigmatic vision of what the future arms industry should look like, and has thus played a crucial role in the contemporary restructuring of the U.S. defense industrial base.

This section also makes the argument that while the pursuit of perpetual innovation has become the defining characteristic of the contemporary arms industry, *affordability* has become an important secondary consideration. During the military-fordist era, production engineers and industrial managers never managed to sever the connection between rate/volume of production and unit cost, despite innovations such as numerically controlled machine tools and other flexibility enhancing innovations. As a result, as the volume of military orders have declined, and as the technological density of weaponry have increased, by the late 1970s unit costs were rising so fast that many feared the United States was on course toward "structural disarmament." Faced with this prospect, during the 1980s state and industrial officials began searching for new ways of manufacturing arms. At first they turned their attention toward the Japanese model of production, which was universally regarded as having solved many of the problems facing the U.S. arms industry (U.S. Department of Commerce 1989). Later they began to look at the lean manufacturing model that was widely perceived to have reversed the sagging fortunes of America's automotive firms. While the new vision of arms production that emerged out of this period of intellectual ferment ultimately transcended the (initially civilian) lean production paradigm, it is clear that this latest cluster of modern methods has exercized a powerful conditioning influence on the contemporary military-industrial restructuring process.

The U.S. Government and the Evolution of Agile Arms Production

The complex edifice of promotion and support underpinning the diffusion of postfordist production techniques through the arms industry began taking shape in the early 1990s with the launching of the Lean Aircraft Initiative (LAI).[6] The LAI began in earnest in 1992 when the U.S. Air Force's Aeronautical Systems Center (AF/ASC) requested that the Massachusetts Institute of Technology (MIT) conduct an initial evaluation of the applicability of lean production practices in the military aircraft industry. MIT, which had earlier identified such postfordist practices as the single most important factor behind the Japanese automobile industry's competitive edge over its American counterpart, conducted an initial assessment of the military aerospace industry, and concluded that the application of lean manufacturing techniques to the manufacture of military aircraft could be expected to result in a number of benefits, including:

- 50 percent reductions in factory labor, factory space, and engineering effort;
- 90 percent reductions in in-process inventory;
- 66 percent reductions in the number of defects;
- 87 percent reductions in suppliers and subcontractors; and
- 50 to 66 percent reductions in aircraft development times.

The assessment also concluded that adopting lean production techniques would improve the "ability of U.S. industry to rapidly develop prototypes and implement product improvements quickly in response to changes in threat and need" (JDW 1995, 45).

As a result of this positive initial evaluation, in August 1993 the AF/ASC launched a more comprehensive three-year program intended to identify and study lean production practices and to promote their diffusion through the military aerospace industry. Under this initiative the U.S. Air Force's Wright Laboratories began collaborating with about twenty military aerospace firms (distributed across the three main subsectors: airframes, avionics, and propulsion) to build and extend the lean production paradigm through an organized program of research, information-sharing, and pilot projects. The LAI was organized under the auspices of MIT's Center for Technology, Policy and Industrial Development (CTPID), which acted as a research hub and clearing house. Funding was provided by both the government (around $950,000 per year) and the participating firms (approximately $75,000 per year per firm). "The whole effort [was] overseen by an advisory board made up of senior officials from the aerospace industry, government and national labour unions" (Hewish and Pohling-Brown 1995, 30).

During its initial stages the LAI focused on evaluating the degree to which lean production practices had diffused through the U.S. military aerospace industry. Subsequently, however, it "sought to identify existing high-performance practices, within and outside the aerospace community, emphasizing those that [could] bring major reductions in both cost and cycle time" (Weiss, Murman, and Roos 1996, 32). To this end the project used integrated research teams (involving government, industry, and labor) to conduct surveys and case studies of relevant industrial organizations. In its final year the LAI concentrated on developing a Lean Enterprise Model (LEM) to aid in the implementation of postfordist production practices throughout the U.S. military aerospace industry.

Several government initiatives resulted from LAI research. For example, the USAF actively encouraged lean manufacturing techniques for the F-22 fighter, JDAM (Joint Direct Attack Munition), and C-17 transport aircraft programs. It has also launched two dedicated pathfinder projects, one in connection with the next-generation Air Force/Navy strike aircraft program (involving seven demonstration projects to pilot the introduction of lean manufacturing techniques), and the other a project related to postfordist modular factories (Hewish and Pohling-Brown 1995, 30–31).

A second, and somewhat more comprehensive, initiative for the promotion of postfordist techniques was also launched in 1991 when the U.S. Department of Defense sponsored a study by an industry-led group to investigate the future of arms production. This study, conducted at Lehigh University's Iacocca Institute, coined the term "agile manufacturing" to describe its vision of America's military-industrial future. As described in the study report *21ˢᵗ Century Manufacturing Enterprise Strategy* (Nagel and Dove 1991), agile manufacturing is a new postfordist production paradigm that is intended to enable the arms industry "to thrive in an environment of continuous and unanticipated change" (McGrath n.d.). Achieving such agility in arms manufacturing requires integrating computer-driven production technologies with the skill base of a knowledgeable workforce using postfordist management structures. It includes elements of both flexible and lean postfordist manufacturing techniques, but it is not synonymous with these approaches. Simply stated, whereas flexible production focuses on process adaptability, and lean production aims at reducing cost and shortening design-to-field times through the use of advanced techniques and technologies, agile production is intended to enhance technology development through the use of rapidly reconfigurable, computer-networked cooperative ventures capable of meeting the changing requirements of knowledge-intensive warfare. In other words, agile manufacturing encompasses the basic postfordist objectives of severing volume/rate of production and cost, reducing waste, and shortening design-to-field cycles, but also emphasizes the rapid creation of "virtual enterprises"—groups of vertically and/or horizontally linked companies that come together via computer networks to fill a specific demand. It is based on the recognition that while programmable automated machine tools and flexible manufacturing techniques are important elements of the new industrial paradigm, they are only part of the picture. True agility requires that the "entire supply chain... be engineered and managed so that manufacturers can work concurrently with their strategic partners, suppliers and customers to reduce costs and improve product design and performance" (Farrell n.d.). Whereas in the automotive industry the tendency has been to organize the supplier chain around semi-permanent "extended enterprise" (supplier-assembler partnerships lasting over twenty years), in the arms industry the vision that has emerged emphasizes the creation of short-term horizontal and vertical teaming arrangements (Whitney et al. 1995).

A key element of the agile manufacturing vision is the creation of an integrated national technology and industrial base (NTIB) comprising agile commercial and military firms, linked by computer networks, that can be assembled quickly to form a virtual enterprise capable of rapid and cost-efficient product realization (Bingaman, Gansler, and Kupperman 1991, ch. 1; Branscombe 1989; Defense Science Board 1989, A13–A18; Nagel and Dove 1991; U.S. Department of Defense 1995). As arms production has become less and less vertically integrated,[7] and as production has come to be based on complex webs of suppliers, assemblers and strategic partners, military-industrial planners, and industry executives have come to recognize that there are considerable benefits to including both commercial and military firms in the pool of potential project participants. Although significant cost savings may derive from including commercial firms in the potential supplier chain (the commercial supplier of a particular technology may be the most cost-efficient), the real military benefit of an integrated NTIB lies in the enhanced access to leading-edge technology that this would afford arms producers. An additional benefit, and one not to be underestimated, would be an expansion of the military supplier base. Over the past few decades, the regulatory burdens associated with defense contracting have driven many of the crucial subtier suppliers (usually small- and medium-sized enterprises) out of the arms industry.[8] This has been a source of concern in military-industrial circles, not only because it threatens the viability and surge capacity of the U.S. arms industry, but because it increases U.S. dependence on foreign sources as well (Bingaman, Gansler, and Kupperman 1991, 6). Creating an integrated NTIB comprising agile firms capable of servicing commercial and military markets with equal facility would assure the continued existence of a robust arms industry at the level of prime contractors, subcontractors, and suppliers.

Inspired by this vision, the U.S. government has recently begun to dismantle many of the regulatory barriers to civil-military integration. There is a growing realization, however, that a truly integrated NTIB will require more than simply removing the regulatory barriers between the commercial technology and industrial base (CTIB) and the defense technology and industrial base (DTIB). While this is an important precondition for integration, the development of an intrinsically dual-use technology and industrial base will require the recomposition of the entire U.S. technology and industrial base into agile firms capable of rapidly forming virtual enterprises in response to constantly evolving commercial and military demand patterns. In essence, the goal is to transcend the distinction between commercial and military firms by creating a single, generic category of industrial enterprise that can be readily incorporated into an industrial web producing either commercial or military goods.[9]

Thus, in a very real sense, the agile manufacturing vision can be said to represent a military-inspired derivative of the postfordist production methods pioneered in the automobile industry. It is clearly rooted in the basic logic of postfordist production, emphasising flexibility, quality, and responsiveness. But it goes beyond this paradigm to include a new vision of interfirm relations, one based on the rapid creation and dissolution of virtual enterprises comprising generic firms (i.e., firms that are neither civil nor military in the traditional sense) that can service the commercial or defense markets with equal ease. While deriving from the military-industrial desiderata generated by the RMA, this vision is not restricted to the arms industry; for, if the agile vision is to be realized, civil industry also has to be transformed. Thus the emergence of this new vision of production has had an important "knock-on" effect: it has triggered a new phase in the restructuring of the commercial technology and industrial base. Increasingly, commercial industry see agile manufacturing as its hope for future competitiveness in a world of fast-paced technical change and intensified global competition (Goldman, Nagel, and Preiss 1995).

Since the publication of *21st Manufacturing Enterprise Strategy*, the vision of agile arms production developed at the Iaccoca Institute has come to enjoy great currency in both government and industry circles. Building on this vision, the U.S. government initiated a number of research programs aimed at infusing an agile manufacturing capability into the defense industrial base: for example, the Manufacturing Automation and Design Environment (MADE) program, the Affordable Multi-Missile Manufacturing (AM^3) program, the Technologies Enabling Agile Manufacturing (TEAM) program, and the Electronic Commerce Resource Center (ECRC) program. The most important of these have been implemented under the auspices of the joint Advanced Research Projects Agency/ National Science Foundation (ARPA/NSF) Agile Manufacturing Initiative (AMI). Initiated in 1993, the AMI's mandate is to "develop, demonstrate and evaluate the advanced design, manufacturing and business transaction processes described in the *21st Century Manufacturing Enterprise Strategy* report" (ARPA n.d.), thus encouraging and facilitating the implementation of agile manufacturing through the arms industry and the broader technology and industrial base upon which the arms industry relies.

In addition to launching the LAI, AMI, and other industrial transformation initiatives, the U.S. government has taken a number of steps to remove the regulatory impediments to agile production and the creation of a unified national technology and industrial base. Until quite recently, of course, many elements of the military acquisition process (even as reformed during the 1980s) worked against the diffusion of postfordist production techniques. The Competition in Contracting Act (CICA), for example, has had a powerful dampening effect on process innovation and the ability of arms producers to adapt their organizational structures to the changing commercial environment. Initially put in place in 1984, the CICA is a Federal statute that required "full and open competition" in all U.S. government procurement programs. While conceived as a means of creating competitive market conditions (and thus reducing prices) in previously noncompetitive markets, CICA acted in a number of ways to slow the proliferation of postfordist techniques that might substantially improve efficiency and productivity in the defense sector. In particular, the requirement that contracts for components and subsystems be tendered on a competitive basis meant that the development of the type of long-term relationships at the heart of many new corporate governance structures is significantly inhibited. In turn, this limited the extent to which concurrent engineering, just-in-time manufacturing (JITM), and total quality management (TQM) practices (all of which are at least partly dependent on these new organizational structures) could be implemented.

Dual/second sourcing[10] practices involving transfers of proprietary technologies, while also rooted in an entirely reasonable impulse to control defense costs, have had similar effects on the proliferation of postfordist manufacturing techniques. In such a situation developers not only run the risk of not being awarded the production contract (which they may be counting on to subsidize development), but of having to transfer technical data and design/development information to competitors. As a result, they are necessarily discouraged from incorporating proprietary production technologies or management techniques in their design proposals. Other regulatory impediments include budget instability, which makes it difficult to employ efficient production planning and control techniques; the nature of military contracts, which stipulate that only approved production processes can be used; and the criminalization of noncompliance, which further reduces flexibility, responsiveness, and risk-taking by forcing managers to fulfil strictly regulatory requirements (Kovacic 1992).

Beyond these direct impediments to the diffusion of postfordist production practices, the regulatory framework governing arms procurement has also impeded the realization of the agile manufacturing vision in that it effectively segregated the defense technology and industrial base from its commercial counterpart, thus blocking the evolution of the kind of unified NTIB required for agile arms production. The regulatory sources of segregation have been well documented in previous studies and need not be rehearsed at length here (Bingaman, Gansler, and Kupperman 1991; Defense Science Board 1989; U.S. Congress 1993; U.S. Congress [OTA] 1994; U.S. Department of Defense [OUDA] 1993; van Opstal 1993). Suffice it to say that during the Cold War factors such as unique accounting requirements, military specifications and standards, state control of technical data rights, and byzantine public contracting procedures has meant that "in many companies, defence products are designed, developed, produced and supported in isolated plants or independent division; and many other companies either maintain separate research facilities for defence and commercial work or simply refuse to accept DOD research contracts" (Gansler 1995, 93). This led to the evolution of two discrete and isolated technology and industrial bases in the United States: one exclusively commercial, the other primarily military (Kelley and Watkins 1995a, 1995b). While this may have made sense even as recently as fifteen years ago, when few firms could meet the technological standards required by DOD, it makes little sense today when the commercial sector is at the forefront of innovation and performance in response to global business competition (Bingaman, Gansler, and Kupperman 1991, ch. 1).

Viewed against this backdrop, it is clear that the American government's ability to realize its vision of an agile arms industry is largely dependent on its ability to eliminate or reduce the barriers separating the commercial and defense technology and industrial bases; for only if these barriers are lowered will it be possible to create the kind of unified technology and industrial base that state and industry officials perceive as being necessary to the future of American arms production. To date, the government has taken a number of steps in the direction of creating such a regulatory framework. Two of these stand out as being particularly important (U.S. Congress [OTA] 1994, 64–66). The first was the passing of the 1994 Federal Acquisition Streamlining Act (FASA), which specifically addressed the purchase of commercial items and services, provided a clearer definition of commercial items and services, eliminated the requirement for cost and pricing data on commercial items, and made it more difficult for the government to acquire rights in technical data for items developed with private funds (U.S. Congress 1994 [OTA], 51).

The second important initiative in this regard involved a significant reduction in the use of military specifications and standards (milspecs) in the defense acquisition process. Milspecs, as a number of government and academic reports have concluded (Bingaman, Gansler, and Kupperman 1991), have long constituted one of the key impediments to the integration of the commercial and defense technology and industrial bases in that they deter many successful commercial firms from undertaking military business. Thus, any movement toward lowering the barriers between the commercial and military technology and industrial bases will require a prior reduction in the use of milspecs. It will also involve "fundamentally altering the incentive structure to promote greater use of commercial goods" (U.S. Congress [OTA] 1994, 84).

In June 1994 Secretary of Defense William Perry took a decisive step in this direction when he circulated a memorandum directing the DOD to implement changes in the use of military specifications and standards (Perry 1994). This memorandum directed military procurement executives "to use performance and commercial specifications and standards instead of military specifications and standards, unless no practical alternative exists to meet the user's needs" (Perry 1994). To be certain, even before 1994 DOD had begun the process of shifting to commercial standards, and by 1993 "had increased the number of adopted nongovernmental [i.e., commercial standards] from 3,279 to 5,617 (a 51 percent increase)" (U.S. Department of Defense [OASD] 1993). Until Perry issued his 1994 memorandum, however, progress had been slow and halting, impeded by a bureaucratic infrastructure not convinced that senior officials were serious about altering the procurement environment so profoundly. Since 1994, however, all this has changed. The Secretary's memorandum has signalled the commitment of senior levels of DOD to procurement reform and the shift to commercial standards. Now there is a clear presumption that commercial standards will be used *except* in narrowly defined circumstances. While the process of integrating the civil and military specifications and standards around the commercial norm is far from complete, it is clear that the process is well underway.

While they mark the beginning of a transformation of the regulatory framework governing arms production, these regulatory and acquisition reform initiatives have thus far failed to create the type of unified technology and industrial base essential to the realization of agile manufacturing. Indeed, in the face of persistent obstacles to commercial purchasing, these restructuring efforts have had only marginal success in promoting commercial-military integration. The process of integration is in its infancy, however, and while the final outcome is difficult to predict precisely, it is clear that the first tentative steps have been taken toward restructuring the regulatory framework in order to realize the state's vision of agile manufacturing.

THE ARMS INDUSTRY IMPLEMENTS AGILE MANUFACTURING

Industry efforts to implement agile manufacturing have taken place along three axes. To begin with, there have been efforts to put in place the technical building blocks of the new production paradigm. The agile vision includes a range of inherently flexible postfordist shop-floor technologies (such as computer-aided design and computer-aided manufacturing [CAD/CAM] systems) intended to facilitate concurrent engineering and flexible manufacturing. Up until the mid-1980s, the application of programmable automation systems was by far the predominant approach to enhancing flexibility in the arms industry. Programmable automation, of course, "began in the 1950s and 1960s, with N/C machining and early computer graphics systems" (Alic et al. 1992, 325). At that time the goal of programmable automation was not flexibility as it is now understood, but improved accuracy and the minimization of the role of skilled labor in the production process (Noble 1984). By the 1980s, however, automated manufacturing systems had evolved considerably as computers and microelectronics had given rise to the computer-based integration of the design, manufacturing, and information-coordination aspects of production in the modern firm. During this period programmable automation had "spread from machine tools to robots, automatically guided vehicles and other materials handling equipment, and inspection equipment, including coordinate measuring machines for checking the dimensions of complex parts" (Alic et al. 1992, 325). Examples of this second generation of programmable automation technologies include:

- *Computer-aided design (CAD)*. CAD systems represent the fusion of computer technology with mechanical drawing. CAD systems not only aid in the production of drawings of parts and components, but allow designs to be stored in databases. This greatly facilitates engineering design changes (which can number in the dozens) as well as electronic data interchange between suppliers and assemblers.
- *Computer-aided manufacturing (CAM)*. CAM involves the use of computers to assist in the planning and production process, from inventory control to the programming of machine tools. CAM has five subsets: production programming (sometimes called computer-aided production planning or CAPP), manufacturing engineering, industrial engineering, facilities engineering, and reliability engineering (DSMC 1989, 8–17).
- *Computer-aided testing (CAT)*. CAT installations are computer-driven systems that test and automatically adjust components and assemblies.

- *Computer-integrated manufacturing (CIM)*. Computer-integrated manufacturing represents the further evolution of CAD/CAM. The goal of CIM is to integrate CAD and CAM into one computer system, thereby enabling the rapid transfer of design data to shop-floor systems.
- *Computer-aided engineering (CAE)*. "CAE uses computational models to simulate the behavior of hypothetical systems" (U.S. Congress [OTA] 1992, 55). CAE systems can dispense with the need to develop hardware prototypes to test new technologies in real-world conditions.

As was the case in the civil sector, throughout the 1980s these second-generation programmable automation systems began to diffuse widely through the U.S. arms sector. But although there are some similarities between the patterns of diffusion in the civil and military sectors, there are also significant differences. Chief among these was the differential *rate* of diffusion of new production technologies. Stated directly, these computer-driven manufacturing systems were adopted by arms producers at a rate far exceeding that at which they were being introduced in the civil sector. Survey data clearly indicate that for each form of postfordist production technology, arms firms have higher rates of employment than their civil counterparts, with the differential reaching more than 15 percent in the area of programmable automated machine tools (Kelley and Watkins 1995a, 531).[11] Moreover, at least one study indicates that during the 1980s arms producers invested 31 percent more per employee and tended to adopt more advanced process technologies. This study also found that "defense contractors have been more innovative in applying computer-aided design, computer-aided manufacturing and computerized quality control" (Kelley and Watkins 1995b, 57).

In addition to programmable automated production systems, agile manufacturing is also dependent on technologies such as tool minimization. As one senior Lockheed official put it,"[t]ool minimization is a key element of [postfordist] lean manufacturing. It can be accomplished via approaches such as designing self-alignment features into a product; constraining product design to the use of common tools; application of common set-up tooling form machining; or using common dies for sheet metal forming operations" (Lang and Hugge 1995, 32).

A good example of the type of tool minimization techniques beginning to diffuse through the U.S. military aerospace industry is the low-rate expandable tooling (LRET) being employed on the McDonnell Douglas Corporation (MDC) F/A-18E/F program. On the forward-fuselage assembly component of this project, MDC is using three static mainframe tools (each of which is a single large tool sharing eighteen auxiliary jigs, known as AJAs or assembly jig accessories), instead of the twenty-seven high-rate specialized tools built for the C/D version of the F/A-18: "The forward fuselage is assembled entirely in the mainframe tools, rather than moving down an assembly line through a series of increasingly complex tools" (Warwick 1995, 60). In fact, there is no production line in the traditional sense: the forward fuselage and nose are being built as a single structure instead of the traditional three subassemblies that are subsequently joined together. MDC officials refer to this as the "car-wash principle," as workers and tools are brought to the work, rather than having the work move down the line to them. McDonnell Douglas claims that the use of LRET on the F/A-18E/F program (forward, center and aft fuselage, wing and empennage) has resulted in a 28 percent reduction in assembly tooling costs.

Another increasingly important new technology that is diffusing through the military aerospace sector is the high-speed machine (HSM) tool. HSM tools make very rapid, very light passes with a small diameter cutter. This results in considerably less stress being placed on the material, allowing the design of thinner, less rigid parts: "For an aileron closure rib manufactured in this way production time has shrunk to just 29 min. Whereas hitherto it took typically 1.7 h just to assemble the rib, and some 232 h to design and fabricate the tools (now zero)" (Hewish and Pohling-Brown 1995, 35). HSM tooling has also allowed MDC to replace sheet-metal assemblies with machined parts, resulting in savings of 30 kg on 154 F/A-18E/F parts and reductions in both tooling costs and cycle time. As the company pursues its goal of "rate-transparent" machining, the ability to produce individual parts on demand, it is moving to augment its existing stock of HSM tools.

As argued above, the agile manufacturing vision emphasizes the importance of information infrastructures that will enable and facilitate the creation of opportunistic partnerships on short notice and of possible short duration (i.e., virtual enterprises). Indeed, perhaps the defining technical element of agile manufacturing is the emerging system of electronic commerce and electronic data interchange linking suppliers and customers via advanced computer systems and networked interfaces.[12] These linkages are expected to serve two purposes. First, they are intended to facilitate the computer-based exchange of information related to the manufacturing process (planning, scheduling, parts ordering, work instructions, job status, machine control, etc.). In this connection, all of the major U.S. military aerospace firms have established or experimented with "paperless factories," and are now moving to create online computer-based linkages with suppliers outside the firm. Thus, firms like Lockheed Martin and Hughes Space and Communications have in the last few years devoted increasing effort to managing the supplier web through the use of standardized or interoperable computer networks. Second, these linkages are intended to facilitate the electronic integration of design activities (in keeping with the principles of concurrent engineering), both within the supply chain and between collaborative partners. Obviously, the creation of a technical infrastructure supporting the development of shared design databases is a necessary precondition for the further evolution of an arms industry comprising rapidly reconfigurable virtual enterprises. Currently, however, there are a number of impediments to the forging of such an agile technology and production base, one of the more important of which is the incompatibility between CAD systems. Since their introduction in the 1970s, there has been a great proliferation of different CAD systems, with the result that it is not unusual to find a number of different (and incompatible) systems in use within both individual firms and across the supplier networks within which they are embedded. As a result, one of the most important thrusts of the current restructuring has been the drive to overcome this problem through the establishment of industry-wide standards and protocols for electronic data interchange. Programmes currently underway include: DOD's CALS (Computer-Assisted Logistics Support) system, the ECRC program, and a range of Agile Manufacturing Network projects taking place under the auspices of the AMI. Though still at an early stage of implementation (with the partial exception of CALS), these initiatives are giving rise to a common set of data interchange standards that are being accepted—at least in principle—by many arms firms.[13] And although there are still many technical, organizational, and commercial barriers to be overcome, the industry has demonstrated a strong commitment to developing shared protocols as quickly as possible. Once in place, these new protocols will become the connective tissue linking the various elements of the national (and perhaps global) technology and industrial bases into an agile manufacturing infrastructure.

A second broad response to the challenges posed by the transformation of the military-industrial environment has been to attempt to implement a number of postfordist lean production methods originally pioneered by Japanese automobile manufacturers and more recently taken up by their American counterparts. These include the introduction of team-based production systems, concurrent engineering practices, integrated product teams, just-in-time supply systems, and continuous process improvement initiatives. Since the early 1990s most of the major American military aerospace firms have decided that these postfordist production techniques— together with new production technologies—offer significant opportunities for cost reduction, technology development, and quality improvement.[14] As a consequence, during this period there has been a rapid acceleration in the pace of process innovation, with firms implementing various restructuring strategies at the intra- and interfirm levels.

A good example of the type of changes in manufacturing process currently underway in the U.S. military aerospace sector is provided by Lockheed Martin Tactical Aircraft Systems (LMTAS). Under its Lean Enterprise Initiative, LMTAS has restructured its manufacturing operations around a number of postfordist production techniques, including integrated product development, design-to-cost, and an automated Manufacturing Assembly Tracking System (handling production planning, scheduling, and machine control). As a result of the application of these postfordist lean production techniques, Lockheed has realized substantial improvements in productivity and cost-containment. At the firm's Government Electronic Systems (GES) facility, for example, the introduction of postfordist techniques have resulted in the following improvements:

- 50 percent reduction in cycle time,
- 25 percent reduction in total cost,
- 26 percent reduction in touch labor,
- 80 percent reduction in inventory,
- 92 percent reduction in defects, and
- 81 percent reduction in scrap (BMPCOE n.d.).

Similarly, through the implementation of lean manufacturing techniques, Lockheed has been able to reduce the fly-away unit cost of the F-16C by $3 million to $20 million a copy. This was achieved despite the reduction in rate of production from 300 per year in 1987 to about 50 per year in 1996, demonstrating the company's success in decoupling rate and volume of production from unit costs (Cook, N. 1994, 30). Using these techniques Lockheed hopes to build the next generation F-22 fighter aircraft at a lower unit cost that the McDonnell F-15 Eagle, even though it will be procured in only about one-third of the numbers (JDW 1995, 42).

In contrast to Lockheed, other firms have chosen to launch "pathfinder" or "incubator" programs to develop and validate all new techniques before they are adopted more widely.[15] McDonnell Douglas's Phantom Works Two is one example of such a program. Phantom Works Two is an advanced engineering unit formally known as McDonnell Douglas Advanced Systems and Technology (MDAS&T). Like its predecessor, the original Phantom Works,[16] Phantom Works Two is spearheading the firm's movement away from the traditional approach to military aerospace production and toward lean manufacturing, rapid prototyping, and quick technology insertion. It is "primarily a facility for trialling technologies and concepts which can be used in production and thus represents the cradle of lean-manufacturing process at [MDC]" (Hewish and Pohling-Brown 1995, 35). Approximately 3,000 people are involved in this new unit, which is supported by an initial investment of $600 million, mostly in the form of advanced research and development contracts from NASA, the USAF, and ARPA.

Thus far, the results achieved through the use of postfordist production technologies and techniques developed at Phantom Works have been impressive. McDonnell Douglas's F/A-18E/F program, for example, has seen remarkable reduction in the number of parts over the earlier C/D variant—from 17,210 to 11,789 (Warwick 1995, 59)—and Northrop Grumman's subcontracting work on the successive F/A-18 models has also shown significant improvements in production after the adoption of lean techniques (Hewish and Pohling-Brown 1995, 31). The techniques developed for the F/A-18E/F model have also been applied to McDonnell Douglas's mature products; for example, the production of the aft radome frame of the AV-8B "took a 27-part, 434-fastener design with 1,295 manufacturing operations and reduced it to a one-piece, 316-fastener, 183-operation design that reduces cost by $5,400 per aircraft" (Lang and Hugge 1995, 31). Lean production principles have also been used to reengineer the manufacturing process used on the firm's F-15 program. As a result, the nose landing-gear door of the F-15, to cite just one example, went from being a "37-part sheet-metal buildup with 822 fasteners that took 207 hr to fabricate and assemble" to a two-part, 90-fastener assembly that takes only 62 hours to manufacture (Lang and Hugge 1995, 31). Similar improvements have been realized on the company's C-17 and AH-64 projects.[17]

In addition to new production technologies and lean manufacturing techniques, industry has also begun to experiment with postfordist organizational structures. In the military-fordist system, U.S. aerospace firms procured most parts and components from their own divisions. These in-house sources were supplemented by purchases from independent suppliers through arms-length transactions. Major prime contractors could deal with between 2,000 and 30,000 suppliers directly. Contracts with independent suppliers were usually negotiated on an annual basis, and the prime contractor relied on hierarchical coordination of information and control over technology in order to manage the task of designing and producing complex systems such as combat aircraft and tactical missiles.

In the late 1990s, rather than managing their entire supply chains directly, prime contractors increasingly opted to deal directly with only a small number of subtier firms, referred to as first-tier suppliers, which supplied entire subsystems or modules rather than individual components and parts. This has involved a shift from short-term to long-term contracts, a decline in multisourcing arrangements and a move toward single-sourcing, and a conscious effort on the part of prime contractors to cut their supplier bases. As a result, the American subcontractor base is in the midst of a severe downsizing. According to industry and government estimates, the number of suppliers has decreased on the order of 60 to 70 percent from 1991 levels. MDC reduced its supplier pool by about 50 percent, from about 7,000 in the early 1990s to around 3,500 in 1997; while Lockheed, Fort Worth, went from about 1,780 to 570 (a decrease of 68 percent) in the same period. First-tier suppliers appear to be following suit, with Pratt & Whitney, to take but one example, cutting its supplier base from about 2,000 to 275 firms (a reduction of 86 percent). These changes suggest that U.S. military aerospace firms are adopting the extended-enterprise strategies favored by Japanese and American automotive firms.

CONCLUSIONS

Many of the findings reported here concerning the diffusion of postfordist production should be regarded as preliminary and, therefore, more indicative of evolutionary tendencies rather than as proof of completed transformation. Nevertheless, based on this broad survey of military-industrial restructuring, four general observations can be made concerning the transition to agile manufacturing. First, the process of experimentation and bricolage that characterizes the current stage of the transformation of arms production is being driven by the need to develop the means to sustain high-quality/low-cost production under conditions of rapidly changing patterns of military demand. The problems experienced by U.S. arms producers in the 1970s and 1980s derived not from a shortage of innovative capacity, but from rising costs that posed a serious threat to their long-term commercial viability. These production problems arose in part from a fundamental tension between the nature of military-fordism (which created an inversely proportional relationship between rate/volume of production and unit costs) and the emergent Revolution in Military Affairs (which involved a shift away from the mass production of simple weapons to an emphasis on smaller numbers of increasingly baroque armaments). Beginning in the 1990s American arms producers began to realize that if they were to maintain their economic viability and technological competitiveness in the context of a changing regulatory framework, they would have to find ways of severing the military-fordist connection between volume and cost, thus achieving affordable low-rate production.

But if the pursuit of affordability is clearly a powerful motive in the current restructuring of arms production, the adoption of agile manufacturing techniques is also being driven by a desire to maintain and enhance the technological vitality of the arms industry. Under conditions of perpetual innovation, extending the technological frontier requires a shift away from an exclusive emphasis on developing radical new technologies in the laboratory and toward a more balanced approach that involves both breakthrough innovations and incremental product and process innovation. Thus, much of the attention of U.S. arms firms seeking to remain at the technological frontier is now focused on "not only the ability to invent new products and technologies [in the R&D laboratory] but also the ability to upgrade and improve those products and manufacture them as efficiently as possible" (Kenney and Florida 1993, 16). As Japanese (and more recently American) automobile and electronics firms have demonstrated, such incremental product and process innovations can be a powerful source of technological dynamism and commercial success. American arms producers are hoping that by introducing agile production they can blur the distinctions between the factory floor and the R&D laboratory, with the result that product and process innovation will be intensified while design-to-field cycles are shortened.

Agile manufacturing is also intended to enhance the technological capacity of the U.S. arms industry by breaking down the barriers separating the civil and military technology and industrial bases. A key element of the agile manufacturing vision is the creation of a unified national technology and industrial base comprising agile firms and virtual enterprises capable of servicing the military and commercial markets with equal facility. Thus, the current restructuring must be seen as extending beyond the arms industry to encompass the civil manufacturing base as well. Indeed, in the long-run agile manufacturing will necessarily involve a blurring of the practical and conceptual lines separating military and civil firms. If the agile manufacturing vision is realized, in the current century there will no longer be distinctive firms servicing segregated markets, only inherently agile "generic" firms capable of rapidly forming virtual enterprises to produce increasingly knowledge-intensive commercial or military goods to order.

A second general conclusion that can be drawn from the literature dealing with the shift to lean production is that the process of military-industrial transformation in the United States is clearly conditioned by civilian best practices. Faced with changes in both the nature of military technology and the regulatory framework governing arms production, American arms firms have not developed a new labor process out of whole cloth. Rather, they have adopted a series of process changes modelled on their perception of the lean-production techniques that had evolved in the Japanese automobile industry during the 1960s and 1970s and that became paradigmatic in the U.S. automotive sector during the mid- to late 1980s. From continuous process improvement to just-in-time manufacturing and concurrent engineering, the "Japanization" of American labor processes has been a defining element of the transformation of the U.S. arms industry.

Third, while the process of transformation is far from complete, the transition to postfordist production techniques in the arms industry appears to have accelerated significantly over the last years, at least at the prime contractor and subcontractor levels.[18] Ten years ago only a handful of arms producers were involved in any sort of restructuring at the shop-floor level beyond the introduction of a few programmable manufacturing technologies. Since the early 1990s, however, all of the top-ten prime contractors, as well as many of the larger subcontractors, have initiated restructuring programs. While the introduction of new manufacturing technologies remains an important part of this process, restructuring initiatives aimed at introducing postfordist labor processes such as JITM, continuous process improvement, and concurrent engineering are proliferating rapidly. Whether adopted at a stroke, or introduced gradually through "pilot" or "pathfinder" programs, postfordist labor processes are increasingly common in all subsectors of the U.S. armaments industry.

A fourth conclusion that can be drawn from this overview is that the U.S. arms industry is somewhere in the late experimental phase of the industrial transition cycle. While progress is being made toward the evolution and implementation of a new arms production paradigm, it is widely recognized that the arms industry is still a long way from realizing the agile vision of a seamless web of military and civil firms, linked by computer-integrated design systems, that are organized to fit a particular market opportunity and can function as an integrated whole capable of responding rapidly to customer needs. In this regard, the most that can be said is that we are now in a period of intense experimentation with new postfordist technologies, techniques, and organizational forms. While the vision of agile manufacturing is guiding this process, and while islands of postfordist production have emerged, it is still too early to claim that the structural transformation of the U.S. arms industry has been completed. A more accurate claim is that the U.S. arms industry is currently in an early phase of what history suggests will be an extended process of industrial transformation.

A final conclusion is that, although the diffusion of lean production practices is being driven primarily by changes in the mode of warfare, and conditioned by the demonstration effect of changes in the automotive industry, it is clear that state military-industrial policy is at least partly responsible for the widespread experimentation with postfordist production techniques that characterizes the current era. Programmes such as the Lean Aircraft Initiative and the Agile Manufacturing Initiative, coupled with changes in the regulatory environment such as the Federal Acquisition Streamlining Act, have acted both to spur and enable the development and diffusion of postfordist production practices through the U.S. arms industry. It is worth noting in this connection that the U.S. government's promotion of a new vision of arms production (agile manufacturing) now seems to be driving a restructuring of the broader civil manufacturing base.

Efforts to improve flexibility, shorten design-to-field cycles, and minimize waste have begun to remove many of the long-standing barriers to cost-efficient batch/custom production in the U.S. armaments sector, even as the technological density of modern weapons continues to increase. While technical and organizational restructurings are still of relatively recent origin (dating primarily from the early 1990s), their effects are already discernible in the forms of reduced unit costs, improved product quality, and accelerated rates of product and process innovation. Continuation of the current trend in restructuring, and the diffusion of agile manufacturing techniques throughout the U.S. arms industry not only constitute the real "quiet revolution" in the arms industry, but also the industrial preconditions for the continued evolution and implementation of the RMA.

NOTES

1. In this chapter, the term "fordism" means a type of production process based on dedicated mechanization, task decomposition and simplification, economies of scale, and moving assembly. "Postfordism," on the other hand, involves technologies and manufacturing practices such as concurrent engineering, flexible manufacturing systems, and just-in-time

inventory techniques. The central innovation of this new cluster of best-practices, however, is its emphasis on flexible volume production; for a good overview see Amin (1994).

2. Elsewhere, I have argued that the history of American arms production can be viewed as comprising four distinct periods (the craft era, the era of the armory system, the era of military-fordism, and the era of military postfordism or agile manufacturing). Each of these conjunctures is separated by a "military-industrial divide"—a period of rapid transition from one arms production paradigm to the next. See Latham (1997).

3. A representative sample of the literature on the RMA includes: Arquilla and Ronfeldt (1993, 1997); Cohen (1996); Dunn (1992); Gouré (1993); Johnson and Libicki (1995); Mazarr, Shaffer, and Ederington (1993); Stix (1995).

4. In the 1950s the United States procured approximately 2,000 fighter aircraft per year; in the 1960s, about 600; and in the 1970s, approximately 300. These numbers (which include several different models in each year) are substantially lower than those of, say, the automobile industry, which typically produced tens of thousands of nearly identical models in any given year (Gansler 1989, 170).

5. This was compounded by the shift away from military use of standard commodities produced in commercial production facilities. As Ann Markusen has noted, in World War I, 80 percent of Army equipment came off standard commercial production lines. During World War II this percentage dropped below 50 percent. By the 1960s, however, "the share of military demand met by specialized equipment made in special facilities had escalated to 90 percent" (Markusen 1991, 399).

6. The term "lean production" was coined by MIT's International Motor Vehicle program in its 1991 report *The Machine That Changed the World*. "Agile manufacturing" now seems to be displacing "lean production" as the most common descriptor of postfordist manufacturing techniques as they are being adapted to arms production (Nagel and Dove 1991). Although there are differences between lean and agile production (especially with respect to the desired characteristics of the supplier chain), broadly speaking, agile manufacturing can be said to encompass and build upon lean production. Thus, the LAI can be said to be an integral part of the U.S. government's effort to develop and promote agile arms production.

7. One indication of this trend is the rise in the subcontracted content of major DOD acquisitions. Subcontracted content increased from 9 percent in 1950, to 41 percent in 1980, to 53 percent in 1990 (AAMRC 1996).

8. Numerous studies have noted this exodus of subtier firms from the defense supplier base, including Augustine (1988) and Blackwell (1989).

9. It is important to note that the agile manufacturing vision effectively supersedes earlier visions of dual use and conversion. Dual use (which originally focused on increasing the ability of defense firms to incorporate commercial product and process technologies) and conversion (which originally focused on redirecting arms production to commercial applications) have both given way to a vision of a fully integrated NTIB comprising agile firms that can be brought together readily to form virtual enterprises to meet either commercial or military demands.

10. Dual sourcing refers to simultaneous production from two sources, typically involving the transfer of technology from the developer to an alternative producer. In such a situation production is split between two firms, with the larger order going to the lower cost producer. Second sourcing is similar except that the entire production contract is put out to tender periodically with the low-cost bidder awarded the entire production contract (Leitzel 1992).

11. These findings are based on data collected in a 1991 survey of 973 randomly selected manufacturing establishments. For a complete description of the methodology used in this study see Kelly and Watkins (1995a, 526).

12. Interview with Agile Infrastructure for Manufacturing Systems (AIMS) official.

13. Interview with DOD officials.

14. Since 1985 the U.S. Navy, through its Best Manufacturing Practices (BMP) program, has sent survey teams to manufacturers to catalogue their best practices and to transfer this knowledge to the rest of the Navy's production base. The most recent survey clearly indicates that many of the leading American arms producers are using postfordist production technologies and techniques (BMPCOE n.d.).

15. Interview with DOD officials.

16. The original Phantom Works was an advanced engineering unit in the New Aircraft and Missile Products (NAMP) Division in St. Louis. Phantom Works Two is larger and more ambitious (comprising the advanced production activities of the firm's space, helicopter, C-17 and tactical aircraft, and missiles projects), but retains the same basic set of objectives.

17. The C-17 cargo door was redesigned for manufacture and assembly with the result that it went from being a 650-part, 12,000 fastener unit to a 77-part unit with no fasteners. The application of lean production techniques on the AH-64 program has reduced assembly time from 23,000 hours to 5,623 hours (Lang and Hugge 1995, 31).

18. Capturing the adoption of postfordist production techniques at the supplier level is a very difficult task given the low public profiles of such firms and the lack of attention they have received in government studies and surveys.

References

Advanced Research Projects Agency (ARPA). n.d. *Agile Manufacturing*. URL <http://www.sei.cmu.edu>.

Agile Aerospace Manufacturing Research Center (AAMRC). 1996. *University of Texas at Arlington*. URL <http://www.utexas.edu/depts/ic2/aamrc/aamrc.html#team>.

Alic, John A., et al. 1992. *Beyond Spinoff. Military and Commercial Technologies in a Changing World*. Boston: Harvard Business School Press.

Amin, Ash. 1994. *Post-Fordism: A Reader*. Oxford: Blackwell Publishers.

Andreski, Stanislaw. 1968. *Military Organization and Society*, 2nd ed. London: Routledge & Kegan Paul.

Andrewes, A. 1956. *The Greek Tyrants*. London: Hutchinson University Library.

Arbatov, Aleksei. 1997a. *The Russian Military in the 21st Century*. Carlisle Barracks, PA: U.S. Army War College, Strategic Studies Institute.

Arbatov, Aleksei. 1997b. Voyennaya reforma: Doktrina, voiska, financy, *Mirovaya ekonomika i mezhdunarodnye otnosheniya*, no. 4 (April): 6–9.

Arnett, Eric. 1998. Military Research and Development. In *SIPRI Yearbook 1998. Armaments, Disarmament and International Security*. Oxford: Oxford University Press/Stockholm International Peace Research Institute.

Arquilla, John, and David Ronfeldt. 1993. Cyberwar is Coming!, *Comparative Strategy* 12, no. 2: 141–65.

Arquilla, John, and David Ronfeldt (eds). 1997. *In Athena's Camp: Preparing for Conflict in the Information Age*. Santa Monica, CA: RAND.

Augustine, Norman. 1988. *Lifeline in Danger: An Assessment of the United States Defense Industrial Base*. Arlington, VA: Aerospace Education Foundation.

Baer, Alain, ed. 1993. *Réflexions sur la nature des futurs systèmes de défense*. Cahiers du CREST no. 12. Paris: Centre de recherche et d'études sur les stratégies et technologies/École Polytechnique.

Ball, Desmond. 1993–94. Military Acquisitions in the Asia-Pacific Region. *International Security* 18, no. 3 (winter): 78–112.

Bartlett, Henry C. et al. 1996. Force Planning, Military Revolutions and the Tyranny of Technology. *Strategic Review* 24, no. 4 (fall): 28–40.

Beaufre, André. 1972. Offensive et défensive. *Stratégie*, no. 30 (April-May-June): 5–31.

Bellamy, Christopher. 1992. "Civilian Experts" and Russian Defence Thinking: The Renewed Relevance of Jan Bloch. *The RUSI Journal* 137, no. 2 (April): 50–55.

Beniger, James R. 1996. *The Control Revolution: Technological and Economic Origins of the Information Society.* Cambridge, MA: Harvard University Press.

Best Manufacturing Practices Center of Excellence (BMPCOE). n.d. BMP Surveys Online. URL <http://www.bmpcoe.org/bestpractices/pdf/index.html>.

Bingaman, Jeff, Jacques Gansler, and Robert Kupperman. 1991. *Integrating Commercial and Military Technologies for National Strength.* Washington, DC: Center for Strategic and International Studies.

Black, Jeremy. 1994. *European Warfare, 1660–1815.* New Haven: Yale University Press.

Black, Jeremy. 1995. A Military Revolution? A 1660–1792 Perspective. In *The Military Revolution Debate*, ed. C. J. Rogers. Boulder: Westiew Press.

Blackwell, James. 1989. *Deterrence in Decay, Report of the CSIS Defense Industrial Base Project.* Washington, DC: Center for Strategic and International Studies.

Blaker, James R. 1997a. Force Structure. In *1997 Strategic Assessment. Flashpoints and Force Structure*, ed. Patrick Clawson. Washington, DC: National Defense University, Institute for National Strategic Studies.

Blaker, James R. 1997b. *Understanding the Revolution in Military Affairs: A Guide to America's 21ˢᵗ Century Defense.* Defense Working Paper no. 3. Washington, DC: Progressive Policy Institute.

Boyle, Roger, the earl of Orrery. 1677. *A Treatise of the Art of War.* London: Henry Herringman.

Bracken, Paul. 1993. The Military After Next. *The Washington Quarterly* 16, no. 3 (autumn): 157–74.

Bracken, Paul. 1994. Future Directions for the Army. In *Whither the RMA: Two Perspectives on Tomorrow's Army*, Paul Bracken and Raoul Henri Alcalá. Carlisle Barracks, PA: U.S. Army War College, Strategic Studies Institute.

Braham, Robert, and Richard Comerford. 1997. Sharing Virtual Worlds. *IEEE Spectrum* [Journal of the Institute of Electrical and Electronics Engineers] 34, no. 3 (March): 18–19.

Branscomb, Anne Wells. 1994. *Who Owns Information? From Privacy to Public Access.* New York: Basic Books.

Branscombe, Lewis. 1989. Dual-Use Technology: Optimizing Economic and Security Interests through National Technology Policy. Distinguished Honeywell W.R. Sweat Lecture on Technology Leadership, 18 May, at the University of Minnesota, Minneapolis.

Brodie, Bernard. 1965. *Strategy in the Missile Age.* Princeton: Princeton University Press.

Buchan, Glenn C. 1994. The Use of Long-Range Bombers in a Changing World: A Classical Exercise in Systems Analysis. In *New Challenges for Defense Planning: Rethinking How Much is Enough*, ed. Paul K. Davis. Santa Monica, CA: RAND, MR-400-RC.

Buchan, Glenn C. 1995a. *The Impact of the Revolution in Military Affairs on Developing States' Military Capability.* Santa Monica, CA: RAND, P-7926.

Buchan, Glenn C. 1995b. *Information War and the Air Force: Wave of the Future? Current Fad?* Santa Monica, CA: RAND, IP-149.

Buchan, Glenn C., and Dave Frelinger. 1994. *Providing an Effective Bomber Force for the Future*, Santa Monica, CA: RAND, CT-119-AF.

Buchan, Glenn C., Dave Frelinger, and Tom Herbert. 1992. *Use of Long-Range Bombers to Counter Armored Invasions.* Santa Monica, CA: RAND, WP-103-AF.

Buchan, Glenn C., et al. (1999) *Potential Vulnerabilities of U.S. Air Force Information Systems: Final Report.* Santa Monica, CA: RAND, MR-816-AF.

Builder, Carl H. 1985. *The Prospects and Implications of Non-nuclear Means for Strategic Conflict.* Adelphi Paper 200. London: International Institute for Strategic Studies.

Builder, Carl H. 1995. Looking in All The Wrong Places? (The Real Revolution in Military Affairs). *Armed Forces Journal International* 132, no. 10 (May): 38–39.

Bunker, Robert J. 1996. Generations, Waves, and Epochs: Modes of Warfare and the RPMA (Revolution in Political and Military Affairs). *Air Power Journal* 10, no. 1 (spring): 18–28.

Burkholder, Peter. 1992. *The Manufacture and Use of Cannons at the Siege of St-Saveur-le-Vicomte, 1375.* Master's thesis, University of Toronto.

Buslenko, N. P. 1964. *Matematicheskoe modelirovanie proizvodstvennykh protsessov na tsifrovykh mashinakh* (Mathematical Modeling of Production Processes on Computers). Moscow: Nauka.

Callaghan, Thomas A. 1988. Pooling Allied and American Resources to Produce a Credible, Collective Conventional Deterrent. Report prepared for the U.S. Department of Defense, MDA903-84-C-0274, August.

Canadian Land Force (CLF). 1996. B-GL-300-001/FP-000, *Conduct of Land Operations—Operational Level Doctrine For The Canadian Army,* (CFP 300-1).

CFP 300 - *Canada's Army (Interim)* 1997, Chapter 1, The Army's Purpose.

Chairman of the Joint Chiefs of Staff (CJCS). 1996. *Joint Vision 2010.* Washington, DC: Department of Defense.

Chen, Youyun. 1997. Junshi jishu geming yu zhanyi lilun fazhan (The Revolution in Military Technology and the Development of Operational Theory). In *Gao jishu tiaojian xia zhanyi lilun yanjiu* (A Study of Operational Theory under High-Tech Conditions), ed. Research Department and Operational Office, National Defense University. Beijing: National Defense University Press.

Cheng, Jian. 1996. Yingjie shijie junshi geming tiaozhan, dali jiaqiang wojun zhiliang jianshe (Meeting the Challenge of the World's Revolution in Military Affairs, Greatly Strengthening the Qualitative Construction of Our Army). In *Kuashiji fazhan de zhizhen, jingshen wenming jianshe de linghun* (The Guide for Transcentury Development, the Soul of Spiritual Civilization Construction), ed. Theoretical Research Center for Building Socialism with Chinese Characteristics, National Defense University. Beijing: National Defense University Press.

Cheng, Mingqun. 1996. Gaojishu tiaojian xia jubu zhanzheng zhanyi houqin baozhang lilun taolunhuai shang de jianghua (Speech at the Conference on Operational Logistical Support under High-Tech Limited War Conditions). In *Gaojishu tiaojian xia jubu zhanzheng zhanyi houqin baozhang yanjiu* (A Study of Operational Logistical Support under High-Tech Limited War Conditions), ed. Research Department, National Defense University. Beijing: National Defense University Press.

Clausewitz. 1984. *On War.* Edited and translated by M. Howard and P. Paret. Princeton: Princeton University Press.

Coakley, Thomas P. 1992. *Command and Control for War and Peace.* Washington, DC: National Defense University.

Cohen, Eliot A. 1990. The Future of Force and American Strategy. *National Interest,* no. 21 (fall): 3–15.

Cohen, Eliot A. 1994. The Mystique of U.S. Air Power. *Foreign Affairs* 73, no. 1 (January-February): 109–24.

Cohen, Eliot A. 1995. Review of *The Military Revolution Debate,* by Clifford J. Rogers. *Foreign Affairs* 74, no. 6 (November/December): 123.

Cohen, Eliot A. 1996. A Revolution in Warfare. *Foreign Affairs* 75, no. 2 (March-April): 37–54.

Cohen, William S. 1997. *Annual Report to the President and the Congress.* Washington, DC: Department of Defense: URL <http://www.dtic.mil:80/execsec/adr97>.

Cook, L. Martin. 1994. Why Serve the State? Moral Foundations of Military Service. The Joseph A. Reich Sr. Distinguished Lecture, Number Seven, 17 November, at the United States Air Force Academy, Colorado.

Cook, Nick. 1994. Building the Lean Machine. *Jane's Defense Weekly* 22, no. 6 (13 August): 29–30.

Cook, Weston F. Jr. 1993. The Cannon Conquest of Nasrid Spain and the End of the Reconquista. *Journal of Military History* 57, no. 1: 43–70.

Cropsey, Seth. 1997. Omniscient, omniprésent, omnipotent: O^3. *Défense nationale* 53 (April): 51–62.

Dahlman, Carl J., and Robert C. Roll. 1997. Trading Butter for Guns: Managing Infrastructure Reductions. In *Strategic Appraisal 1997. Strategy and Defense Planning for the 21st Century,* eds. Zalmay M. Khalilzad and David A. Ochmanek. Santa Monica, CA: RAND.

Dai, Jinyu. 1993. Gaojishu jubu chenggui zhanzheng duice de jidian sikao (Reflections on Solutions for Conventional High-Tech Limited War). In *Gaojishu jubu zhanzheng yu zhanyi zhanfa* (High-Tech Limited War and Operational Art), ed. Research Department, National Defense University. Beijing: National Defense University Press.

Dai, Jinyu. 1995. Zhongguo kongjun zhanlue lilun de xingcheng he fazhan (The Formulation and Development of China's Air Strategy). In *Kongjun zhanlue xue* (The Science of the Air Force Strategy), ed. Dai, Jinyu. Beijing: National Defense University Press.

de Bloch, Jean. 1993. *Jean de Bloch: Selected Articles.* Fort Leavenworth, KS: Combat Studies Institute, US Army Command and General Staff College.

de Commines, Philip. 1906. *Memoirs of Philip de Commines,* vol. 1. Edited by A. R. Scoble. London: George Bell and Sons.

de Rose, François, ESECS, and Yves Boyer. 1985. *Nouvelles technologies et défense de l'Europe.* Paris: Institut français de relations internationales/Économica.

Defence Efficiency Review. 1997. *Future Directions for the Management of Australia's Defence. Report of the Defence Efficiency Review.* Canberra: Department of Defence, URL <http://www.defence.gov.au/minister/der/report.pdf>.

Defence Science & Technology Organisation (DSTO). 1997. *The Takari Program—An Introduction.* URL <http://www.dsto.defence.gov.au/esrl/takari/takexint.html>.

Defense Manpower Data Center (DMDC). 1996. *Active Duty Officers, Ad Hoc Report.* Report DMDC–3035 (December). Arlington, VA: Defense Manpower Data Center.

Defense Science Board. 1989. *Use of Commercial Components in Military Equipment.* Washington, DC: U.S. Department of Defense, Office of the Undersecretary of Defense (Acquisition).

Defense Systems Management College (DSMC). 1989. *Defense Manufacturing Management: Guide for Program Managers.* 3rd ed. Fort Belvoir, VA: DSMC.

Deng, Lianfang. 1994. Gaojishu jubu zhanzheng tiaojian xia wojun zhanyi zuozhan ying caiqu 'xianpanhoujian' de jiben zhanfa (Our Operations Should Adopt Operational Art of "Exhaustion First, Annihilation Second" under High-Tech Conditions). In *Mao Zedong junshi sijiang zai Zhongguo de shenli yu fazhan* (Victory and Development of Mao Zedong's Military Thought in China), ed. Research Department, National Defense University. Beijing: National Defense University Press.

Department of Defence [Australia]. 1997a. *Australia's Strategic Policy. Paying for Force Structure Priorities*: URL <http://www.defence.gov.au/minister/sr97/pri.html>.

Department of Defence [Australia]. 1997b. *Australia's Strategic Policy.* Canberra: Department of Defence, URL <http://www.defence.gov.au/minister/sr97/SR97.pdf>.

Desch, Michael C. 1996. War and Strong States, Peace and Weak States? *International Organization* 50, no. 2 (spring): 237–68.

DeVries, Kelly. 1998. Gunpowder Weaponry and the Rise of the Early Modern State. *War in History* 5: 134–37.

Dibb, Paul. 1997–98. The Revolution in Military Affairs and Asian Security. *Survival* 39, no. 4 (winter): 93–116.

DiNardo, R. L., and Daniel J. Hughes. 1995. Some Cautionary Thoughts on Information Warfare. *Airpower Journal* 9, no. 4 (winter): 69–79.

Doughty, Robert A. 1998. Myth of the Blitzkrieg. In *Challenging the United States Symmetrically and Asymmetrically: Can America be Defeated?*, ed. Lloyd J. Matthews, Carlisle Barracks, PA: U.S. Army War College.

Douglas, David C. 1969. *The Norman Achievement*. Berkeley: University of California Press.

Douhet, Giulio. [1942] 1983. *The Command of the Air*. Translated by Dino Ferrari. New York: Coward-McCann; reprint Washington, DC: Office of Air Force History.

Druzhinin, V. V., and D. S. Kontorov. 1972. *Ideaya, algoritm, reshenie* (Concept, Algorithm, Decision). Moscow: Voyennoe Izdatel'stvo.

Druzhinin, V. V., and D. S. Kontorov. 1976. *Voprosy voyennoy sistemotekhniki* (Issues of Military Systems Engineering). Moscow: Voyennoe Izdatel'stvo.

Dubled, H. 1976. L'artillerie royale française a l'époque de Charles VII et au début du règne de Louis XI (1437–69); les frères Bureau. *Mémorial de l'Artillerie Française* 50: 555–637.

DuBois, Pierre. 1936. *Summaria Brevis et Compendiosa Doctrina Felicis Expedicionis et Abreviacionis Guerrarum ac Litum Regni Francorum*, edited by Hellmut Kämpf. Leipzig: Teubner.

Dugin, Aleksandr. 1994. *Konservativnaya revolyutsiya*. Moscow: Arktogeya.

Dugin, Aleksandr. 1997. *Osnovy geopolitiki: Geopoliticheskoe budushchee Rossii*. Series Bol'shoe prostranstvo. Moscow: Arktogeya.

Dunn, Martin. 1996. RMA = Revolution in Military Acronyms? A Contrary View. *Research and Analysis*, no. 5 (March), URL <http://www.adfa.oz.au/DOD/dara/issue05.htm>.

Dunn, Richard J. III. 1992. *From Gettysburg to the Gulf and Beyond: Coping with Revolutionary Technological Change in Land Warfare*. McNair Papers no. 13. Washington, DC: National Defense University Press.

European Security Study (ESECS). 1983. *Strengthening Conventional Deterrence in Europe. Proposals for the 1980s*. London: Macmillan.

Farrell, Tim. n.d. *Agile Manufacturing*. URL <http://www.niit.org/sha/amfg/amfg.html>.

Feng, Yujun, and Feng Yujun. 1997. Shuaixiang shixian zhanyi xuenlian de zhuanbien (Taking the Lead in Transforming Operational Training). *Jiefangjun Bao* (People's Liberation Army Daily), 19 August: p. 6.

Finer, Samuel E. 1975. State and Nation-Building in Europe: The Role of the Military. In *The Formation of National States in Western Europe*, ed. Charles Tilly. Princeton: Princeton University Press.

Fiorini, Pierre. n.d. *CORI: Conséquences opérationnelles de la Révolution de l'Information*. Recherches et documents no. 4. Paris: Centre de recherche et d'études sur les stratégies et technologies.

Fitzsimonds, James R., and Jan M. van Tol. 1994. Revolutions in Military Affairs. *Joint Force Quarterly*, no. 4 (spring): 24–31.

Forrest, W. G. 1966. *The Emergence of Greek Democracy*. London: Weidenfeld and Nicholson.

Freedman, Lawrence. 1998. *The Revolution in Strategic Affairs*. Adelphi Paper 318. London: Oxford University Press/International Institute for Strategic Studies.

Freedman, Lawrence, and Efraim Karsh. 1991. How Kuwait Was Won: Strategy in the Gulf War, *International Security* 16, no. 2 (fall): 5–41.

Friedman, Thomas L. 1995. The No-Dead War. *The New York Times*, 23 August, p. A21.

Fukuyama, Francis, and Abram N. Shulsky. 1999. Military Organization in the Information Age: Lessons from the World of Business. In *The Changing Role of Information in*

Warfare, eds. Zalmay M. Khalilzad and John P. White. Santa Monica, CA: RAND/ Project Air Force.

Galvin, John General (ret.). 1993. The Face of Conflict in the Year 2010. Paper read at the TRADOC's 20th Anniversary Seminar on Future Warfare, 20 June-1 July, at Fort Monroe, Virginia.

Gansler, Jacques. 1980. *The Defense Industry*. Cambridge, MA: MIT Press.

Gansler, Jacques. 1989. *Affording Defense*. Cambridge, MA: MIT Press.

Gansler, Jacques. 1995. The Future of the Defence Firm: Integrating Civil and Military Technologies. In *The Future of the Defence Firm: New Challenges, New Directions*, eds. Andrew Latham and Nick Hooper. Dordrecht: Kluwer Academic Publishers.

Gao, Rui. 1988. Guanyu zhanshu fazhan he yanjiu de jige wenti (Views on Tactics Development and Research). In *Zhanshu fazhan xintan* (New Explorations of Tactics Development), vol. I, ed. Hao, Zizhou. Beijing: Academy of Military Science Press.

Gareev, Makhmut A. 1985. *M. V. Frunze—voyennyy teoretik*. Moscow: Voyenizdat.

Gareev, Makhmut A. 1994. Metodologicheskie problemy voyennykh nauk. *Voyennaya mysl'*, no. 8 (September-October): 40–54.

Gareev, Makhmut A. 1995. *Esli zavtra voyna? (Chto izmenitsya v kharaktere vooruzhennoy bor'by v blizhayshie 20–25 let)*. Moscow: VlaDar.

Gareev, Makhmut A. 1998. *If War Comes Tomorrow? The Contours of Future Armed Conflict*. London: Frank Cass.

Garnier, Joseph. 1895. *L'Artillerie des Ducs de Bourgogne, d'après les documents conservés aux archives de la Côte-d'Or*. Paris: Honoré Champion.

Godwin, Paul H.B. 1992. Chinese Military Strategy Revisited. *Annals of the American Academy of Political and Social Sciences* 519: 191–201.

Goldman, Steve, Roger Nagel, and Kenneth Preiss. 1995. *Agile Competitors and Virtual Organizations*. New York: Van Nostrand Reinhold.

Gongora, Thierry. 1998. The Revolution in Military Affairs: What should the CF do about it? *[The Defence Associations] National Network News* 5, no. 2 (summer): 6–8.

Gouré, Dan. 1993. Is there a Military-Technical Revolution in America's Future? *The Washington Quarterly* 16, no. 4 (autumn): 175–92.

Gray, Colin S. 1995. The Changing Nature of Warfare? *Naval War College Review* 49, no. 2 (spring): 7–22.

Gray, Thomas. 1836. *Scalacronica*. Edited by J. Stevenson. Edinburgh: Maitland Club.

Guan, Jixian. 1993a. *Gaojishu jubu zhanzheng zhanyi* (Operations in High-Tech Limited War). Beijing: National Defense University Press.

Guan, Jixian. 1993b. Gaojishu tiaojian xia zhanyi tedian jiqi dui yixie zhanyi wenti de zhongda yingxiang (The Operational Caracteristics of High-Tech Limited War and Their Great Impacts on Operations). In *Gaojishu jubu zhanzheng yu zhanyi zhanfa* (High-Tech Limited War and Operational Art), ed. Research Department, National Defense University. Beijing: National Defense University Press.

Guiccardini, Francesco. 1964. *History of Italy and History of Florence*. Translated by Cecil Grayson and edited by J. R. Hale. New York: Washington Square Press.

Gumahad, Arsenio T. Lt. Col. 1997. The Profession of Arms in the Information Age. *Joint Force Quarterly*, no. 15 (spring): 14–20.

Gurtov, Mel, and Byong-Moo Hwang. 1998. *China's Security. The New Roles of the Military*. Boulder: Lynne Rienner Publishers.

Haas, Richard N. 1995. Paradigm Lost. *Foreign Affairs* 74, no. 1 (January-February): 43–58.

Hagerman, Edward. 1988. *The American Civil War and the Origins of Modern Warfare*. Bloomington, IN: Indiana University Press.

Hashim, Ahmed S. 1998. The Revolution in Military Affairs Outside the West. *Journal of International Affairs* 51, no. 2 (spring): 431–45.

Heisbourg, François. 1997. L'Évolution doctrinale et les réformes en cours. In *La France et sa défense*, ed. Philippe Tronquoy. Paris: La Documentation française, Cahiers français no. 283.

Henderson, Nicholas. 1964. *Prince Eugen of Savoy*. New York: Praeger.

Hewish, Mark. 1996. At the Sword's Point. Specialized Equipment for Early-Entry Forces. *International Defense Review* 29, no. 11 (November): 36–43.

Hewish, Mark. 1998. US Army Marches Towards a Digital Horizon. *International Defense Review* 31, no. 1 (January): 11.

Hewish, Mark, and Pamela Pohling-Brown. 1995. Making Change a Positive Force: Revolution in U.S. Aircraft Factories. *International Defence Review* 28, no. 4 (April): 30–35.

Howard, Michael Sir. 1994. How Much Can Technology Change Warfare? In *Two Historians in Technology and War*, Sir Michael Howard and John F. Guilmartin Jr. Carlisle Barracks, PA: U.S. Army War College, Strategic Studies Institute.

Howard, Michael. 1986. Men against Fire: The Doctrine of the Offensive in 1914. In *Makers of Modern Strategy from Machiavelli to the Nuclear Age*, ed. Peter Paret. Princeton: Princeton University Press.

Hu, Jianming. 1994. Luetan Mao Zedong junshi sijiang dui wojun zai gaojishu tiaojian xia zuozhan de zhidao (Preliminary Discussions of Mao Zedong's Military Thought for Directing our Combat under High-Tech conditions). In *Mao Zedong junshi sijiang zai Zhongguo de shenli yu fazhan* (Victory and Development of Mao Zedong's Military Thought in China), ed. Research Department, National Defense University. Beijing: National Defense University Press.

Hu, Siyun. 1993. Shiying liti zhanzheng xuyao fahui zenti zuozhan weili: hetong zhanyi zhong kongjun zuozhan shiyong weiti tantao (Adaptation to the Requirements of Three-Dimentional Warfare and Increases in Comprehensive Combat Effectiveness: Explorations of Air Combat in Combined Operations). In *Gao jishu tiaojian xia zhanyi lilun yanjiu* (High-Tech Limited War and Operational Art), ed. Research Department and Operational Office, National Defense University. Beijing: National Defense University Press.

Huang, Xinting. 1984. Renzhen zongjie zuozhan jingyan jiasu zhuangjiabing xiandaihua jianshe (A Serious Summary of Combat Experiences for Speeding-up Modernization of Armor Troops). In *Junshi xueshu lunwen xun* (Selected Military Papers from Military Studies), vol. I, ed. Journal of Military Studies. Beijing: Academy of Military Science Press.

Huang, Xuejun, Li Xiaolin, and Xiao Yuehong. 1988. 2000 nian wojun zhanshu fazhan chuyi (Opinions on the Tactics Development of our Army in 2000). In *Zhanshu fazhan xintan* (New Explorations of Tactics Development), vol. I., ed. Hao Zizhou. Beijing: Academy of Military Science Press.

Huntington, Samuel. 1993. The Clash of Civilizations? *Foreign Affairs* 72, no. 3 (summer): 22–49.

Hura, Myron, and Gary McLeod. 1993a. *Route Planning Issues for Low Observable Aircraft and Cruise Missiles: Implications for the Intelligence Community*. Santa Monica, CA: RAND, MR–187–AF.

Hura, Myron, and Gary McLeod. 1993b. *Intelligence Support and Mission Planning for Autonomous Precision-Guided Weapons: Implications for Intelligence Support Plan Development*. Santa Monica, CA: RAND, MR-230-AF.

Hura, Myron, and Gary McLeod. 1995. *Ensuring Adequate Intelligence Support for the Acquisition of New Weapon Systems*. Santa Monica, CA: RAND, DB-125-CMS.

Huxley, Tim, and Susan Willett. 1999. *Arming East Asia*. Adelphi Paper 329. London: Oxford University Press/International Institute for Strategic Studies.

International Institute for Strategic Studies (IISS). 1998. *The Military Balance 1998/99.* London: Oxford University Press/International Institute for Strategic Studies.

Isaev, Vladimir, and Aleksandr Filonik. 1996. Russiya i Arabskiy mir: V poiskakh sposobov realizatsii dolgovremennykh interesov. *Nezavisimaya gazeta*, 29 February, p. 5.

Jacobsen, Carl G. 1990. *Strategic Power: USA/USSR.* London: Macmillan.

JDW. 1995. Valuable Lessons Home to Roost.1995. *Jane's Defence Weekly* 23, no. 20 (20 May): 41–45.

Johansen, Anatol, and Sybe Rispens. 1999. Augen im All. *Die Zeit*, 10 June, p. 32.

Johnson, Stuart E, and Martin C. Libicki. 1995. *Dominant Battlespace Knowledge: The Winning Edge.* Washington, DC: National Defense University Press.

Johnston, Alastair I. 1995–96. China's New "Old Thinking". *International Security* 20, no. 3 (winter): 5–42.

Joxe, Alain. 1996. État des lieux de la RAM: deux antinomies structurelles en limitent l'efficacité stratégique. *L'Armement* 51 (March): 137–42.

Juvenal des Ursins, Jean. 1838. Histoire de Charles VI. In *Choix des chroniques et mémoires sur l'histoire de France. XIVe siècle.* Paris: Panthéon Littéraire.

Kaldor, Mary. 1981. *The Baroque Arsenal.* New York: Hill and Wang.

Keegan John. 1993. *A History of Warfare.* New York: Alfred A. Knopf.

Kelley, Maryellen R., and Todd A. Watkins. 1995a. In from the Cold: Prospects for Conversion of the Defense Industrial Base. *Science* 268, no. 5210 (28 April): 525–32.

Kelley, Maryellen R., and Todd A. Watkins. 1995b. The Myth of the Specialized Military Contractor. *Technology Review* 98, no. 3 (April): 52–58.

Kendall, Frank. 1992. Exploiting the Military Technical Revolution: A Concept for Joint Warfare. *Strategic Review* 20, no. 2 (spring): 23–30.

Kenney, Martin, and Richard Florida. 1993. *Beyond Mass Production: The Japanese System and its Transfer to the U.S.* Oxford: Oxford University Press.

Khalilzad, Zalmay. 1995. Losing the Moment? The United States and the World After the Cold War. *The Washington Quarterly* 18, no. 2 (spring): 87–107.

Khalilzad, Zalmay, and David Ochmanek. 1997. Introduction. In *Strategic Appraisal 1997. Strategy and Defense Planning for the 21ˢᵗ Century*, eds. Zalmay M. Khalilzad and David A. Ochmanek. Santa Monica, CA: RAND.

Kipp, Jacob W. 1987. Conventional Force Modernization and the Asymmetries of Military Doctrine: Historical Reflections on Air/Land Battle and the Operational Maneuver Group. In *The Uncertain Course: New Weapons, Strategies, and Mind-sets*, ed. Carl G. Jacobsen, Oxford: Oxford University Press.

Kipp, Jacob W. 1996a. The Nature of Future War: Russian Military Forecasting and the Revolution in Military Affairs: A Case of the Oracle of Delphi or Cassandra? *The Journal of Soviet Military Studies* 9, no. 1 (March): 1–45.

Kipp, Jacob W. 1996b. Soldiers and Civilians Confronting Future War: Lev Tolstoy, Jan Bloch, and Their Russian Military Critics. In *Tooling for War: Military Transformation in the Industrial Age*, ed. Stephen D. Chiabotti. Chicago: Imprint Publications.

Kipp, Jacob W. 1998. *Russian Military Reform: Status and Prospects (Views of a Western Military Historian).* Fort Leavenworth, KS: Foreign Military Studies Office: URL <http://call.army.mil//call/fmso/fmsopubs/issues/rusrform.htm>.

Kir'yan, M. M. 1982. *Voyenno-tekhnicheskiy progress i vooruzhennye sily SSSR (Analiz razvitiya vooruzheniya, organizatsii i sposobov deystvii.* Moscow: Voyenizdat.

Kirshin, Yu. Ya. et al. 1985. *Sovetskiye Vooruzhennyye Sily v usloviyakh razvitogo sotsializma.* Moscow: Nauka.

Kokoshin, Andrei A. 1995. *Armiya i politika: Sovetskaya voyenno-politicheskaya i voyenno-strategicheskaya mysl'.* Moscow: Mezhdunarodnye Otnosheniya.

Kokoshin, Andrei A. 1996. Voyenno-politicheskie i ekonomicheskie aspekty reformy Vooruzhennykh Sil Rossii. *Voyennaya mysl'* 6 (November-December): 2–11.

Kovacic, William E. 1992. Regulatory Controls as Barriers to Entry in Government Procurement. *Policy Sciences* 25, no. 1 (February): 36–37.

Krause, Keith. 1992. *Arms and the State: Patterns of Military Production and Trade.* Cambridge, UK: Cambridge University Press.

Krepinevich Andrew F. 1994a. Une révolution dans les conflits: une perspective américaine. *Défense nationale* 50 (January): 57–71.

Krepinevich, Andrew. 1994b. From Cavalry to Computers. The Pattern of Military Revolutions. *The National Interest* 37 (fall): 30–42.

Lang, James D., and Paul B. Hugge 1995. Lean Manufacturing for Lean Times. *Aerospace America* 33, no. 5 (May): 28–36.

Larionov, V. V. 1996. Interv'yu: Voyenno-tekhnicheskaya politika: Retrospektivnyy analiz. *Problemy prognozirovaniya*, no. 3: 170–74.

Larionov, Valentin, and Andrei Kokoshin. 1991. *Prevention of War: Doctrines, Concepts and Prospects.* Moscow: Progress Publishers.

Larson, Eric V. 1996. *Casualties and Consensus: The Historical Role of Casualties in Domestic Support for U.S. Military Operations.* Santa Monica, CA: RAND, MR–726–RC.

Latham, Andrew. 1997. From the "armory system" to "agile manufacturing": Industrial divides in the history of American arms production. Ph.D. diss., York University.

Laurent, Jacques and René Ernould. 1989. Vers une nouvelle "Révolution dans les affaires militaires." *Stratégique*, no. 42: 11–53.

le Baker, Geoffrey. 1889. *Chronicon*, edited by E. M. Thompson. Oxford: Clarendon.

Lebed, Aleksandr. 1996. Zhestkiy kontrol' i usilenie otvetstvennosti. *Nezavisimaya gazeta*, 29 June, p. 1, 3.

Leggat, John. 1998. Executive Summary. Paper read at the DGIIP/DRAB Symposium on the Implications of the Revolution in Business Affairs for DND in 2010–2020, Department of National Defence, 25 June, at Ottawa.

Leitzel, Jim. 1992. Competition in Procurement. *Policy Sciences* 25, no. 1 (February): 43–56.

Lewis, John W., and Litai Xue. 1988. *China Builds the Bomb.* Stanford: Stanford University Press.

Li, Desheng. 1984. Yaoshi xunlian laiyige datupo (Making a Big Breaking through in Training). In *Junshi xueshu lunwen xun* (Selected Military Papers from Military Studies), vol. I, ed. Journal of Military Studies. Beijing: Academy of Military Science Press.

Li, Jihong. 1994. Lizhu xianyou zhuangbei zengqiang daying gaojishu tianjian xia renmin zhanzheng de xinxin (Strengthening Confidence in Winning People's Limited War under High-Tech Conditions with Available Weapons). In *Gaojishu tiaojian xia jubu zhanzheng zhengzhi gongzuo yanjiu* (A Study of Political Work in High-Tech Limited War), ed. Li, Jihong. Beijing: National Defense University Press.

Li, Jijun. 1994. *Junshi lilun yu zhanzheng shijian* (Military Theory and War Practice). Beijing: Academy of Military Science Press.

Libicki, Martin C. 1996a. The Emerging Primacy of Information. *Orbis* 40, no. 2 (spring): 261–74.

Libicki, Martin C. 1996b. Information and Nuclear RMA Compared. *Strategic Forum*, no. 82 (July), URL <http://www.ndu.edu/inss/strforum/forum82.html>.

Libicki, Martin C. 1998. Information War, Information Peace. *Journal of International Affairs* 51, no. 2 (spring): 411–28.

Libicki, Martin C, and Cdr James A. Hazlett. 1993. Do We Need an Information Corps? *Joint Force Quarterly*, no. 2 (autumn): 88–97.

Liu, Jingsong. 1992. Dui zhanqu zhu junbing zhong lianhe zuozhan zhihui wenti de tantiao (Explorations of Command Issues related to Combined Services and Arms Combat at the War Zone Level). In *Jundui zhihui lilun jijin* (Collected Papers on Military Command Theory), ed. National Defense University. Beijing: National Defense University Press.

Liu, Weiguo. 1995. *Zhanzheng zhidao yu zhanzheng zhidao guilu* (War Guidance and Laws for Directing War). Beijing: People's Liberation Army Press.

Lomov, I. A., ed. 1973. *Nauchno-tekhnicheskiy progress i revolyutsiya v voyennom dele*. Moscow: Voyenizdat.

Long, Houchun. 1992. Redai shanyue conglin di zhanyi zuozhan zong de zhengzhi gongzuo (Political Work in Tropical Jungle and Mountainous Operations). In *Jubu zhanzheng zhanyi zhengzhi gongzuo* (Political Work in Local War and Operations), ed. Li Jihong. Beijing: National Defense University Press.

Luttwak, Edward N. 1993. *The Endangered American Dream. How to Stop the United States from Becoming a Third-World Country and How to Win the Geo-Economic Struggle for Industrial Supremacy*. New York: Simon and Schuster.

Luttwak, Edward N. 1996. A Post-Heroic Military Policy. *Foreign Affairs* 75, no. 4 (July-August): 33–44.

Malik, J. Mohan. 1990. Chinese Debate on Military Strategy. *Journal of Northeast Asian Studies* 9, no. 2 (summer): 3–32.

Markusen, Ann. 1991. The Military-Industrial Divide. *Environment and Planning D: Society and Space*, no. 9: 391–416.

Massie, Robert K. 1991. *Dreadnought. Britain, Germany, and the Coming of the Great War*. New York: Ballantine Books.

Mathews, Jessica Tuchman. 1989. Redefining Security. *Foreign Affairs* 68, no. 2 (spring): 162–77.

Maynes, Charles W. 1993-94. A Workable Clinton Doctrine. *Foreign Policy*, no. 93 (winter): 3–20.

Mazarr, Michael J. 1994. *The Revolution in Military Affairs: A Framework for Defense Planning*. Carlisle Barracks, PA: U.S. Army War College, Strategic Studies Institute.

Mazarr, Michael J., Jeffrey Shaffer, and Benjamin Ederington. 1993. *The Military Technical Revolution: A Structural Framework*. Washington, DC: Center for Strategic and International Studies.McGrath, Mike. n.d. *Agile Manufacturing Program*. URL <http://www.arpa.mil/sisto/overview/agile.html>.

McInnes, Colin. 1998. Labour's Strategic Defence Review. *International Affairs* 74, no. 4 (October): 823–45.

McKitrick, Jeffrey et al. 1994. *The Revolution in Military Affairs*. McLean, VA: Science Applications International Corporation.

McKitrick, Jeffrey, James Blackwell, Fred Littlepage, George Kraus, Richard Blanchfield, and Dale Hill. 1995. The Revolution in Military Affairs. In *Battlefield of the Future. 21ˢᵗ Century Warfare Issues*, eds. Barry Schneider and Lawrence E. Grinter. Maxwell Air Force Base, AL: Air University Press.

McNeill, William H. 1982. *The Pursuit of Power. Technology, Armed Force, and Society since A.D. 1000*. Chicago: University of Chicago Press.

Meng, Jinxi. 1988. Lun jingong zhandou de zongshen daji (On Deep Strikes of Offensive Operations). In *Zhanshu fazhan xintan* (New Explorations of Tactics Development), vol. I., ed. Hao Zizhou. Beijing: Academy of Military Science Press.

Metz, Steven, and James Kievit. 1995. *Strategy and the Revolution in Military Affairs: From Theory to Policy*. Carlisle Barracks, PA: U.S. Army War College, Strategic Studies Institute.

Millett, Allan R., and Peter Maslowski. 1984. *For the Common Defense*. New York: The Free Press.

Ministerstvo Oborony Rossiyskoy Federatsii (MORF), Institut voyennoy istorii. 1994. *Voyennaya entsiklopediya*. Moscow: Voyennoe Izdatel'stvo.

Ministry of Defence [United Kingdom]. 1998. *Strategic Defence Review. Modern Forces for the Modern World*. London: Ministry of Defence, URL <http://www.mod.uk/policy/sdr/wpconts.htm>.

Moiseev, N. N. 1988. *Sotsializm i informatika*. Moscow: Izdatel'stvo politicheskoy literatury.

Mork, Gordon R. 1967. Flint and Steel: A Study in Military Technology and Tactics in the Seventeenth Century in Europe. *Smithsonian Journal of History* 2, no. 2 (summer): 25–52.

Mueller, John. 1989. *Retreat from Doomsday: The Obsolescence of Major War*. New York: Basic Books.

Murawiec, Laurent. 1998. La Révolution dans les affaires militaires aux États-Unis: puissance de l'innovation. *Défense nationale* 54 (July): 62–77.

Murray, Williamson. 1997a. Thinking About Revolutions in Military Affairs. *Joint Force Quarterly*, no. 16 (summer): 69–76.

Murray, Williamson. 1997b. Clausewitz Out, Computer In: Military Culture and Technological Hubris. *The National Interest*, no. 48 (summer): 57–64.

Nagel, Roger N., and Rick Dove. 1991. *21st Century Manufacturing Enterprise Strategy*, vols. 1 and 2. Bethlehem, PA: Iaccoca Institute, Lehigh University.

National Research Council (NRC). 1992. *Strategic Technologies for the Army of the Twenty-first Century / Board on Army Science and Technology, Commission on Engineering and Technical Systems*. Washington, DC: National Academy Press.

Noble, David F. 1984. *Forces of Production: A Social History of Industrial Automation*. New York: Alfred A. Knopf.

Nosworthy, Brent. 1990. *The Anatomy of Victory. Battle Tactics, 1689-1763*. New York: Hippocrene Books.

Nye, Joseph S. Jr., and William A. Owens. America's Information Edge. 1996. *Foreign Affairs* 75, no. 2 (March-April): 20–36.

O'Hanlon, Michael. 1997. Transforming NATO: The Role of European Forces. *Survival* 39, no. 3 (autumn): 5–15.

Ogarkov, N. V. 1982. *Vsegda v gotovnosti k zashchite otechestva*. Moscow: Voyenizdat.

Ogarkov, N. V. 1985. *Istoriya uchit bditel'nosti*. Moscow: Voyenizdat.

Osgood, Robert E. 1979. *Limited War Revisited*. Boulder: Westview Press.

Owens, William A. 1994. JROC: Harnessing the Revolution in Military. *Joint Force Quarterly*, no. 5 (summer): 55–57.

Owens, William A. 1995a. The Emerging System of Systems. *U.S. Naval Institute Proceedings* 121, no. 5 (May): 35–39.

Owens, William A. 1995b. *High Seas: The Naval Passage to an Uncharted World*. Annapolis, MD: Naval Institute Press.

Owens, William A. 1995–96. The American Revolution in Military Affairs. *Joint Force Quarterly* 10 (winter): 37–38.

Owens, William A. 1996. The Emerging U.S. System-of-Systems. *Strategic Forum*, no. 63 (February), URL <http://www.ndu.edu/inss/strforum/forum63.html>.

Palmer, Diego Ruiz. 1995. *De Metz à Creil: les structures de commandement françaises de l'après-guerre froide*. Recherches et documents no. 1. Paris: Centre de recherche et d'études sur les stratégies et technologies.

Parker, Geoffrey. 1988. *The Military Revolution. Military Innovation and the Rise of the West, 1500-1800*. Cambridge, UK: Cambridge University Press.

Peitgen, Heinz-Otto, Hartmut Jurgens, and Dietmar Saupe. 1992. *Chaos and Fractals: New Frontiers of Science*. New York: Springer-Verlag Inc.

Perry, William J. Secretary of Defense. 1994. *Memorandum for Secretaries of Military Departments, Subject: Specifications and Standards—A New Way of Doing Business*. 29 June.

Peters, Ralph Maj. 1995. After the Revolution. *Parameters* 25, no. 2 (summer): 7–14.

Petersen, M. J. Maj. 1995. Review of *The Military Revolution Debate*, by Clifford J. Rogers. *Airpower Journal* 9, no. 4: 116–17.

Pirumov, V. S. 1994. Some Elements of Research Methodology Related to the Problem of National Security under Present Conditions. In *Military Doctrine and Military Reconstruction in Post-Confrontational Europe*, General Staff of the Czech Armed Forces. Prague: Vojenske rozhledy/Czech Military Review.

Pirumov, V. S. 1996. Nekotorye aspekty informatsionnoy voyny, Paper presented at NATO Conference on Information Operations, May, in Brussels, Belgium.

Pozhidaev, D. 1996. Informatsionnaya voyna v planakh pentagona. *Zarubezhnoe voyennoe obozrenie*, no. 2 (February): 2–4.

Qiu, Guijin, 1994. Shunying gaojishu zhanzheng qushi jicheng he fayang wojun junshi lilun de jige wenti (Several Issues related to the Following and Developing of Our Military Theories in Accordance with High-Tech War). In *Mao Zedong junshi sijiang zai Zhongguo de shenli yu fazhan* (Victory and Development of Mao Zedong's Military Thought in China), ed. Research Department, National Defense University. Beijing: National Defense University Press.

Radzikhovskiy, Leonid. 1997. A Wolf of War or a Fox of Politics? *Ogonek*, no. 27 (14–20 July): 20–21.

Ralston, David B. 1990. *Importing the European Army. The Introduction of European Military Techniques and Institutions into the Extra-European World, 1600–1914*. Chicago: The University of Chicago Press.

Reimer, Dennis J. General. 1996. Training: Our Army's Top Priority and Don't You Forget it! *Military Review* 76, no.4 (July-August): 55–62.

Richter, Andrew. 1999. *The Revolution in Military Affairs and its Impact on Canada: The Challenge and the Consequences.* Working Paper 28. Vancouver: University of British Columbia, Institute of International Relations.

Ricks, Thomas E. 1994. Warning Shot: How Wars Are Fought Will Change Radically Pentagon Planner Says. *Wall Street Journal*, 15 July, p. A1, A5.

Ricks, Thomas E, and Roy J. Harris Jr. 1994. Marshall's Ideas Help to Change Defense Industry. *The Wall Street Journal*, 15 July, p. A5.

Rikhye, Ravi, and Pushpindar Singh. 1994. External Threats and India's Conventional Capabilities: Perspectives Till 2010. In *Future Imperilled. India's Security in the 1990s and Beyond*, ed. Bharat Karnad. New Delhi: Viking.

Rockwell, Robert. 1997. An Infrastructure for Social Software. *IEEE Spectrum* [Journal of the Institute of Electrical and Electronics Engineers] 34, no. 3 (March): 26–31.

Rogers, Clifford J., ed. 1995a. *The Military Revolution Debate. Readings on the Military Transformation of Early Modern Europe*. Boulder: Westview Press.

Rogers, Clifford J. 1995b. The Military Revolutions of the Hundred Years War. In *The Military Revolution Debate. Readings on the Military Transformation of Early Modern Europe*, ed. Clifford J. Rogers. Boulder: Westview Press.

Rosecrance, Richard. 1996. The Rise of the Virtual State. *Foreign Affairs* 75, no. 4 (July-August): 45–61.

Rosen, Stephen Peter. 1982. Vietnam and the American Theory of Limited War. *International Security* 7, no. 2 (fall): 83–113.

Rowell, Jan. 1996. *Intel's ASCI Red Project Hits 200 GFLOPS Milestone (28 November)*. URL <http://www.ssd.intel.com/tflop2.html>.

Russett, Bruce. 1993. *Grasping the Democratic Peace. Principles for a Post-Cold War World*. Princeton: Princeton University Press.

Ryabchuk, V. D. 1994. Nauka, obrazovanie, reforma. *Voyennaya mysl'*, no. 2 (February): 39–41.

Ryabchuk, V. D. et al. 1995. *Elementy voyennoy sistemologii primenitel'no k reshenyu problem operativnogo iskusstva i takitiki obshchevoyskobykh ob'edineniy, soyedineniy i chastey: Voyenno-teoreticheskiy trud*. Moscow: Izdatel'stvo Akademii.

Sakharov, Andrei. 1996. Smuty i avtoritarizm v Rossii, polemicheskie zametki (Troubles and Authoritarianism in Russia, Polemical Comments). *Svobodnaya mysl'*, no. 9 (September) : 89–101.

Salmon, J. 1977. Political Hoplites. *Journal of Hellenic Studies* 97: 93–101.

Scales, Robert H. 1993. *Certain Victory: The U.S. Army in the Gulf War*. Fort Leavenworth, KS: U.S. Army Command and General Staff College Press.

Schake, Kori, Amaya Bloch-Lainé, and Charles Grant. 1999. Building a European Defence Capability. *Survival* 41, no. 1 (spring); 20–40.

Schmidt, Christian, and Pierre Dussauge. 1997. Les Mutations du système français d'armement. In *La France et sa défense*, ed. Philippe Tronquoy. Paris: La Documentation française, Cahiers français no. 283.

Schwartau, Winn. 1994. *Information Warfare*. New York: Thunder's Mouth Press.

Sergievskiy, V. 1993. "Klyuchevye tekhnologii" ministerstva oborony SshA. *Zarubezhnoe voyennoe obozrenie*, no. 5 (May): 9–11.

Shadwick, Martin. 1998. Executive Summary. DGIIP/DRAB Symposium on the Implications of the Revolution in Business Affairs for DND in 2010–2020, Department of National Defence, 25 June, at Ottawa.

Shambaugh, David. 1996. China's Military in Transition. *The China Quarterly*, no. 146, June: 265–98.

Shavrov, I. E, and M. I. Galkin, eds. 1977. *Metodologiya voyenno-nauchnogo poznaniya*. Moscow: Voyenizdat.

Shearer, David. 1998. *Private Armies and Military Intervention*. Adelphi Paper 316. London: Oxford University Press/International Institute for Strategic Studies.

Shevelev, E. G. 1996. Sistemologiya natsional'noy bezopasnosti Rossii: sovremennoe sostoyanie I perspektivy razvitiya, *Voyennaya mysl'*, no. 6 (November-December).

Shlykov, Vitaly. 1996. Interv'yu: Ugrozy real'nye i mnimye, Beseda s polkovnikom v otstavke V. V. Shylkovym, *Problemy prognozirovaniya*, no. 4: 131–41.

Shumeyko, Vladimir. 1996. Neobkhodimo samoobnovlenie presidentskoy politiki. *Nezavisimaya gazeta,* 17 January, p. 1, 3.

Snead, J. Michael. 1995. *United States Aerospace Forces 1.1.2020*. U.S. Air Force Material Command, URL <http://www.afmc/wpafb.mil/STBBS/strev/2020/contents.htm>.

Sokolovskiy, Marshal S.V. 1962. *Voyennaya strategiya*, 1ˢᵗ ed. Moscow: Voyenizdat.

Song, Chengzhi. 1984. Nuli jianshe xiandaihua de renmin paobing (Striving to Build Modernized People's Artillery Troops). In *Junshi xueshu lunwen xun* (Selected Military Papers from Military Studies), vol. I, ed. Journal of Military Studies. Beijing: Academy of Military Science Press.

Song, Shilun. 1984. Guanyu jinhou fanqinlue zuozhan jige wenti de chubu tantao (Preliminary Discussions of Several Issues Related to Future Anti-Aggression Combat). In *Junshi xueshu lunwen xun* (Selected Military Papers from Military Studies) vol. II, ed. Journal of Military Studies. Beijing: Academy of Military Science Press.

Sovetskaya voyennaya entsiklopediya. 1977. Moscow: Voyenizdat.

Sovetskaya voyennaya entsiklopediya. 1979. Moscow: Voyenizdat.

Soviet Military Encyclopedia. 1979. Moscow: Voyenizdat, s.v. "The Revolution in Military Affairs."

Stix, Gary. 1995. Fighting Future Wars. *Scientific American* 273, no. 6 (December): 92–98.

Strange, Susan. 1996. *The Retreat of the State. The Diffusion of Power in the World Economy*. Cambridge, UK: Cambridge University Press.

Strange, Susan. 1997. The Erosion of the State. *Current History* 96, no. 613 (November): 365–69.

Su, Yu. 1984. Dui weilai fanqinlue zhanzheng chuqi zuozhan fangfa jige wenti de tantao (Preliminary Discussions of Combat Issues in the Early Stage of Future Anti-Aggression War). In *Junshi xueshu lunwen xun* (Selected Military Papers from Military Studies), vol. II, ed. Journal of Military Studies. Beijing: Academy of Military Science Press.

Sullivan, Brian R. 1996. Future National Security Environment: Possible Consequences for Army SOF (Special Operations Forces). *Special Warfare* 9, no. 3 (August): 1–12.

Sullivan, Gordon R., and James M. Dubik. 1993. *Land Warfare in the 21ˢᵗ Century*. Carlisle Barracks, PA: U.S. Army War College, Strategic Studies Institute.

Sun, Jizhang. 1990. *Zhanyi xue jichu* (Introduction to Operational Science). Beijing: National Defense University Press.

Szafranski, Richard. 1996. Peer Competitors, the RMA, and New Concepts: Some Questions. *Naval War College Review* 49, no. 2 (spring): 113–19.

Thomas, Timothy L. 1998. *Behind the Great Firewall of China: A Look at RMA/IW Theory from 1996–1998*. Fort Leavenworth, KS: Foreign Military Studies Office, URL <http://call.army.mil//call/fmso/fmsopubs/issues/Chinarma.htm>.

Tiroch, Bertrand. 1997. Les Armées françaises à l'horizon 2015. In *La France et sa défense*, ed. Philippe Tronquoy. Paris: La Documentation française, Cahiers français no. 283.

Toffler Alvin, and Heidi Toffler. 1993. *War and Anti-War. Survival at the Dawn of the 21ˢᵗ Century*. Boston: Little, Brown.

Tsvylev, R. I. 1996. *Postindustrial'noe razvitie: Uroki dlya Rossii*. Moscow: Nauka.

U.S. Congress. 1993. *Streamlining Defense Acquisition Laws: Report of the Acquisition Law Advisory Panel to the United States Congress*. Washington, DC: U.S. Government Printing Office, January.

U.S. Congress, Office of Technology Assessment (OTA). 1992. *Building Future Security: Strategies for Restructuring the Defense Technology and Industrial Base*, OTA-ISC-350. Washington, DC: U.S. Government Printing Office.

U.S. Congress, Office of Technology Assessment (OTA). 1994. *Assessing the Potential for Civil-Military Integration: Technologies, Processes and Practices*, OTA-ISS-611. Washington, DC: U.S. Government Printing Office.

U.S. Department of Commerce. 1989. *Findings of the U.S. Department of Defense Technology Assessment Team on Japanese Manufacturing Technology*. Washington, DC: National Technical Information Service.

U.S. Department of Defense, Office of the Assistant Secretary of Defense(OASD) (Public Affairs). 1993. DOD's Acquisition Reform Recommendations to the 800 Panel Report. *News Release* 28 (October).

U.S. Department of Defense, Office of the Undersecretary of Defense for Acquisition (OUDA). 1993. *Report of the Defense Science Board Task Force on Defense Acquisition Reform*. Washington, DC: U.S. Government Printing Office.

U.S. Department of Defense. 1995. *Dual Use Technology: A Defense Strategy for Affordable, Leading-Edge Technology*. Washington, DC: U.S. Government Printing Office.

U.S. House. 1996. National Authorization Act for Fiscal Year 1997: Conference Report to Accompany H.R. 3230, Subtitle B - Force Structure, 104ᵗʰ Cong. 2ⁿᵈ session, H.R. 104-724, Sec 923.

van Creveld, Martin. 1985. *Command in War*. Cambridge, MA: Harvard University Press.

van Creveld, Martin. 1989. *Technology and War. From 2000 B.C. to the Present*. New York: Free Press.

van Creveld, Martin. 1991. *The Transformation of War*. New York: Free Press.

van Creveld, Martin. 1996. The Fate of the State. *Parameters* 26, no. 1 (spring): 4–18.

van Opstal, Debra. 1993. *Integrating Civilian and Military Technologies: An Industry Survey*. Washington, DC: Center for Strategic and International Studies.

Verbruggen, J. F. 1997. *The Art of Warfare in Western Europe During the Middle Ages. From the Eighth Century to 1340*. translated by S. Willard and R. W. Southern, 2ⁿᵈ English ed. Woodbridge: The Boydell Press.

Vigor, Peter H. 1988. The Soviet Union and the Future of Land Warfare. In *Emerging Doctrines and Technologies*, ed. Robert L. Pfaltzgraff, Jr. Lexington, MA: Lexington Books.

Voyennaya Akademiya General'nogo Shtaba Vooruzhennykh Sil Rossiyskoy Federatsii, Kafedra istorii voyn i voyennogo iskusstva. 1995. *Problemy voyennogo iskusstva vo Vtoroy mirovoy voyne i v poslevoyennyy period (Strategiya i operativnoe iskusstvo): Uchebnik dlya slushateley Voyennoy akademii General'nogo Shtaba.* Moscow: Tipografiya VAGSh.

Voyennyy entsiklopedicheskiy slovar'. 1983. Moscow: Voyenizdat.

Wagner, Arthur L. 1899. *The Campaign of Koniggratz, a study of the Austro-Prussian conflict in the light of the American Civil War.* 2nd ed. Kansas City: Hudson-Kimberly.

Wang, Baofu. 1989. Sujun zaoqi yanjiu he gaige zhanyi lilun de jingyan jaoxun (The Experiences and Lessons of Soviet Military Early Research on Reformulating Operational Art). *Junshi lishi* (Military History) 2: 25–28.

Warwick, Graham. 1995. Bigger and Better. *Flight International* 147, no. 4457 (February): 59–62.

Watts, Barry, and Williamson Murray. 1996. Military Innovation in Peacetime. In *Military Innovation in the Interwar Period*, eds. Williamson Murray and Allan R. Millett. Cambridge, UK: Cambridge University Press: 369–415.

Weiss, Stanley I., Earll M. Murman, and Daniel Roos. 1996. The Air Force and Industry Think Lean. *Aerospace America* 34, no. 5 (May): 32–39.

Whitney, Daniel, et al. 1995. *Agile Pathfinders in the Aircraft and Automobile Industries— a Progress Report.* Cambridge, MA: Massachusetts Institute of Technology, URL: <http://web.mit.edu/ctpid/www/agile/atlanta.html>.

Xiong, Deyu. 1996. Lun zhanqu gaojishu zhanzheng tiaojian xia de jundi liangong dixi (On the Military-Civilian Joint Logistics Supply System of the War Zone under High-Tech War Conditions). In *Gaojishu tiaojian xia jubu zhanzheng zhanyi houqin baozhang yanjiu* (A Study of Operational Logistical Support under High-Tech Limited War Conditions), ed. Research Department, National Defense University. Beijing: National Defense University Press.

Xu, Zhilong. 1988. Shilun zongshen gongji zhanshu (Preliminary Discussions of Deep Offensive Tactics). In *Zhanshu fazhan xintan* (New Explorations of Tactics Development), vol. I, ed. Hao Zizhou. Beijing: Academy of Military Science Press.

Yang, Yi, and Yin Pelun. 1988. Zhanshu xiandai hua he wojun teshe (Modernized Tactics and Our Army's Characteristics). In *Zhanshu fazhan xintan* (New Explorations of Tactics Development), vol. I, ed. Hao Zizhou. Beijing: Academy of Military Science Press.

Yanov, Aleksandr. 1995. *Posle El'tsina: "Veymarskaya" Rossiya.* Moscow: Kruk.

Yao, Hongde. 1988. Sujun zhanshu de fazhan (Soviet Tactics Development). In *Zhanshu fazhan xintan* (New Explorations of Tactics Development), vol. II. ed. Hao Zizhou. Beijing: Academy of Military Science Press.

Zhang, Caiqian. 1984. Dui zhanzheng chuqi guanche jiji fangyu zhanlue fangzen de xiangfa (Thoughts on the Application of Active Defense Strategic Principles at the Early Stage of War). In *Junshi xueshu lunwen xun* (Selected Military Papers from Military Studies), vol. I, ed. Journal of Military Studies. Beijing: Academy of Military Science Press: 123–29.

Zhang, Honghai. 1993. Gaojishu tiaojian xia de zhanyi zuozhan kongjun zuozhan fangfa tantao (Explorations of Air Force Combat Methods in Operations under High-Tech Conditions). In *Gao jishu tiaojian xia zhanyi lilun yanjiu* (A Study of Operational Theory under High-Tech Conditions), ed. Research Department, National Defense University. Beijing: National Defense University Press.

Zhang, Mingyou. 1997. Jiaqiang zongshen kangji zhuzhong fanji zhishen (Reinforcing Deep-Resistance and Winning through Counterstrikes). In *Gao jishu tiaojian xia zhanyi lilun yanjiu* (A Study of Operational Theory under High-Tech Conditions), ed. Research Department and Operational Office, National Defense University. Beijing: National Defense University Press.

Zhang, Xinsheng. 1997. Shiji zijiao de junshi lilun geming (The Revolution in Military Theory at the Turn of Century). *Jiefangjun Bao* (People's Liberation Army Daily), 2 September, p. 6.

Zhang, Xiucai. 1988. Shilun quanzongshen liti fangyu de zhuzhi xietong (A Preliminary Discussion of Organizational Coordination of Total, Deep, Three-Dimentional Defense). In *Zhanshu fazhan xintan* (New Explorations of Tactics Development), vol. II, ed. Hao Zizhou. Beijing: Academy of Military Science Press.

Zhang, Youxia. 1994. Lun xiandai tiaojian xia de yezhan (On Night Combat under Modern Conditions). In *Mao Zedong junshi sijiang zai Zhongguo de shenli yu fazhan* (Victory and Development of Mao Zedong's Military Thought in China), ed. Research Department, National Defense University. Beijing: National Defense University Press.

Zhang, Zhixiu. 1984. Cong zhiwei huanji kan jinhou zuozhan zhide zhuyi de jige wenti (Several Issues Relevant to Future Operations in Light of Self-Defense Counterstrikes). In *Junshi xueshu lunwen xun* (Selected Military Papers from Military Studies) vol. II, ed. Journal of Military Studies. Beijing: Academy of Military Science Press.

Zhao, Kaizhong. 1992. Dui kongjun zuozhan zhihui guilu de sikao (Reflections on Air Combat Command Laws). In *Jundui zhihui lilun jijin* (Collected Papers on Military Command Theory), ed. National Defense University. Beijing: National Defense University Press.

Zhongguo dabaike quanshu bianjibu (Editorial Board, Chinese Encyclopedia). 1989. *Zhongguo dabaike quanshu: junshi* (The Chinese Encyclopedia: the Military), vol. II. Beijing: Chinese Encyclopedia Press.

Zhou, Lide. 1984. Dui Gaoping diqu zuozhan jihua wenti de tantiao (Revisiting Gaoping Combat Plans). In *Junshi xueshu lunxen xun* (Selected Military Papers from Military Studies) vol. II, ed. Journal of Military Studies Press. Beijing: Academy of Military Science.

Zhou, Tienhong. 1995. *Ludi bianjing zuozhan zhanshou yanjiu* (A Study of Land Border Combat Tactics). Beijing: Academy of Military Science Press.

Zhu, Yinliang. 1996. Renmin zhanzheng cixiang zai xin Zhongguo chengli hou junshi douzheng de yunyong he fazhan (The Application and Development of People's War in Operations after the Founding of New China). In *Xiandai jubu zhanzheng tiaojian xia de renmin zhanzheng* (People's War Under Contemporary Local War Conditions), ed. Liu Shene. Beijing: Academy of Military Science Press.

Index

Revolution in Operational Art: as an alternative concept to the RMA, 3; domestic political ramifications of, 114, 119, 126; foreign analysis of, 105-6; incorporation of Soviet doctrine in, 119; initiation of, 108; obstacles to implementation, 126; and superpower invasion of China, 115; and the United States as a threat, 120, 125. *See also* People's Liberation Army; C^{3}I, as weak elements of the Chinese ROA

RMA (revolution in military affairs): arms manufacturing as dimension of, 5-6; challenges of implementation, 149-53, 157; and conventional invasions, 3, 144-45, 157; and defense industrial base, 82, 137 (*see also* Defense Industry; National technology and industrial base); definition of, 1, 3, 17, 22, 84, 88, 93-94, 131, 140-41, 160-61; and doctrinal developments, 62-63, 70-72, 75, 82; diffusion of, 2, 28, 33, 137-38; and force (or power) projection, 15, 80; and gains in military efficiency, 4, 6, 140, 145, 154, 157; historical classification and examples of, 22, 24; impact on alliances, 7-8, 17, 136-37; impact on hierarchy of power, 8, 28-29, 32, 139, 153-56, 157; and low-intensity conflicts, 3, 79-80, 100, 138, 140, 146-49, 157; (non-) revolutionary character, 2-4, 5, 17, 30-32, 34, 61-62, 75, 83, 84, 132, 139, 143, 157; and organizational innovation (or adaptability), 79, 82, 140, 151-52, 157; and post–Cold War geopolitics, 79-81, 98-99, 132-33; potential for developing countries, 14-15, 144, 156; potential for variation through adaptation, 139, 154-56; and revolution in business affairs, 6, 10, 11, 12; as a rupture in operational art, 132-33; shaped in the past by great power rivalries, 16; and the shift from quantity to quality, 32, 33, 87, 93, 145, 162; social and political implications, 2, 3, 29-30, 33-34; and space systems or operations, 142-43, 155; strategic utility of (or lack thereof), 3, 79-80, 138

Roche, James, 82
Rokhlin, Colonel-General Lev, 102
Russia: and conflict in Chechnya, 100, 102; delayed adoption of the RMA, 13,

100, 102-3; and information warfare, 94, 96, 99-100; and military forecasting, 88-89, 91-92, 104; military reform in, 101-3; "Time of Troubles" in, 87, 100-101, 104; transition to information society in, 95-96, 97-98; views on post–Cold War geopolitics from, 100-101, 103-4; views on the RMA from, 93-94, 96-97, 98. *See also* Soviet Union

Sakharov, Andrei, 101
Satellite: and direct broadcast, 46, 52; and electronic countermeasures, 40, 44, 156; and European access to information from U.S., 8; and information blockade, 52; and military communications, 66; and nuclear antisatellite weapons, 143; and the PLA, 121; relevance for developing countries seeking global reach, 155, 156; and Russia, 13; as space-based sensor platform, 65; useful in Bosnia, 138; U.S. use of, 151-52

Sensors: concealment and deception against, 154; cost of system of, 150; and electronic warfare, 44-45; importance in information gathering, 65; and information corps, 55; and intelligence-based warfare, 41-43; and monitoring by a global government, 74; as part of the RMA, 93, 122; and precision strike, 141; and premature use during Vietnam War, 149; semantic attack against, 54; on soldiers and vehicles, 69

Shalikashvili, General John, 85
Simulation, 54, 73-74. *See also* DVE
Situational awareness, 4, 7, 41, 67, 141, 154. *See also* Dominant battlespace knowledge (or awareness)
Somalia, 130, 133, 148, 153, 155. *See also* Aideed, Mohammed
Sokolovskiy, Marshal S. V., 92
Soviet Union: its inability to meet the challenges of the RMA and of defense reform, 90-91; losing the Cold War for lack of "think tanks", 93; and mass industrial war, 94-95; and origins of the RMA concept, 12, 77-78, 81, 87-88, 90, 129-30, 161; views on the RMA in, 88, 90-91; and war in Afghanistan, 91, 95
Special forces, 123, 134, 161
Stalin, Josef, 72, 91, 101
State, decline of, 3, 61, 74-75, 80

About the Editors and Contributors

JIANXIANG BI holds a Ph.D. in Political Science from Carleton University (Ottawa, Canada). He is a defense consultant and specialist in the Chinese military.

YVES BOYER is Associate Director of the *Fondation pour la recherche stratégique*, a research center on defense issues based in Paris, France. He has published widely on American defense issues and European security for more than ten years. He has been Guest Scholar at the Woodrow Wilson Center (Washington, D.C.) and Research Associate with the IISS (London).

GLENN C. BUCHAN is a Senior Defense Analyst with the RAND Corporation. He was Associate Program Director for Force Modernization and Employment in Project Air Force.

FRANÇOIS GÉRÉ is Scientific Director at the *Fondation pour la recherche stratégique*, a research center on defense issues based in Paris, France. He has been Visiting Professor at the SAIS, Johns Hopkins University, Washington, D.C. In recent years he has written on the future of war, nuclear proliferation, and psychological warfare.

THIERRY GONGORA is Research Associate with the *Institut québécois des hautes études internationales*, an international affairs research center affiliated to *Université Laval*, Quebec City. He has published on defense issues and Middle East affairs in such journals as *Defense Analysis* and the *International Journal of Middle East Studies*.

JACOB W. KIPP is Senior Analyst at the Foreign Military Studies Office, Fort Leavenworth, Kansas. He has published widely on Soviet and Russian military affairs.

ANDREW LATHAM is Assistant Professor of Political Science at Macalester College (St. Paul, Minnesota). He has published widely on the U.S. arms industry and on issues of arms proliferation. He will soon publish *Industrial Divides in the History of US Arms Production: From the 'Armory System' to 'Agile Manufacturing.'*

MARTIN C. LIBICKI was Senior Fellow at the Institute for National Strategic Studies (National Defense University, Washington D.C.). He now works for the RAND Corporation in Washington, D.C. He has published extensively in recent years on the subject of information warfare.

Col. HOWARD J. MARSH is a former Department Head of Applied Military Science at the Royal Military College of Canada and works at the National Defence Headquarters in Ottawa, Canada.

CLIFFORD J. ROGERS is Assistant Professor of History, United States Military Academy, West Point. He has written extensively on medieval and early modern military history and he is the editor of *The Military Revolution Debate.*

HARALD VON RIEKHOFF is Professor of Political Science, Carleton University (Ottawa, Canada). He is the author and editor of several books dealing with German foreign policy, NATO, arms control, and Canada-U.S. relations.

ISBN 0-313-31037-8

90000>

EAN

9 780313 310379

HARDCOVER BAR CODE